IRISH FOLK & FAIRY TALES

IRISH FOLK & FAIRY TALES

Edited by Sean Kelly

GALLEY PRESS
A Division of W. H. Smith Publishers Inc.
112 Madison Avenue
New York City 10016

The Rutledge Press

Published by Galley Press
An imprint of W. H. Smith Publishers Inc.
112 Madison Avenue
New York, New York 10016
Manufactured in U.S.A.

Designed by Allan Mogel

1 2 3 4 5 6 7 8 9 10

Library of Congress Cataloging in Publication Data

Main entry under title:

Irish folk and fairy tales.

    1. Tales—Ireland. 2. Fairy tales—Ireland.
3. Legends—Ireland. I. Kelly, Sean, 1940–
GR153.5.I74 1982   398.2'09415   82-11963
ISBN 0-8317-5001-4

We'd like to thank the following publishers and authors for granting permission to reprint stories from their books:

B.T. Batsford, Ltd., 4 Fitzhardinge St., London WIH OAH, England, *The Folklore of Ireland*, by Sean O'Sullivan, ("Diarmaid and Grainne," "Cromwell and O'Donnell," "The Everlasting Fight").

The Mercier Press, 4 Bridge Street, Cork, Ireland, *Folktales of the Irish Countryside*, by Kevin Danaher, ("The World Underground," "The Soupstone").

University of Chicago Press, 5801 Ellis Avenue, Chicago, IL 60637, U.S.A., *Folktales of Ireland*, by Sean O'Sullivan, ("Three Laughs of the Leprachaun").

The Bodley Head, Ltd., 9 Bow Street, London WC2E 7AL, England, *The Hound of Ulster*, by Rosemary Sutcliff, ("Deidre & the Sons of Usna").

The Macmillan Company, 866 Third Avenue, New York, NY 10022, U.S.A., *Irish Fairy Tales*, by James Stephens, ("The Story of Tuan MacCairill").

Irish Academic Press, Ltd., 3 Serpentine Avenue, Dublin, Ireland, *Beside the Fire*, by Douglas Hyde, ("The Well O' The World's End," "William of the Tree").

Colin Smythe, Ltd., P.O. Box 6, Gerrards Cross, Buckinghamshire SL9 7AE, England, *Gods and Fighting Men*, by Lady Gregory, ("Midhir and Etain").

CONTENTS

Introduction

The illustrations in this book are taken from an old edition of Crofton Croker's *Legends of the South of Ireland*. Croker began collecting stories under the inspiration of the brothers Grimm, whose "Children's and Household Tales" had just been published. It was generally believed that the folk tales gathered by the Grimm's had established the reality of a German *folk*—a separate, distinct German race and culture which was entitled to be a "Nation."

The Irish, whose right to Nationhood was then, as now, in question, quite understandably began to collect and publish their own folk tales; and some of the greatest anthologies were edited by staunch Irish patriots—Lady Wilde, Douglas Hyde, and W.B. Yeats.

(In our time—ironically enough—collectors and students of folk lore are struck by the universality of the tales—the plots, characters and symbols that occur and re-occur in all lands, on all people—which argues not for the separate destinies of nations but the brotherhood of Man.)

There are, nonetheless, qualities unique to Irish folk tales, and one of them is the pervasive presence of the supernatural. (It was this, more than any search for an Irish *volksgeist* that appealed to the mystic Yeats.) The stories gathered by the Grimms are quite eroneously called "Fairy Tales." There are Giants, Dwarfs and Talking Beasts aplenty, but very few Fairies. Irish folklore, on the other hand, almost exclusively concerns the doings of the "Little People," 'Gentry," the Ould Ones, the *Sidhe*.

The Irish seem, simply and naturally, to *assume* the presence of another world, beneath, above, or beyond our own, affecting us, affected by us, a world much older than ours, and forever young. Small wonder that the Gaels were so quickly and firmly converted to Christianity!

Since Yeat's collection, Irish Folk Stories and Fairy Tales, (published in 1888), there have been many anthologies of Irish folklore published, but none so popular as the Archpoet's. Literally millions of tales, in English and Gaelic, have been collected, recorded, and filed away in libraries. Scholars such as Sean O'Sullivan and Kevin Danaher have gathered, sifted, and published lovely books of these tales and legends. In making this selection, I have been (a cliché come true) embarrassed by riches.

I hope this selection of tales—from myths to jokes, from the distant past to the present—is representative. Obviously, it is very subjective, and such faults of ommission or transcription are my own.

The source of each tale is indicated in its introduction, and to the books listed there (too many, alas, out of print!) the reader is invited to turn for more of the same. I have many people to thank for their help in making this collection, including the many typists who had to work from manuscripts as indecipherable as any ogham stone . . . but I must single out Hedy Caplan, of The Rutledge Press, for her patience and research, Patty Brown, ditto, and the Irish American Historical Society for the use of their library.

Sean Kelly
New York 1982

I. BEFORE MAN AND TIME

Before Time and Man

Even they that walked on the high cliffs,
  High as the clouds were then,
Gods of unbearable beauty
  That broke the hearts of men . . .

G. K. Chesterton
"The Ballad of the White Horse"

Caesar divided all Gaul into three parts, and conquered. By the first century of the Christian era, the Gauls, a people whose territory had extended from Germany through northern Italy, France, Spain, and Britain, had ceased to exist as a people with their own language and culture. The Gaelic language was spoken, Gaelic gods worshipped, Gaelic life lived, only in the wild west of Europe—in Brittany, Wales, and Ireland.

The branch of the Gaulic nation in Ireland was called the Celts; and for fifteen centuries, despite invasions by Viking raiders and Christian missionaries, Ireland was a Celtic nation, where the most respected men were the *filidh*, the priest-poet-teacher-seers; myth makers, rhyme spinners, storytellers. Delight in and respect for the *word*, spoken or sung, remains a feature of the Irish character.

The Celtic language—Gaelic—was first written down in the fifth century. (The missionaries introduced the natives to that arcane skill.) There exist manuscripts dating from as far back as the eighth century, in which we find the stories the *filidh* told—tales of the Tuatha De Danann, the godlike inhabitants of the island before the Celts themselves invaded, before Time and Man.

This story Joseph Jacobs calls "the earliest Fairy Tale of modern Europe;" it was first written down twelve hundred years ago.

Conn of the Hundred Battles was indeed High King of Ireland at Tara, from A.D. 123 to 157. It is a matter of historical record that his first-born son was named Connla, but that a younger brother succeeded to the throne.

HOW CONNLA WAS CALLED AWAY

Conn of the Hundred Battles had a son, Connla Red Hair. And one day when the lad was out hunting with his father in the mountains of Usna, he saw a woman, whose dress was a wonder.

"Where do you come from?" Connla asked her.

"From the Land of the Ever Living," she answered, "where there is neither death nor sorrow, and where we are forever feasting, with no need of servants for our feasts. Our life is play without quarrel. Because our homes are under the round green hills, we are called the People of the Hills."

"Who's that talking?" shouted Conn, and he drew his blade, for although he heard her voice, no one but Connla could see the fairy woman standing there.

Then the woman answered Conn, "Your son is speaking to a maiden who is beautiful, and of a noble race. It is I who will never grow old, nor die. And because Connla Red Hair is my own true love, I am calling him away now, to the Land of Delight, where Broadag is king forever over a country without weeping or woe.

"Come away, Connla Red Hair, bright-eyed and fair of face! Come away to the place where a golden crown is waiting, where your youth and beauty will never fade, till the day of Doom!"

When all the company had heard this speech from the woman whom none could see, Conn cried to his Druid, "Help me, oh Wise Man, Song-Maker, Spell-Caster! For here is a power beyond my understanding, and strength greater than my own! A woman, invisible as air, is stealing away my darling, my royal son!"

Then the Druid began to chant a charm against the voice of the woman, until she was silent, and even Connla could see her no longer. But as she vanished before the might of the Druid's song, she threw an apple to Connla.

For the length of a month from that day, Connla went without food or drink, except for his apple. However much he ate of it, the apple was whole all the while; and all the while a terrible yearning was upon him for the fairy woman he alone had seen.

The last day of that month, Connla was with his father the king, on the Plain of Arcomin, when he saw the same woman coming to him again, and calling him by name.

"Connla, who sits on a high throne here, among Dying People, with nothing but death before you; we who have watched you day by day in your home and among your dear ones, we the Ever Living bid you away with us now to the Land of Delight."

When Conn heard that voice, he gave orders to his company. "Bring me the Druid here, quickly, for the fairy woman has the power of speech on her again!"

But then he heard the woman say, "Conn of the Hundred Battles, it is small love or honor the Druids' power has among the Fair People, for the time is coming when all their Black Magic will be scattered like darkness in the dawn."

Conn knew, none better, that his Connla Red Hair had spoken to not a soul but that woman, since he first heard her voice. Now he turned to his son and asked him, "Is it that her words have touched your heart, Connla?"

"It goes hard with me, Father," the boy answered him, "for I love my home and my people above all things, and yet, and yet . . . I feel a great longing in me, because of this woman."

Then the woman spoke again, and her speech was like singing. "That longing is like the waves of the sea, Connla Red Hair, and you

15

struggle against it even as it carries you off and away. Sail with me now, in my swift crystal ship, to Broadag's kingdom, beneath the Fairy Hill!

"And there is yet another country, beyond that, where we could be by fall of night, though the bright sun is setting here. It is an island to delight the heart, where women and girls live only."

When the woman had finished her song, Connla suddenly rushed away from his companions and leapt into her crystal ship. The king and all could only stand and watch, as he rowed away across the bright sea, toward the setting sun, until he was lost to their sight.

And Connla Red Hair was never seen again by mortal man, from that time to this.

Now, Conn of the Hundred Battles was a mortal man, an historical figure, if you like. He was of the race we call Celtic, and the language he spoke was Gaelic.

But the woman who called his son Connla away was of an older race, it seems. She was a fairy, of the people the Celts called the Sidhe (it's pronounced "shee," as in banshee, *and any Irishman or woman named Sheehan or Sheehy or Shea or O'Shea probably has fairy blood; just ask them).*

But Sidhe is only our word for them. They called themselves the Tuatha De Danaan, and they themselves were not native to Ireland, but came in great ships and conquered a race called Fir Bolgs, and before that . . .

It's, as they say, a long story and probably best told by the only person who was an eyewitness to it all, Tuan Mac Cairill.

(This version of Tuan's tale was written by the great Irish poet and novelist James Stephens.)

THE STORY OF TUAN MAC CAIRILL

Chapter I

Finnian, the Abbot of Moville, went southwards and eastwards in great haste. News had come to him in Donegal that there were yet people in his own province who believed in gods that he did not approve of, and the gods that we do not approve of are treated scurvily, even by saintly men.

He was told of a powerful gentleman who observed neither Saint's day nor Sunday.

"A powerful person!" said Finnian.

"All that," was the reply.

"We shall try this person's power," said Finnian.

"He is reputed to be a wise and hardy man," said his informant.

"We shall test his wisdom and his hardihood."

"He is," that gossip whispered, "—he is a magician."

"I will magician him!" cried Finnian angrily. "Where does that man live?"

He was informed, and he proceeded to that direction without delay.

17

In no great time he came to the stronghold of the gentleman who followed ancient ways, and he demanded admittance in order that he might preach and prove the new God, and exorcise and terrify and banish even the memory of the old one; for to a god grown old Time is as ruthless as to a beggarman grown old.

But the Ulster gentleman refused Finnian admittance.

He barricaded his house, he shuttered his windows, and in a gloom of indignation and protest he continued the practices of ten thousand years, and would not hearken to Finnian calling at the window or to Time knocking at his door.

But of those adversaries it was the first he redoubted.

Finnian loomed on him as a portent and a terror; but he had no fear of time. Indeed he was the foster-brother of Time, and so disdainful of the bitter god that he did not even disdain him; he leaped over the scythe, he dodged under it, and the sole occasions on which Time laughs is where he chances on Tuan, the son of Cairill, the son of Mauredac Red-neck.

Chapter II

Now Finnian could not abide that any person should resist both the Gospel and himself, and he proceeded to force the stronghold by peaceful but powerful methods. He fasted on the gentleman, and he did so to such purpose that he was admitted to the house; for to an hospitable heart the idea that a stranger may expire on your doorstep from sheer famine cannot be tolerated. The gentleman, however, did not give in without a struggle: he thought that when Finnian had grown sufficiently hungry he would lift the siege and take himself off to some place where he might get food. But he did not know Finnian. The great abbot sat down on a spot just beyond the door, and composed himself to all that might follow him from his action. He bent his gaze on the ground between his feet, and entered into a meditation from which he would only be released by admission or death.

The first day passed quietly.

Often the gentleman would send a servitor to spy if that deserter of the gods was still before his door, and each time the servant replied that he was still there.

"He will be gone in the morning," said the hopeful master.

On the morrow the state of siege continued, and through that day

18

the servants were sent many times to observe through spy-holes.

"Go," he would say, "and find out if the worshiper of new gods has taken himself away."

But the servants returned each time with the same information.

"The new Druid is still there," they said.

All through that day no one could leave the stronghold. And the enforced seclusion wrought on the minds of the servants, while the cessation of all work banded them together in small groups that whispered and discussed and disputed. Then these groups would disperse to peep through the spy-hole at the patient, immobile figure seated before the door, wrapped in a meditation that was timeless and unconcerned. They took fright at the spectacle, and once or twice a woman screamed hysterically, and was bundled away with a companion's hand clapped on her mouth, so that the ear of their master should not be affronted.

"He has his own troubles," they said. "It is a combat of the gods that is taking place."

So much for the women; but the men also were uneasy. They prowled up and down, tramping from the spy-hole to the kitchen, and from the kitchen to the turreted roof. And from the roof they would look down on the motionless figure below, and speculate on many things, including the staunchness of man, the qualities of their master, and even the possibility that the new gods might be as powerful as the old. From these peepings and discussions they would return languid and discouraged.

"If," said one irritable guard, "if we buzzed a spear at the persistent stranger, or if one slung at him with a jagged pebble!"

"What!" his master demanded wrathfully, "is a spear to be thrown at an unarmed stranger? And from this house?"

And he soundly cuffed that indelicate servant.

"Be at peace, all of you," he said, "for hunger has a whip, and he will drive the stranger away in the night."

The household retired to wretched beds; but for the master of the house there was no sleep. He marched his halls all night, going often to the spy-hole to see if that shadow was still in the shade, and pacing thence, tormented, preoccupied, refusing even the nose of his favourite dog as it pressed lovingly into his closed palm.

On the morrow he gave in.

19

The great door was swung wide, and two of his servants carried Finnian into the house, for the saint could no longer walk or stand upright by reason of the hunger and exposure to which he had submitted. But his frame was tough as the unconquerable spirit that dwelt within it, and in no long time he was ready for whatever might come of dispute or anathema.

Being quite re-established, he undertook the conversion of the master of the house, and the siege he laid against that notable intelligence was long spoken of among those who are interested in such things.

He had beaten the disease of Mugain; he had beaten his own pupil the great Colm Cille; he beat Tuan also, and just as the latter's door had opened to the persistent stranger, so his heart opened, and Finnian marched there to do the will of God, and his own will.

Chapter III

One day they were talking together about the majesty of God and His love, for although Tuan had now received much instruction on this subject he yet needed more, and he laid as close as a siege on Finnian as Finnian had before that laid on him. But man works outwardly and inwardly. After rest he has energy, after energy he needs repose; so, when we have given instruction for a time, we need instruction, and must receive it or the spirit faints and wisdom herself grows bitter.

Therefore Finnian said: "Tell me now about yourself, dear heart."

But Tuan was avid of information about the True God.

"No, no," he said, "the past has nothing more of interest for me, and I do not wish anything to come between my soul and its instruction; continue to teach me, dear friend and saintly father."

"I will do that," Finnian replied, "but I must first meditate deeply on you, and must know you well. Tell me your past, my beloved, for a man is his past, and is to be known by it."

But Tuan pleaded:

"Let the past be content with itself, for man needs forgetfulness as well as memory."

"My son," said Finnian, "all that has ever been done has been done for the glory of God, and to confess our good and evil deeds is part

20

of instruction; for the soul must recall its acts and abide by them, or renounce them by confession and penitence. Tell me your genealogy first, and by what descent you occupy these lands and stronghold, and then I will examine your acts and your conscience."

Tuan replied obediently:

"I am known as Tuan, son of Cairill, son of Mauredac Red-neck, and these are the hereditary lands of my father."

The saint nodded.

"I am not as well acquainted with Ulster genealogies as I should be, yet I know something of them. I am by blood a Leinsterman," he continued.

"Mine is a long pedigree," Tuan murmured.

Finnian received that information with respect and interest.

"I also," he said, "have an honourable record."

His host continued:

"I am indeed Tuan, the son of Starn, the son of Sera, who was brother to Partholon."

"But," said Finnian in bewilderment, "there is an error here, for you have recited two different genealogies.

"I do not understand this," Finnian declared roundly.

"I am now known as Tuan Mac Cairill," the other replied, "but in the days of old I was known as Tuan Mac Starn, Mac Sera."

"The brother of Partholon," the saint gasped.

"That is my pedigree," Tuan said.

"But," Finnian objected in bewilderment, "Partholon came to Ireland not long after the Flood."

"I came with him," said Tuan mildly.

The saint pushed his chair back hastily, and sat staring at his host, and as he stared the blood grew chill in his veins, and his hair crept along his scalp and stood on end.

Chapter IV

But Finnian was not one who remained long in bewilderment. He thought on the might of God and he became that might, and was tranquil.

He was one who loved God and Ireland, and to the person who could instruct him in these great themes he gave all the interest of his mind and the sympathy of his heart.

"It is a wonder you tell me, my beloved," he said. "And now you must tell me more."

"What must I tell?" asked Tuan resignedly.

"Tell me of the beginning of time in Ireland, and of the bearing of Partholon, the son of Noah's son."

"I have almost forgotten him," said Tuan. "A greatly bearded, greatly shouldered man he was. A man of sweet deeds and sweet ways."

"Continue, my love," said Finnian.

"He came to Ireland in a ship. Twenty-four men and twenty-four women came with him. But before that time no man had come to Ireland, and in the western parts of the world no human being lived or moved. As we drew on Ireland from the sea the country seemed like an unending forest. Far as the eye could reach, and in whatever direction, there were trees; and from these there came the unceasing singing of birds. Over all that land the sun shone warm and beautiful, so that to our sea-weary eyes, our wind-tormented ears, it seemed as if we were driving on Paradise.

"We landed and we heard the rumble of water going gloomily through the darkness of the forest. Following the water we came to a glade where the sun shone and where the earth was warmed, and there Partholon rested with his twenty-four couples, and made a city and a livelihood.

"There were fish in the rivers of Eire, there were animals in her coverts. Wild and shy and monstrous creatures ranged in her plains and forests. Creatures that one could see through and walk through. Long we lived in ease, and we saw new animals grow—the bear, the wolf, the badger, the deer, and the boar.

"Partholon's people increased until from twenty-four couples there came five thousand people, who lived in amity and contentment although they had no wits."

"They had no wits!" Finnian commented.

"They had no needs of wits," Tuan said.

"I have heard that the first-born were mindless," said Finnian. "Continue your story, my beloved."

"Then, sudden as a rising wind, between one night and a morning,

22

there came a sickness that bloated the stomach and purpled the skin, and on the seventh day all of the race of Partholon were dead, save one man only."

"There always escapes one man," said Finnian thoughtfully.

"And I am that man," his companion affirmed.

Tuan shaded his brow with his hand, and he remembered backwards through incredible ages to the beginning of the world and the first days of Eire. And Finnian, with his blood again running chill and his scalp crawling uneasily, stared backwards with him.

Chapter V

"Tell on, my love," Finnian murmured.

"I was alone," said Tuan. "I was so alone that my own shadow frightened me. I was so alone that the sound of a bird in flight, or the creaking of a dew-drenched bough, whipped me to cover as a rabbit is scared to his burrow.

"The creatures of the forest scented me and knew I was alone. They stole with silken pad behind my back and snarled when I faced them; the long, grey wolves with hanging tongues and staring eyes chased me to my cleft rock; there was no creature so weak but it might hunt me; there was no creature so timid but it might outface me. And so I lived for two tens of years and two years, until I knew all that a beast surmises and had forgotten all that a man had known.

"I could pad as gently as any; I could run as tirelessly. I could be invisible and patient as a wild cat crouching among leaves; I could smell danger in my sleep and leap at it with wakeful claws; I could bark and growl and clash with my teeth and tear with them."

"Tell on, my beloved," said Finnian, "you shall rest in God, dear heart."

"At the end of that time," said Tuan, "Nemed the son of Agnoman came to Ireland with a fleet of thirty-four barques, and in each barque there were thirty couple of people."

"I have heard it," said Finnian.

"My heart leaped for joy when I saw the great fleet rounding the land, and I followed them along scarped cliffs, leaping from rock to rock like a wild goat, while the ships tacked and swung seeking a harbour. There I stooped to drink at a pool, and I saw myself in the chill water.

"I saw that I was hairy and tufty and bristled as a savage boar; that I was lean as a stripped bush; that I was greyer than a badger; withered and wrinkled like an empty sack; naked as a fish; wretched as a starving crow in winter; and on my fingers and toes there were great curving claws, so that I looked like nothing that was known, like nothing that was animal or divine. And I sat by the pool weeping my loneliness and wildness and my stern old age; and I could do no more than cry and lament between the earth and sky, while the beasts that tracked me listened from behind the trees, or crouched among bushes to stare at me from their drowsy covert.

"A storm arose, and when I looked again from my tall cliff I saw that great fleet rolling as in a giant's hand. At times they were pitched against the sky and staggered aloft, spinning gustily there like wind-blown leaves. Then they were hurled from these dizzy tops to the flat, moaning gulf, to the glassy, inky horror that swirled and whirled between ten waves. At times a wave leaped howling under a ship, and with a buffet dashed it into air, and chased it upwards with thunder stroke on stroke, and followed again, close as a chasing wolf, trying with hammering on hammering to beat in the wide-wombed bottom and suck out the frightened lives through one black gape. A wave fell on a ship and sunk it down with a thrust, stern as though a whole sky had tumbled at it, and the barque did not cease to go down until it crashed and sank in the sand at the bottom of the sea.

"The night came, and with it a thousand darknesses fell from the screeching sky. Not a round-eyed creature of the night might pierce an inch of that multiplied gloom. Not a creature dared creep or stand. For a great wind stroke the world lashing its league-long whips in cracks of thunder, and singing to itself, now in a world-wide yell, now in an ear-dizzying hum and buzz; or with a long snarl and whine it hovered over the world searching for life to destroy.

"And at times, from the moaning and yelping blackness of the sea, there came a sound—thin-drawn as from millions of miles away, distinct as though uttered in the ear like a whisper of confidence—and I knew that a drowning man was calling on his God as he thrashed and was battered into silence, and that a blue-lipped woman was calling on her man as her hair whipped round her brows and she whirled about like a top.

"Around me the trees were dragged from earth with dying groans; they leaped into the air and flew like birds. Great waves whizzed from the sea; spinning across the cliffs and hurtling to the earth in monstrous clots of foam; the very rocks came trundling and sliding and grinding among the trees; and in that rage, and in that horror of blackness, I fell asleep, or I was beaten into slumber."

Chapter VI

"There I dreamed, and I saw myself changing into a stag in dream, and I felt in dream the beating of a new heart within me, and in dream I arched my neck and braced my powerful limbs.

"I awoke from the dream, and I was that which I had dreamed.

"I stood a while stamping upon a rock, with my bristling head swung high, breathing through wide nostrils all the savour of the world. For I had come marvellously from decrepitude to strength. I had writhed from the bonds of age and was young again. I smelled the turf and knew for the first time how sweet that smelled. And like lightning my moving nose sniffed all things to my heart and separated them into knowledge.

"Long I stood there, ringing my iron hoof on stone, and learning all things through my nose. Each breeze that came from the right hand or the left brought me a tale. A wind carried me the tang of wolf, and against that smell I stared and stamped. And on a wind there came the scent of my own kind, and at that I belled. Oh, loud and clear and sweet was the voice of the great stag. With what ease my lovely note went lilting. With what joy I heard the answering call. With what delight I bounded, bounded; light as a bird's plume, powerful as a storm, untiring as the sea.

"Here now was ease in ten-yard springings, with a swinging head, with the rise and fall of a swallow, with a curve and flow and urge of an otter of the sea. What a tingle dwelt about my heart! What a thrill spun to the lofty points of my antlers! How the world was new! How the sun was new! How the wind caressed me!

"With unswerving forehead and steady eye I met all that came. The old, lone wolf leaped sideways, snarling, and slunk away. The lumbering bear swung his head of hesitations and thought again; he trotted his small red eye away with him to a near-by brake. The stags of my race fled from my rocky forehead, or were pushed back and back until their legs broke under them and I trampled them to death. I was the beloved, the well known, the leader of the herd of Ireland.

25

"And at times I came back from my boundings about Eire, for the strings of my heart were drawn to Ulster; and, standing away, my wide nose took the air, while I knew with joy, with terror, that men were blown on the wind. A proud head hung to the turf then, and the tears of memory rolled from a large bright eye.

"At times I drew near, delicately, standing among thick leaves or crouched in long grown grasses, and I stared and mourned as I looked on men. For Nemed and four couples had been saved from that fierce storm, and I saw them increase and multiply until four thousand couples lived and laughed and were riotous in the sun, for the people of Nemed had small minds but great activity. They were savage fighters and hunters.

"But one time I came, drawn by that intolerable anguish of memory, and all of these people were gone: the place that knew them was silent: in the land where they had moved there was nothing of them but their bones that glinted in the sun.

"Old age came on me there. Among these bones weariness crept into my limbs. My head grew heavy, my eyes dim, my knees jerked and trembled, and there the wolves dared chase me.

"I went again to the cave that had been my home when I was an old man.

"One day I stole from the cave to snatch a mouthful of grass, for I was closely besieged by wolves. They made their rush, and I barely escaped from them. They sat beyond the cave staring at me.

"I knew their tongue. I knew all that they said to each other, and all that they said to me. But here was yet a thud left in my forehead, a deadly trample in my hoof. They did not dare come into the cave.

"'Tomorrow,' they said, 'we will tear out your throat, and gnaw on your living haunch'."

Chapter VII

"Then my soul rose to the height of Doom, and I intended all that might happen to me, and agreed to it.

"'Tomorrow,' I said, "I will go out among ye, and I will die,' and at that the wolves howled joyfully, hungrily, impatiently.

"I slept, and I saw myself changing into a boar in dream, and I felt in dream the beating of a new heart within me, and in dream I

26

stretched my powerful neck and braced my eager limbs. I awoke from my dream, and I was that which I had dreamed.

"The night wore away, the darkness lifted, the day came; and from without the cave the wolves called to me:

" 'Come out, O Skinny Stag. Come out and die.'

"And I, with joyful heart, thrust a black bristle through the hole of the cave, and when they saw that wriggling snout, those curving tusks, that red fierce eye, the wolves fled yelping, tumbling over each other, frantic with terror; and I behind them, a wild cat for leaping, a giant for strength, a devil for ferocity; a madness and gladness of lusty, unsparing life; a killer, a champion, a boar who could not be defied.

"I took the lordship of the boars of Ireland.

"Wherever I looked among my tribes I saw love and obedience; whenever I appeared among the strangers they fled away. And the wolves feared me then, and the great, grim bear went bounding on heavy paws. I charged him at the head of my troop and rolled him over and over; but it is not easy to kill the bear, so deeply is his life packed under that stinking pelt. He picked himself up and ran, and was knocked down and ran again blindly, butting into trees and stones. Not a claw did the big bear flash, not a tooth did he show, as he ran whimpering like a baby, or as he stood with my nose rammed against his mouth, snarling up into his nostrils.

"I challenged all that moved. All creatures but one. For men had again come to Ireland. Semion, the son of Stariath, with his people, from whom the men of Domnann and the Fir Bolg and the Galiuin are descended. These I did not chase, and when they chased me I fled.

"Often I would go, drawn by my memoried heart, to look at them as they moved among their fields; and I spoke to my mind in bitterness:

"When the people of Partholon were gathered in counsel my voice was heard; it was sweet to all who heard it, and the words I spoke were wise. The eyes of women brightened and softened when they looked at me. They loved to hear him when he sang who now wanders in the forest with a tusky herd."

Chapter VIII

"Old age again overtook me. Weariness stole into my limbs, and anguish dozed into my mind. I went to my Ulster cave and dreamed my dream, and I changed into a hawk.

"I left the ground. The sweet air was my kingdom, and my bright eye stared on a hundred miles. I soared, I swooped; I hung, motionless as a living stone, over the abyss; I lived in joy and slept in peace, and had my fill of the sweetness of life.

"During that time, Beothach, the son of Iarbonel the Prophet, came to Ireland with his people, and there was a great battle between his men and the children of Semion. Long I hung over that combat, seeing every spear that hurtled, every stone that whizzed from a sling, every sword that flashed up and down, and the endless glittering of the shields. And at the end I saw that the victory was with Iarbonel. And from his people the Tuatha De and the Ande came, although their origin is forgotten, and learned people, because of their excellent wisdom and intelligence, say that they came from heaven.

"These are the people of Faery. All these are the gods.

"For long, long years I was a hawk. I knew every hill and stream; every field and glen of Ireland. I knew the shape of cliffs and coasts, and how all places looked under the sun or moon. And I was still a hawk when the sons of Mil drove the Tuatha De Danann under the ground, and held Ireland against arms or wizardry; and this was the coming of men and the beginning of genealogies.

"Then I grew old, and in my Ulster cave close to the sea I dreamed my dream, and in it I became a salmon. The green tides of ocean rose over me and my dream, so that I droned in the sea and did not die, for I awoke in deep waters, and I was that which I dreamed.

"I had been a man, a stag, a boar, a bird, and now I was a fish. In all my changes I had joy and fulness of life. But in the water joy lay deeper, life pulsed deeper. For on land or air there is always something excessive hindering; as arms that swing at the sides of a man, and which the mind must remember. The stag has legs to be tucked away for sleep, and untucked for movement; and the bird has wings that must be folded and pecked and cared for. But the fish has but one piece from his nose to his tail. He is complete, single and unencumbered. He turns in one turn, and goes up and down and round in one sole movement.

"How I flew through the soft element: how I joyed in the country where there is no harshness: in the element which upholds and gives way; which caresses and lets go, and will not let you fall. For man may stumble in a furrow; the stag tumble from a cliff; the hawk, wing-weary and beaten, with darkness around him and the storm behind, may dash his brains against a tree. But the home of the salmon is his delight, and the sea guards all her creatures."

Chapter IX

"I became the king of the salmon, and with my multitudes, I ranged on the tides of the world. Green and purple distances were under me: green and gold the sunlit regions above. In these latitudes I moved through a world of amber, myself amber and gold; in those others, in a sparkle of lucent blue, I curved, lit like a living jewel: and in these again, through dusks of ebony all mazed with silver, I shot and shone, the wonder of the sea.

"I saw the monsters of the uttermost ocean go heaving by; and the long lithe brutes that are toothed to their tails; and below, where gloom dipped down on gloom, vast, livid tangles that coiled and uncoiled, and lapsed down steeps and hells of the sea where even the salmon could not go.

"I knew the sea. I knew the secret caves where ocean roars to ocean; the floods that are icy cold, from which the nose of a salmon leaps back as a sting; and the warm streams in which we rocked and dozed and were carried forward without motion. I swam on the outer-most rim of the great world, where nothing was but the sea and the sky and the salmon; where even the wind was silent, and the water was clear as clean grey rock.

"And then, far away in the sea, I remembered Ulster, and there came on me an instant, uncontrollable anguish to be there. I turned, and through days and nights I swam tirelessly, jubilantly; with terror wakening in me, too, and a whisper through my being that I must reach Ireland or die.

"I fought my way to Ulster from the sea.

"Ah, how that end of the journey was hard! A sickness was racking in every one of my bones, a languor and weariness creeping through my every fibre and muscle. The waves held me back and held me back; the soft waters seemed to have grown hard; and it was as though I were urging through a rock as I strained toward Ulster from the sea.

29

"So tired I was! I could have loosened my frame and been swept away; I could have slept and been drifted and wafted away; swinging on grey-green billows that had turned from the land and were heaving and mounting and surging to the far blue water.

"Only the unconquerable heart of the salmon could brave that end of toil. The sound of the rivers of Ireland racing down to the sea came to me in the last numb effort: the love of Ireland bore me up: the gods of the rivers trod to me in the white-curled breakers, so that I left the sea at long, long last; and I lay in sweet water in the curve of a crannied rock, exhausted, three parts dead, triumphant."

Chapter X

"Delight and strength came to me again, and now I explored all the inland ways, the great lakes of Ireland, and her swift brown rivers.

"What a joy to lie under an inch of water basking in the sun, or beneath a shady ledge to watch the small creatures that speed like lightning on the rippling top. I saw the dragon-flies flash and dart and turn, with a poise, with a speed that no other winged thing knows; I saw the hawk hover and stare and swoop; he fell like a falling stone, but he could not catch the king of the salmon: I saw the cold-eyed cat stretching along a bough level with the water eager to hook and lift the creatures of the river. And I saw men.

"They saw me also. They came to know me and look for me. They lay in wait at the waterfalls up which I leaped like a silver flash. They held out nets for me; they hid traps under leaves; they made cords of the colour of water, of the colour of weeds—but this salmon had a nose that knew how a weed felt and how a string—they drifted meat on a sightless string, but I knew of the hook; they thrust spears at me, and threw lances which they drew back again with a cord.

"Many a wound I got from men, many a sorrowful scar.

"Every beast pursued me in the waters and along the banks; the barking, black-skinned otter came after me in lust and gust and swirl; the wild cat fished for me; the hawk and the steep-winged, spear-beaked birds dived down on me, and men crept on me with nets the width of a river, so that I got no rest. My life became a ceaseless scurry and wound and escape, a burden and anguish of watchfulness—and then I was caught."

Chapter XI

"The fisherman of Cairil, the King of Ulster, took me in his net. Ah, that was a happy man when he saw me! He shouted for joy when he saw the great salmon in his net.

"I was still in the water as he hauled delicately. I was still in the water as he pulled me to the bank. My nose touched air and spun from it as from fire, and I dived with all my might against the bottom of the net, holding yet to the water, loving it, mad with terror that I must quit that loveliness. But the net held and I came up.

" 'Be quiet, King of the River,' said the fisherman; 'give in to Doom,' said he.

"I was in air, and it was as though I was in fire. The air pressed on me like a fiery mountain. It beat on my scales and scorched them. It rushed down my throat and scalded me. It weighed on me and squeezed me, so that my eyes felt as though they must burst from my head, my head as though it would leap from my body, and my body as though it would swell and expand and fly in a thousand pieces.

"The light blinded me, the heat tormented me, the dry air made me shrivel and gasp; and as he lay on the grass, the great salmon whirled his desperate nose once more to the river, and leaped, leaped, leaped, even under the mountain of air. He could leap upwards, but not forwards, and yet he leaped, for in each rise he could see the twinkling waves, the rippling and curling waters.

" 'Be at ease, O King' said the fisherman. 'Be at rest, my beloved. Let go the stream. Let the oozy marge be forgotten, and the sandy bed where the shades dance all in green and gloom, and the brown flood sings along.'

"And as he carried me to the palace, he sang a song of the river, and a song of Doom, and a song in praise of the King of the Waters.

"When the king's wife saw me she desired me. I was put over a fire and roasted, and she ate me. And when time passed, she gave birth to me, and I was her son and the son of Cairill the king. I remember warmth and darkness and movement and unseen sounds. All that happened I remember, from the time I was on the gridiron until the time I was born. I forget nothing of these things."

"And now," said Finnian, "you will be born again, for I shall baptize you into the family of the Living God."

31

＊　＊　＊　＊　＊

So far the story of Tuan, the son of Cairill.

No man knows if he died in those distant ages when Finnian was abbot of Moville, or if he still keeps his fort in Ulster, watching all things, and remembering them for the glory of God and the honour of Ireland.

Angus (The Wandering Aengus, Yeats called him) is the Irish god of love. His proper name is Oenghus Mac ind Og, and he was the son of the Fairy King and the goddess of the River Boyne.

He has played a part in many a happy—and sad—love story. It was Angus who sheltered the passionate runaways, Diarmuid and Grania, from the wrath of her husband, Finn McCool. They hid away in his home, Bruigh na Boinne, in what is now called Newgrange, County Meath. It is an acre in size, entirely underground, and fully seventeen feet from floor to wood-beamed ceiling.

Visitors—especially lovers, I suppose—are welcome there still.

This, Angus's own love story, had great consequences. Because Queen Maeve helped him in his quest, Angus took her side against Cuchulain and Ulster in the War of the Bull.

THE DREAM OF ANGUS

Angus was fast asleep one night in his bed when he saw a girl coming toward him. He thought she must surely be the most beautiful in all Ireland.

But when Angus reached out his hand, to bring her to him, she vanished away. He lay in his bed awake till morning, heartsick for the loss of her.

He got no rest that day, thinking how she had gone from him without a word spoken between them, and no food passed his lips.

That night, she appeared to him again. In her hand was a little harp, the sweetest he had ever heard, and she played it and sang him to sleep. He woke at dawn, and remembered that he still had not spoken a word to the girl, nor she to him. He would eat nothing again that day, fretting for the night to come.

In this way, a whole year passed, so that Angus grew pale and thin, and fell into a wasting sickness. But he never told a soul about the girl, so that not one of all the physicians of Ireland could say what was wrong with him.

Finally, they sent for Fingen, the king's own physician, to attend him. That one would name a man's illness from the look on his face, and could tell from the drift of chimney smoke how many were sick in the house below.

33

Fingen gazed down on Angus, then bent and whispered to him, "I think this sickness of yours goes by the name of Love-in-Vain."

"You have guessed well," said Angus. "Each night, a beautiful girl comes to me, the most beautiful girl in all Ireland. She brings with her a little harp, and she plays . . ."

"Enough!" said Fingen. "She shall be yours. Send someone now to your mother, to come and speak with you."

So Boyne, the mother of Angus, came to them, and the physician told her of her son's illness, and of its cause. "Have all Ireland searched for this girl your son has seen," he advised her, and he left Angus in her care.

And for the length of a year, she had all Ireland searched, but no trace of the girl could be found, so she sent for Fingen to come once more.

"Let his father the Dagda come and speak to his son," he instructed her. Then together they summoned the Dagda, king of the fairies, until he himself, the Lord of All Powers, was obliged to appear before them.

"Why have I been called here?" he asked, in his usual bad temper. "To speak to your son, and to help him," answered Fingen, most respectfully, "for he is lying near death for the love of a girl he saw in a dream, and who cannot be found."

"What of that?" growled the Dagda. "You know as much about such matters as I, wizard!"

"Ah, well," said Fingen sadly, "perhaps I do. And here I thought I was addressing the king of all the fairy folk of Ireland. . . ."

"That I am!" roared the Dagda.

"Well then," said the sly physician, "it would be a small thing for you to come with us over to Munster. They say that Bauve, who is chieftan of the fairies there, can be very helpful in matters such as this."

So to Munster they went, all three, and Bauve, who was chieftain over the fairy hill there, welcomed them graciously, bowing low before the Dagda, and asking how he might serve him.

"My son Angus," said the Faiy King, "has been wasting away these last two years for the love of a girl he saw in a dream. I command you to seek out this young woman, and find her for his sake."

35

"It shall be done," said Bauve, "if it takes me all of a year."

And so another twelve months passed, and they went again to Bauve's house in the fairy hill of Munster. "I have good news for you," the chieftain told them. "I went round the whole of Ireland, until I found her. The girl is at Loch Bel Dragon, in the Galtee mountains."

"Well done," said the Dagda. "Now let Angus go with you there, and we'll see if this is the same girl he saw in his dreams."

Then Angus was brought in a chariot to Bauve's house, and made welcome with a feast that lasted three days and three nights. At the end of that, Bauve said to him, "Come away with me now, and we'll see whether this is the same girl that came to you in your dream."

They journeyed far, across the plains and through high mountains, until they came to the shores of a great lake, and there they saw three times fifty young women, and the girl herself was among them; but she was taller and lovelier than them all. There was a silver chain between each two of them, but about her own throat was a necklace of silver and a chain of bright beaten gold.

"Do you see her?" asked Bauve.

"I do," whispered Angus. "What is her name?"

"She is Caer, the daughter of Ethal, who is chieftain over the fairy hills of Connacht," answered Bauve. "I have no power over her, Angus. You cannot take her with you this time."

"I know that," said Angus. "But she is the one who came to me in my dream."

Then Angus returned to his home country, and Bauve went with him. They told the Dagda and Boyne their news—that they had seen the girl, that she was beautiful as ever Angus had said, and they told her name, and her father's name.

"Well," grumbled the Dagda, "what can we do now?"

"I think," said Bauve," that the best thing to do is to go to Connacht and ask for the aid of King Aelill and Queen Maeve, for the girl is of their province."

With threescore chariots to escort him, the Dagda set out for Cruachan, the palace of Aelill and Maeve, and there he was made welcome with a great feast, so that they were eating and drinking for the length of a week. At the end of that, Aelill politely asked the Fairy King the purpose of his visit.

"My son Angus," said the Dagda, who was becoming impatient

with telling the tale, "has fallen in love with a girl of your province and become sick because of it. I have come to ask you to let the lad have her."

"We will!" said Maeve.

"Who is she?" asked Aelill.

"The daughter of Ethal," said the Dagda.

Maeve and her husband exchanged a long glance, until he spoke. "If she were ours to give, she would be given," he said. "But we have no power over her."

The Dagda stared hard into his cup of ale, and thought hard about the advice he had received from court physicians and Munster chieftains.

"What we might do," said Maeve, "is summon her father here to us."

"Let it be done," said the Dagda.

A steward of Aelill was sent to Ethal, the father of Caer, to invite him to the palace; but the man soon returned, with this message from that proud fairy: "I will not come to Aelill and Maeve, nor will I give my daughter to the son of the Dagda!"

Aelill was angry, hearing that. "He will come, nevertheless," said he, "and the heads of his warriors with him!" Then Aelill and the Dagda, together with their warriors, rode out against the Fairy Hill of Ethal. They took the hill in a terrible fight, and Ethal was brought before them, a captive. Aelill commanded him, "Give your daughter now to the son of the Dagda here, who is king over all the fairies of Ireland!" And the Dagda smiled.

"That is not in my power to do," Ethal answered, and the Dagda stopped smiling. "There is an enchantment upon my daughter," Ethal continued, "which is beyond all my magic."

"And what manner of enchantment might that be?" asked the Dagda softly, clenching his fists tight as though he were holding his temper inside them.

"The spell over her is that she must take the shape of a bird for one year, and her own true human form the next," said Ethal.

"What form is on her this year?" aske Aelill.

Now Caer's father was unwilling to betray her. "I cannot say," he answered.

"Your head from you if you cannot say!" shouted Maeve.

37

"This much I will tell you," said Ethal then. "All Hallows' Eve, she will be in the shape of a swan, at Loch Bel Dragon, and three times fifty swans with her, for she told me as much herself."

Then peace was made between them, the mortal king and queen and the fairy chieftain, and the Dagda bade farewell to all of them, and returned to his home, where he told his son, "Go you to Loch Bel Dragon upon All Hallows' Eve, and call her to you from the water."

When it was down in the autumn, Angus went again to the mountain lake, and there he saw three times fifty white birds, linked two by two with the silver chains around their necks. He stood on the shore, in his human form, and called the girl to him. "Come and speak to me, Caer!"

"Who calls me?" came the answer.

"Angus calls you."

"I will go to you," she said, "if you swear by your honor that I can come back to the water again."

"My word upon it," said he.

So she went to him, a tall white swan with a necklace of silver and a chain of bright beaten gold about her neck. He held her fast in his arms, and took upon himself the shape of a swan; and, that his word might not be broken, they went together into the loch, and around it three times, swimming.

Then they spread their wings and rose up over the water, two graceful white birds, linked together by a golden chain, and they flew away to his own country.

So sweet was the music they made in their flight that the mortals below who heard it fell smiling to sleep for three days and three nights.

And Caer stayed with Angus forever after.

When the Tuatha De Danann (the Irish call them the Sidhe, but the rest of the world calls them fairies) came "through the air and the high air" into Ireland, they tried to live in peace with the native Fir Bolg people.

But because of the love of Midhir for Etain, the truce was broken, and the Fir Bolgs were doomed. Once, they were giants. Soon, they were to be Little People—the leprechauns, some say, are scattered and solitary remnants of the tribe.

But when the story of Midhir and Etain begins, the Sidhe, and their king the Dagda, are sharing the land with the Fir Bolg and their king, Eochaid.

The tale of Midhir and Etain has been told and retold. Fiona Macleod made a play of it, called The Immortal Hour, *and Michael MacLiammor modernized it in* The Stars Are Walking. *This version (slightly edited) is taken from Lady Augusta Gregory's wonderful book,* Gods & Fighting Men.

MIDHIR AND ETAIN

After a while Midhir took Etain to be his wife. And there was great jealousy on Fuamach, the wife he had before, when she saw the love that Midhir gave to Etain, and she called to the Druid, to help her, and he put spells on Etain so that Fuamach was able to drive her away.

And when she was driven out, Angus Og, son of the Dagda, took her into his keeping; and when Midhir asked her back, he would not give her up, but he brought her about with him to every place he went. And wherever they rested, he made a sunny house for her, and put sweet-smelling flowers in it, and he made invisible walls about it, that no one could see through and that could not be seen.

But when news came to Fuamach that Etain was so well cared for by Angus, anger and jealousy came on her again, and she searched her mind for a way to destroy Etain altogether.

And it is what she did: she persuaded Midhir and Angus to go out and meet one another and to make peace, for there had been a quarrel between them ever since the time Etain was sent away. And when Angus was away, Fuamach went and found Etain there, in her sunny house. And she turned her with Druid spells into a fly, and then she sent a blast of wind into the house, that swept her away through the window.

But as to Midhir and Angus, they waited a while for Fuamach to come and join them. And when she did not come they were uneasy in their minds, and Angus hurried back. When he found the sunny house empty, he went in search of Fuamach, and it was along with the Druid he found her, and he struck her head off there and then.

And for seven years Etain was blown to and fro through Ireland in great misery. And at last she came to the house of Etar, of Inver Cechmaine, where there was a feast going on, and she fell from a beam of the roof into the golden cup that was beside Etar's wife. And Etar's wife drank her down with the wine, and at the end of nine months she was born again as Etar's daughter.

And she had the same name as before, Etain; and she was reared as a king's daughter, and there were fifty young girls, daughters of princes, brought up with her to keep her company.

And it happened one day Etain and all the rest of the young girls were out bathing in the bay at Inver Cechmaine, and they saw from the water a man, with very high looks, coming towards them over the plain, and he riding a bay horse with mane and tail curled. A long green cloak he had on him, and a shirt woven with threads of red gold, and a brooch of gold that reached across to his shoulders on each side. And he had on his back a shield of silver with a rim of gold and a boss of gold, and in his hand a sharp-pointed spear covered with rings of gold from heel to socket. Fair yellow hair he had, coming over his forehead, and it bound with a golden band to keep it from loosening.

And when he came near them he got down from his horse, and sat down on the bank, and this is what he said:

"It is here Etain is today, at the Mount of Fair Women. It is among little children is her life on the strand of Inver Cechmaine.

"Many great battles will happen for your sake to Eochaid of Midhe; destruction will fall upon the Sidhe, and war on thousands of men."

And when he had said that, he vanished, and no one knew where he went. And they did not know the man that had come to them was Midhir.

And when Etain was grown to be a beautiful young woman, she

was seen by Eochaid Feidlech, High King of Ireland, and this is the way that happened.

He was going one time over the fair green of Bri Leith, and he saw at the side of a well a woman, with a bright comb of gold and silver, and she washing in a silver basin having four golden birds on it, and little bright purple stones set in the rim of the basin. A beautiful purple cloak she had, and silver fringes to it, and a gold brooch; and she had on her a dress of green silk with a long hood, embroidered in red gold, and wonderful clasps of gold and silver on her breasts and on her shoulder. The sunlight was falling on her, so that the gold and the green silk were shining out. Two plaits of hair she had, four locks in each plait, and a bead at the point of every lock, and the colour of her hair was like yellow flags in summer, or like red gold after it is rubbed.

There she was, letting down her hair to wash it, and her arms out through the sleeve-holes of her shift. Her soft hands were as white as the snow of a single night, and her eyes as blue as any blue flower, and her lips as red as the berries of the rowan-tree, and her body as white as the foam of a wave. The bright light of the moon was in her face, the highness of pride in her eyebrows, a dimple of delight in each of her cheeks, the light of wooing in her eyes, and when she walked she had a step that was steady and even like the walk of a queen.

And Eochaid sent his people to bring her to him, and he asked her name, and she told him her name was Etain, daughter of Etar, king of the Riders of the Sidhe. And Eochaid gave her his love, and he paid the bride-price, and brought her home to Tara as his wife, and there was a great welcome before her there.

It was a good while after that, there was a great fair held at Tara, and Etain was out on the green looking at the games and the races. And she saw a rider coming towards her, but no one could see him but herself; and when he came near she saw he had the same appearance as the man that came and spoke with her and her young girls the times they were out in the sea at Inver Cechmaine. And when he came up to her he began to sing words to her that no one could hear but herself. And this is what he said:

"O beautiful woman, will you come with me to the wonderful country that is mine? It is pleasant to be looking at the people there, beautiful people without any blemish; their hair is of the colour of the flag-flower, their fair body is as white as snow, the colour of the foxglove is on every cheek. The young never grow old there; the fields and the flowers are as pleasant to be looking at as the blackbird's eggs; warm, sweet streams of mead and of wine flow through that country; there is no care and no sorrow on any person; we see others, but we ourselves are not seen.

"Though the plains of Ireland are beautiful, it is little you would think of them after our great plain; though the ale of Ireland is heady, the ale of the great country is still more heady. O beautiful woman, if you come to my proud people it is the flesh of pigs newly killed I will give you for food; it is ale and new milk I will give you for drink; it is feasting you will have with me there; it is a crown of gold you will have upon your hair, O beautiful woman!

"And will you come there with me, Etain?" he said. But Etain said she would not leave Eochaid the High King. "Will you come if Eochaid gives you leave?" Midhir said then. "I will do that," said Etain.

One day, after that time, Eochaid the High King was looking out from his palace at Tara, and he saw a strange man coming across the plain. Yellow hair he had, and eyes blue and shining like the flame of a candle, and purple dress on him, and in his hand a five-pronged spear and a shield having gold knobs on it.

He came up to the king, and the king bade him welcome. "Who are you yourself?" the king said; "and what are you come for, for you are a stranger to me?" "If I am a stranger to you, you are no stranger to me, for I have known you this long time," said the strange man. "What is your name?" said the king. "It is nothing very great," said he; "I am called Midhir." "What is it brings you here?" said Eochaid. "I am come to play a game of chess with you," said the stranger. "Are you a good player?" said the king. "A trial will tell you that," said Midhir. "The chess-board is in the queen's house, and she is in her sleep at this time," said Eochaid. "That is not matter," said Midhir, "for I have with me a chess-board, and it made of silver, and precious stones shining in every corner of it." And then he brought out the chessmen, and they made of gold, from a bag that was of shining gold threads.

"Let us play now," said Midhir. "I will not play without a stake," said the king. "What stake shall we play for?" said Midhir. "We can settle that after the game is over," said the king.

They played together then, and Midhir was beaten, and this is what the king asked of him, fifty brown horses to be given to him. And then they played the second time, and Midhir was beaten again, and this time the king gave him four hard things to do: to make a road over Moin Lamraide, and to clear Midhe of stones, and to cover the district of Tethra with rushes, and the district of Darbrech with trees.

So Midhir brought his people to do those things, and it is hard work they had doing them. And Eochaid used to be out watching them, and he took notice that when the men of the Sidhe yoked their oxen, it was by the neck and the shoulder they used to yoke them, and not by the forehead and the head. And it was after Eochaid taught his people to yoke them that way, he was given the name of Eochaid Airem, that is, of the Plough.

And when all was done, Midhir came to Eochaid again, looking thin and wasted enough with the dint of the hard work he had been doing, and he asked Eochaid to play the third game with him. Eochaid agreed, and it was settled as before, the stake to be settled by the winner. It was Midhir won the game that time, and when the king asked him what he wanted, "It is Etain, your wife, I want," said he. "I will not give her to you," said the king. "All I will ask then," said Midhir, "is to put my arms about her and to kiss her once." "You may do that," said the king, "if you will wait to the end of a month." So Midhir agreed to that, and went away for that time.

At the end of the month he came back again, and stood in the great hall at Tara, and no one had ever seen him look so comely as he did that night. And Eochaid had all his best fighting men gathered in the hall, and he shut all the doors of the palace when he saw Midhir come in, for fear he would try to bring away Etain by force.

"I am come to be paid what is due to me," said Midhir. "I have not been thinking of it up to this time," said Eochaid, and there was anger on him. "You promised me Etain, your wife," said Midhir. The redness of shame came on Etain when she heard that, but Midhir said, "Let there be no shame on you, Etain, for it is through the length of a year I have been asking your love and I have offered you every sort of treasure and riches, and you refused to come to me till such a time as your husband would give you leave." "It is true I said that," said Etain. "I will go if Eochaid gives me up to you." "I will not give you up," said Eochaid; "I will let him do no more than put his arms about you in this place, as was promised him." "I will do that," said Midhir.

With that he took his sword in his left hand, and he took Etain in his right arm and kissed her. All the armed men in the house made a rush at him then, but he rose up through the roof bringing Etain with him, and when they rushed out of the house to follow him, all they could see were two swans high up in the air, linked together by a chain of gold.

There was great anger on Eochaid then, and he went and searched all through Ireland, but there were no tidings of them to be had, for they were in the houses of the Sidhe.

It was to the house of Angus on the Boyne they went first, and after they had stopped there a while they went to a hill of the Sidhe in Connacht.

Then they went to Leith; and Etain's daughter Esa came to them there, and she brought a hundred of every sort of cattle with her, and Midhir fostered her for seven years. And all through that time Eochaid the High King was making a search for them.

But at last Codal of the Withered Breast took four rods of yew and wrote Oghams on them, and through them and through his enchantments he found out that Etain was with Midhir in Leith.

So Eochaid went there, and made an attack on the place, and he was for nine years besieging it, and Midhir was driving him away. And then his people began digging through the hill; and when they were getting near to where Etain was, Midhir sent three times twenty beautiful women, having all of them the appearance of Etain, and he bade the king choose her out from among them. And the first he chose was his own daughter Esa. But then Etain called to him, and he knew her, and he brought her home to Tara.

But there was great anger on Midhir and his people because of their hill being attacked and dug into. And it was in revenge for that insult they brought Conaire, High King of Ireland, that was grandson of Eochaid and of Etain, to his death afterwards at Da Derga's Inn.

Cormac, son of Art the lonely, grandson of Conn of the Hundred
Battles, was the greatest of ancient Ireland's High Kings. His was a
golden reign and according to the Book of Ballymote, *"The world was*
replete with all that was good in his time: the food and the fat of the
land, and the fish of the sea were in abundance. There were neither
woundings nor robberies, but everyone enjoyed his own, in peace."

Cormac had all the attributes of the perfect king. In his youth, he
was a shepherd. He built the magnificent palace at Tara. He was wise in
judgment, and generous; he was a lawmaker, warrior, and poet; and
after his death (in A.D. *267) it was natural for his subjects to ascribe his*
power and glory to fairy influence. After all, wasn't it his own uncle,
Connla Red Hair, who was called away by the fairy maiden?

(Manannan, the fairy king Cormac meets in this tale, is the sea
god of the Celts. They say that the flying white foam of the waves of
the ocean is the manes of his mighty horses as they gallop and
plunge.)

HOW CORMAC MAC ART WENT TO FAIRY

One day, Cormac saw a youth upon the green having in his hand a glittering fairy branch with nine apples of red. And whensoever the branch was shaken, wounded men and women enfeebled by illness would be lulled to sleep by the sound of the very sweet fairy music which those apples uttered, nor could any one upon earth bear in mind any want, woe, or weariness of soul when that branch was shaken for him.

"Is that branch thy own?" said Cormac.

"It is indeed mine."

"Wouldst thou sell it? and what wouldst thou require for it?"

"Will you give me what I ask?" said the youth.

The king promised, and the youth then claimed his wife, his daughter, and his son. Sorrowful of heart was the king; heaviness of heart filled his wife and children when they learned that they must part from him. But Cormac shook the branch amongst them, and when they heard the soft, sweet music of the branch they forgot all care and sorrow and went forth to meet the youth, and he and they took their departure and were seen no more. Loud cries of weeping and mourning were made throughout Erin when this was known; but Cormac

46

shook the branch so that there was no longer any grief or heaviness of heart upon any one.

After a year Cormac said: "It is a year to-day since my wife, my son, and my daughter were taken from me. I will follow them by the same path that they took."

Cormac went off, and a dark magical mist rose about him, and he chanced to come upon a wonderful marvelous plain. Many horsemen were there, busy thatching a house with the feathers of foreign birds; when one side was thatched they would go and seek more, and when they returned not a feather was on the roof. Cormac gazed at them for a while and then went forward.

Again, he saw a youth dragging up trees to make a fire; but before he could find a second tree the first one would be burnt, and it seemed to Cormac that his labor would never end.

Cormac journeyed onwards until he saw three immense wells on the border of the plain, and on each well was a head. From out the mouth of the first head there flowed two streams, and into it there flowed one; the second head had a stream flowing out of and another stream into its mouth, whilst three streams were flowing from the mouth of the third head. Great wonder seized Cormac, and he said: "I will stay and gaze upon these wells, for I should find no man to tell me your story." Then he set onwards till he came to a house in the middle of a field. He entered and greeted the inmates. There sat within a tall couple clad in many-hued garments, and they greeted the king, and bade him welcome for the night.

Then the wife bade her husband seek food, and he arose and returned with a huge wild boar upon his back and a log in his hand. He cast down the swine and the log upon the floor and said: "There is meat; cook it for yourselves."

"How can I do that?" said Cormac.

"I will teach you," said the man. "Split this great log, make four pieces of it, and make four quarters of the hog; put a log under each quarter; tell a true story, and the meat will be cooked."

"Tell the first story yourself," said Cormac.

"Seven pigs I have of the same kind as the one I brought, and I could feed the world with them. For if a pig is killed I have but to put its bones into the sty again, and it will be found alive the next morning."

The story was true, and a quarter of the pig was cooked.

Then Cormac begged the woman of the house to tell a story.

"I have seven white cows, and they fill seven cauldrons with milk every day, and I give my word that they yield as much milk as would satisfy the men of the whole world if they were out on yonder plain drinking it."

That story was true, and a second quarter of the pig was cooked.

Cormac was bidden now to tell a story for his quarter, and he told how he was upon a search for his wife, his son, and his daughter that had been borne away from him a year before by a youth with a fairy branch.

"If what thou says be true," said the man of the house, "thou art indeed Cormac, son of Art, son of Conn of the Hundred Battles."

"Truly I am," quoth Cormac.

That story was true, and a third quarter of the pig was cooked.

"Eat thy meal now," said the man of the house.

"I never ate before," said Cormac, "having only two people in my company."

"Wouldst thou eat it with three others?"

"If they were dear to me, I would," said Cormac.

Then the door opened, and there entered the wife and children of Cormac: great was his joy and his exultation.

Then Manannan Mac Lir, lord of the fairy cavalcade, appeared before him in his own true form, and said thus:

"I it was, Cormac, who bore away these three from thee. I it was who gave thee this branch, all that I might bring thee here. Eat now and drink."

"I would do so," said Cormac, "could I learn the meaning of the wonders I saw today."

"Thou shalt learn them," said Manannan. "The horsemen thatching the roof with feathers are a likeness of people who go forth into the world to seek riches and fortune; when they return, their houses are bare, and so they go on forever. The young man dragging up the trees to make a fire is a likeness of those who labor for others; much trouble they have, but they never warm themselves at the fire. The three heads in the wells are three kinds of men. Some there are who give freely

48

when they get freely; some who give freely though they get little; some who get much and give little and they are the worst of the three, Cormac," said Manannan.

After that Cormac and his wife and his children sat down, and a tablecloth was spread before them.

"That is a very precious thing before thee," said Manannan; "There is no food however delicate that shall be asked of it but it shall be had without doubt."

"That is well," quoth Cormac.

After that Manannan thrust his hand into his girdle and brought out a goblet and set it upon his palm. "This cup has this virtue," said he, "that when a false story is told before it, it makes four pieces of it, and when a true story is related it is made whole again."

"Those are very precious things you have, Manannan," said the king.

"They shall all be thine," said Manannan; "the goblet, the branch, and the tablecloth."

Then they ate their meal, and that meal was good, for they could not think of any meat but they got it upon the tablecloth, nor of any drink but they got it in the cup. Great thanks did they give to Manannan.

When they had eaten their meal a couch was prepared for them and they lay down to slumber and sweet sleep.

Where they rose on the morrow morn was in Tara of the kings, and by their side were tablecloth, cup, and branch.

Thus did Cormac fare at the court of Manannan, and this is how he got the fairy branch.

The missionaries who carried Christianity to the ends of Europe were usually both clever and generous-spirited enough to respect local beliefs. Was there a spring with resident water-nymph on the neighborhood? Certainly, they said. That's Saint (Somebody)'s Well! Was there a nature god in the forest nearby, a mischievous fellow with horned brow and cloven hoofs? They did not deny Pan his existence or power—but they gave him another name, and new responsibilities.

After Ireland was converted, many of the high deeds of the old heroes were ascribed to saints. And as for the Sidhe, the fairy folk in the water, in the air, beneath the hills—what would they be but fallen angels?

Here is one version of the story of Angelic Rebellion and Fairy Origin—quite believable, to any one once forbidden to cross the threshold into that dark, silent chamber of polished oak and lace doilies: the parlor . . . especially a parlor like my Grandma's, dominated by a big, framed, reproduction of a Raphael madonna . . . .

FALLEN ANGELS

Before there was Christian or Jew, before there was Adam or Eve or anyone at all living in Ireland or the rest of the world, there was a war in Heaven. This is what happened.

God the Father had a parlor, and no angel had leave to go into it, not even Lucifer, who was God's favorite, and the chief of the angels. But Lucifer was a proud one, and one day he made up his mind he'd have a look into God's parlor, to see what was in it. So he did that, and what he saw was, over the mantlepiece a picture of the Blessed Virgin, the Holy Mother of God, that wouldn't be coming into the world for thousands of years!

That's what started the war in Heaven—when God, who knows all things, found out what Lucifer had done. Half of creation took God's side in the war, and the rest of them were for Lucifer.

Back in those times, everything could talk, the sun and the moon and all. The sun was for God, and when the war was won, it was left shining bright as before. But the moon backed Lucifer's faction, and was turned into a dull and changeable light, that will be always shrinking down to the size of a silken thread, then growing to its fullness, and shrinking again.

The sea came out for Lucifer, as well. Before that time, the sea was settled and steady; but to punish it, God set it to tossing and heaving, ebbing away six hours, then six hours flowing in to strike itself against the rocks.

The bad angels that were on the side of Lucifer were thrown out of Heaven, and for a long time there were angels falling as thick as a storm of snow, until Saint Michael the archangel was afraid that Heaven would be empty entirely, and spoke to God about it.

God said, "Close the gates, then. Those that are in are in, and those that are out are out. And let every angel remain where he is, till the Day of Judgment!"

Some angels had fallen into the sea, and there they live to this day, in palaces beneath the waves. Some had managed to land on their feet, and it's they who still go on top of the ground and under it, the people of the hills, the fairy folk. Those that were not done falling through the sky are up there still, blown about by every gust of wind, wailing and whispering. Those are the Powers of the Air.

As for Lucifer, we call him the devil now, because he and the worst of his followers fell straight down through the earth into hell. God grant they stay there.

II. HIGH
DEEDS

High Deeds

Many and many a son of Conn, the Hundred Fighter,
  In the red earth lies at rest;
Many a blue eye of Clan Colman the turf covers;
  Many a swan-white breast.

Angus of Gillan
"The Dead at Clonmacnois"
(trans. Rolleston)

There was a sufficiency of kings in ancient Erin; every Irish person who claims to be of royal descent might well be speaking the truth.

Scholars guess at the century in which the Gaels came to Ireland; it was sometime between 1000 and 300 B.C. All are agreed upon the *day*—May 1, the Druidic feast of Beltane.

Dazzled by what Standish O'Grady calls "a blaze of Bardic light," we read of a thousand kings, and their deeds and their wisdom and their laws, their battles upon land and sea . . . until, at the time of Christ, Conaire Mor is High King over Ireland, and Conor Mac Nessa king of the province of Ulster.

It is from this period that the first great cycle of tales comes to us—the heroic saga of a war between all the other kings (and queens) of Ireland and Conor's Red Branch knights of Ulster, led by the legendary Cuchulain.

By a kind of mad Irish irony, Ulster remains outside the Republic of Ireland to this day, and a statue of the dying warrior Cuchulain marks the spot, in Dublin, where the 1916 war of independence from Britain began.

Three centuries (and another thousand or so kings) later, Cormac Mac Art was High King at Tara, and under him served Finn McCool, and his troops, the Fianna. The many stories of Finn's adventures depict him as a less godlike hero than Cuchulain—Finn seems part Paul Bunyan and part Robin Hood, a natural leader, a fierce and skillful warrior, quick to anger, a sentimental lover, and a proud father, and, even in his time, something of an anachronism—the archetypal Irish cop.

The story of Cuchulain, called in Irish *Tain bo Cuailnge*, has been translated many times into English—most recently, and beautifully, by Thomas Kinsella.

Lady Augusta Gregory's *Gods and Fighting Men* contains the most complete retelling of the Finn saga; but stories of Finn may be found in collections by Rolleston, Curtin, others . . . and wherever, in Ireland, tall tales are still told.

When the race of mortal men (called Milesians or, after the Gaelic tongue they spoke, Gaels) came to Ireland, they met the host of the Sidhe in the terrible battle of Taillte. At the end of the long fight, so the story goes, the two great nations parleyed, and agreed to share the land equally. They left the terms of the division to the judgment of Amergin, the poet of the Gaels.

He dictated that his people would live in Erin above the ground, and the Sidhe below it; thus were the fairies condemned to live forever beneath the hills and lakes. (It might well be the result of fairy anger at this trick that the mortal Irish have never since had much luck with truces and boundaries, so that their country remains divided to this day.)

Tain Bo Culaigne, the heroic saga which Yeats called "the Irish Iliad," concerns a border war between the Gaels of Ulster and the forces of the rest of Ireland in the first century A.D.—*five hundred years after anthropologists believe the Gaelic-speaking Celts arrived in Ireland.*

The hero of the Tain *is Cuchulain, and it is, in the main, the tale of his deeds and death; but its most famous chapter describes an incident that began the war, and altered its alliances. It is the tale of love and treachery about the king of Ulster, Conor Mac Nessa, and the woman known as Deirdre of the Sorrows.*

J. M. Synge made a great drama of it; James Stephens a wonderful novel. This version is taken from Rosemary Suthcliffe's book, Hound of Ulster.

DEIRDRE AND THE SONS OF USNA

Now when Cuchulain and Emer had been together a few years in the sunny house that he had built at Dun Dealgan, a great sorrow and the shadow of a great threat fell upon Ulster. But the beginning of that wild story was long before, in the year that Cuchulain first went to the Boys' House.

In that year a certain Ulster chieftain called Felim made a great feast for the King and the Red Branch Warriors. And when the feasting was at its height, and the Greek wine was going round and the harp song shimmering through the hall, word was brought to Felim from the women's quarters that his wife had borne him a daughter.

The warriors sprang to their feet to drink health and happiness upon the bairn, and then the King, half laughing, bade Cathbad, who was with him to foretell the babe's fortune and make it a bright one. Cathbad went to the door of the hall and stood for a long while gazing up at the summer stars that were big and pollen-soft in the sky, and when he came back into the torchlight there was shadow in his face, and for a while he would not answer when they asked him the meaning of it. But at last he said, 'Call her Deirdre, for that name has the sound of sorrow, and sorrow will by her to all Ulster. Bright-haired she will be, a flame of beauty; warriors will go into exile for her sake, and many shall fight and die because of her, yet in the end she shall lie in a little grave apart by herself, and better it would be that she had never been born.'

Then the warriors would have had the babe killed there and then, and even Felim, standing grey-faced among them, had nothing to say against it; but Conor Mac Nessa, his own Queen having died a while since in bearing Follaman their youngest son, had another thought, and he said, 'Ach now, there shall be no slaying, for clearly this fate that Cathbad reads in the stars can only mean that some chieftain of another province or even maybe of the Islands or the Pict Lands over the water will take her for his wife and for some cause that has to do with her, will make war on us. Therefore, she shall grow up in some place where no man may set eyes on her, and when she is of age to marry, then I myself will take her for Queen. In that way the doom will be averted, for no harm can come to Ulster through her marriage to me.'

So Conor Mac Nessa took charge of the child, and gave her to Levarcham his old nurse who was one of the wisest women in all Emain Macha. And in a hidden glen of Slieve Gallion he had a little house built, with a roof of green sods so that above ground it would look no more than one of the little green hillocks of the Sidhe, and a turf wall ringing it round, and a garden with apple trees for shade and fruit and pleasure. And there he set the two of them, to have no more sight of men, save that once a year his own most trusted warriors should bring them supplies of food and clothing, until the child was fifteen and ready to become his Queen.

So in the little secret homestead with her foster mother, Deirdre grew up from a baby into a child and from a child into a maiden, knowing no world beyond the glen, and seeing no man in all that time, for every year when the warriors came, Levarcham would shut her within doors until they were gone again. Every year the King would send her some gift, a silver rattle hung with tiny bells of green glass, a coral-footed dove in a wicker cage, a length of wonderfully patterned silk that had come in a ship from half the world away. 'What *is* a ship?' said Deirdre to her foster mother, 'and how far is half the world away? Could I get there if I set out very early in the morning and walked all day until the first stars came out?' And at that, Levarcham grew anxious, knowing that her charge was beginning to wonder about the world beyond the glen.

In the year that she was fourteen, her gift was a string of yellow amber that smelled fragrant as a flower when she warmed it between her hands, and that year the King brought it himself, and came with it into the house under the sheltering turf. And so for the first time, he saw Deirdre, and he with the first gray hairs already in his beard. And sorrow upon it, from that moment he gave her his heart's love, and she could never be free of it again.

That was in the summer, and before the cuckoo was gone, and before the last scarlet leaves fell from the wild cherry trees, and before the first snow came, the King returned to the glen for another sight of Deirdre. She knew that she was to be his Queen, but 'twas little enough that meant to her for good or ill, for it was a thing that belonged to the outside world, and the outside world as yet seemed very far away.

And then one winter night the outside world came to her threshold.

A wild night it was, with the wind roaring up through the woods and the sleety rain of it hushing across the turf roof, and Deirdre was sitting at old Levarcham's feet, spinning saffron wool by the light of the burning peats, when she thought she heard a strange cry, mingled with the voices of the storm, and lifted her head to listen. 'What was that, my Mother?'

'Only a bird calling to its mate through the storm. Nothing that need concern you,' said Levarcham.

But the cry came again, nearer now, and Deirdre said, 'It sounded like a human voice—and the voice of one in sore trouble.'

'It is only the wild geese flying over. Bide by the fire and go on spinning.'

And then between gust and gust of the wind there came a fumbling and a thumping against the timbers of the small strong door, and the voice cried, 'Let me in! In the name of the sun and the moon let me in!'

And heedless of the old woman crying out to stop her, Deirdre leapt up and ran to unbar and lift the rowan-wood pin; and the door swung open and the wind and rain leapt in upon her, and with the wind and the rain, a man stumbled into the house place, and his sodden cloak like spread wings about him, as though he were indeed some great storm-driven bird.

He aided Deirdre to force shut the door. And as he came into the firelight that shone on his rain-drenched hair that was black as a crow's wing and on his face, and on the great height of him, Levarcham took one look at him and said, 'Naisi, Son of Usna, it is not the time to be bringing up the year's supplies. You have no right in this place.'

'Myself not being the King,' Naisi said, and let his sodden cloak fall from his shoulders, though indeed he was as wet within it as without. 'A storm-driven man has a right to any shelter that opens to him.'

'And shall we have your brothers at the door next? Seldom it is that you three are apart!'

'We have been hunting together, but Ardan and Ainle turned homward before I did,' said the tall man, and swayed. 'Give me leave to sit by your fire until the storm sinks, for I have been lost and wandering a long while until I saw your light and—it is weary I am.'

'Ach well, if you tell no man that you have been here, there'll be no harm done, maybe,' said Levarcham. 'Sit, then, and eat and drink while you're here, for by the looks of you, if I turn you away now, the Red Branch will be one fewer by morning.'

So Naisi sank down with a sigh upon the piled sheepskins, almost into the warm peat ash, and sat there with hanging head, the sodden hunting-leathers steaming upon him. Deirdre brought barley bread, and curd from their little black cow, and a cup of pale Greek wine, and set all beside him. He had been careful until then not to look at her, but when she gave him the cup into his hands he looked up to thank her; and having looked, could not look away again. And Deirdre could not look away either.

And Levarcham, watching both of them out of her small bright eyes, while she went on with Deirdre's abandoned spinning, saw how it was with them, and how the blood came back into Naisi's face that had been grey as a skull, and how the girl's face answered his, and thought to herself, 'Trouble! Grief upon me! I see such trouble coming, for there's no gray in *his* beard, and she with all the candles lit behind her eyes for him! I should have turned him away to die in the storm.' But there was a little smile on her, all the same, for despite her loyalty to Conor Mac Nessa who had been her nursling, she had felt it always a sad thing that Deirdre should be wed to the King who was old enough to have fathered her.

After that, King Conor was not the only one to come visiting Deirdre, for again and again Naisi would come to speak with her, and Levarcham knew that she should tell this to the King, but the time went by and the time went by and she listened to Deirdre's pleading and did not tell him.

Then one evening when the wind blew over the shoulder of Slieve Gallion from the south and the first cold smell of spring was in the air, Deirdre said to Naisi when it was time for him to go, 'Let you take me with you, and not leave me to be Queen beside a King that has grey hairs in his beard.'

And Naisi groaned, 'How can I do as you ask? I that am one of the King's own bodyguard, his hearth companion?'

And he went away, vowing in his heart that he would come no more to the turf house in the hidden glen. But always he came again, and always Deirdre would plead, 'Naisi, Naisi, take me away with you, it is you that I love. I have given no troth to the King, for none has ever been asked of me, and it is yours that I am.'

For a long while he held out against her, and against his own heart. But at last, when the apple trees behind the house were white with blossom, and Deirdre's wedding to the King no more than a few weeks away, the time came when he could hold out no longer. And he said, 'So be it then, bird-of-my-heart; there are other lands across the sea and other kings to serve. For your sake I will live disgraced and die dishonoured, and not think the price too high to pay, if you love me, Deirdre.'

In the darkness of the next night he came with horses, and with Ardan and Ainle his brothers; and they carried off both Deirdre and Levarcham, for the old woman said, 'Grief upon me! I have done ill for your sakes, and let you not leave me now to the King's wrath!'

They fled to the coast and took ship for Scotland, and there Naisi and his brothers took service with the Pictish King. But after a while the King cast his looks too eagerly in Deirdre's direction, and they knew that the time had come to be moving on again.

After that they wandered for a long while, until they came at last to Glen Etive, and there they built a little huddle of turf bothies on the loch shore, and the men hunted and Deirdre and the old nurse cooked for them and spun and wove the wool of their few mountain sheep; and so the years went by.

And in all those years, three, maybe, or four, Conor Mac Nessa made no sign, but sat in his palace at Emain Macha, and did not forget. And from time to time some ragged herdsman or wandering harper would pass through Glen Etive and beg shelter for the night, and afterwards return to Conor the King and tell him all that there was to tell of Deirdre and the sons of Usna—and they thinking themselves safe hidden all the while.

At last it seemed to the King, from the things told him by his spies, that the sons of Usna were growing restless in their solitudes; their thoughts turning back, maybe, to the life in a king's hall, and the feasting and the fighting to which they had been bred. Then he sent for Conall of the Victories, and Cuchulain, and old Fergus Mac Roy, and said to them, 'It is in my mind that the sons of Usna have served long enough in exile, and the time comes to call them home.'

'In friendship?' said Cuchulain, for he had never judged his kinsman one who would easily forgive a wrong, even after so long time.

'In friendship,' said the King. 'I had a fool's fondness for the girl, but that is over long since. More it means to me to have the young men of my bodyguard about me. Therefore, one of you three shall go to Glen Etive, and tell them that the past is past, and bring them again to Emain Macha.'

'And which of us three?' said Conall.

And the King considered, turning his frowning gaze from one to the other. 'Conall, what would you do if I were to choose you, and harm came to them through me, after all?'

And Conall returned his gaze as frowningly. 'I should know how to avenge them, and my own honour that would die dead with them.'

'That sounds like a threat,' said the King, 'but it makes no matter, since the question is but an empty one.' and he turned to Cuchulain.

'I can answer only as Conall has answered,' Cuchulain said, 'but I think that after the revenge was over, men would no longer call me the Hound of Ulster but the Wolf of Ulster.' And he looked long and hard into the King's eyes. 'Therefore, it is as well, I think, that it is not myself that you will be sending to bring home the sons of Usna.'

'No, it is not yourself, but Fergus Mac Roy, that I shall send,' said Conor the King. And Fergus, who was no fool in the general way of things, was so filled with gladness—for he loved Naisi and his brothers almost as much as he did Cuchulain, as much as he loved his own sons, and his heart had wearied for them in their exile—that he lost his judgment and he did not see the look that Cuchulain had turned upon the King.

So Fergus went down to the coast and took ship for Scotland and at last he came on a quiet evening to the cluster of green bothies on the shore of Glen Etive; and when Naisi and his brothers, who were but just returned from their hunting, saw him drawing near along the shore, they came racing to meet him and fling their arms about his shoulders, greeting him and marvelling at his coming, and demanding what would be the latest news out of Ireland.

'The news out of Ireland is this,' said Fergus, as they turned back towards the bothies together. 'That Conor the King has put from his mind the thing that happened four springs ago between you and Deirdre and himself, and can no longer get the full pleasure of his mead-horn nor the full sweetness of harp song unless you return in friendship to enjoy them with him as you used to do.'

Now at this the three brothers set up a shout, for they were as joyful to hear his news as he was to tell it. But Deirdre, who had come from the bothies to join them, said, 'The sons of Usna do well enough here in Scotland. Let you be welcome here at our hearth, and then go back and tell King Conor that.'

'We do well enough here,' said Naisi, 'but each man does best in the land that bred him, for it is there that the roots of his heart are struck.'

'Ah, Naisi, Naisi, I have seen you and Ardan and Ainle growing weary of this happy Glen Etive; I know how you have longed for the King's Hall, and to be driving again like the wind behind the swift horses of Ulster. Yet I have had evil dreams of late and there is a shadow on my heart.'

'Deirdre, what is it that you are afraid of?'

'I scarcely know,' said Deirdre. 'I find it hard to believe in the King's forgiveness. What safeguard have we if we give ourselves back into his power?'

And Fergus Mac Roy said, 'Mine. And I think that no king in all Ireland would dare to violate that.'

Then while they ate the evening meal about the peat fire in the house place, Naisi laughed at her for her fears, swaggering a little with his thumbs in his belt, because the King had sent for him to come back to his old place again. And next day they gathered up all that they had of goods and gear, and went down to the coast, to where the ship that had brought Fergus from Ireland lay waiting on the tide line. And the bothies by the loch shore were left empty and forsaken.

The rowers bent to their oars and the long corach slipped seaward; and sitting in the stern with old Levarcham against her knee, Deirdre looked back past the man at the steering oar towards the shores of Scotland, and a lament rose in her, and would not be held back.

'My love to you, oh land of Alban; pleasant are your harbours and your clear green-sided hills. Glen Archan, my grief! High its hart's tongue and bright its flowers; never were young men lighter hearted than the three sons of Usna in Glen Archan. Glen-da-Rua, my grief! Glen-da-Rua! Sweet is the voice of the cuckoo in the woods of Glen-da-Rua. Glen Etive, my grief! Ochone! Glen Etive! It was there I built my first house, and slept under soft coverings with Naisi's hand beneath my head. And never would I have left you, Glen Etive, but that I go with Naisi my love.'

Scarcely had they set foot in Ulster once more, when Baruch, a veteran of the Red Branch, came to meet them, and bade Fergus, as an old friend, to feast with him that night in his Dun close by. And with him were Fergus's two sons, Illan the Fair and Buinne the Red, come to greet him on his return. Now Fergus did not know that the King had ordered that feast, but he knew that his oath to Conor Mac Nessa bound him to bring Deirdre and the sons of Usna straight from their landing place to Emain Macha, and he tried to win clear of the thing, saying that he could not turn aside from his way until he had brought Deirdre and the three brothers under safe conduct to the King's presence. But Baruch would not be denied, and bade him remember that his geise

forbade him ever to refuse when bidden to a feast, and so at last despite
Deirdre's pleading (for no warrior might go against his geise) he bade
his sons to take charge of the party, and himself went with Baruch.

When the six of them drew near to Emain Macha, Deirdre said,
'See now, how it will be. If Conor the King bids us to his own hall and
his own hearth-side, then he means us no ill; but if we are lodged apart
in the Red Branch Hostel, then grief upon us! For all that I fear will
come to pass.'

And when they came into the Royal Dun they were lodged in the
Red Branch Hostel, to wait until the King should send for them. And
Deirdre said, without hope of being heeded, 'Did I not tell you how it
would be?'

But Naisi only laughed and held her warm in his arms, saying,
'Soon the King will send for us in friendship, and all things will be as
they used to be.'

But first the King sent for old Levarcham, and she went and made
her peace with him where he sat moodily in his sleeping-chamber with
his favourite hound at his feet. And he asked her how it was with
Deirdre, and if her beauty was on her yet, after so many years in the
wilderness.

'Ach now, what would you be expecting? Life in the wilderness
deals hardly with a woman,' said Levarcham. 'The skin that was so
white is brown now, and the wind has chapped her lips and the sun has
faded her hair. Her beauty is all gone from her and if you were to see
her now you would think her any farmer's woman.'

'Then I will not send for her when I send for the sons of Usna,' said
the King, and he sighed. 'Since Naisi has had her beauty, let him keep
her. I will not see her again.'

But when Levarcham had been gone a while he began to doubt in
his heart whether she had told him the truth, and he called to him his
shield-bearer, and said, 'Go you and find some means to look secretly at
the woman that is in the Red Branch Guest House, and come back and
tell me whether she is yet fair to look upon.'

So it was that when those within the Guest House were taking their
ease after the evening meal, Deirdre and Naisi playing chess together
while the others lay about the fire, Ardan cried out suddenly and
sprang to his feet, pointing to the high window in the gable wall. And
looking where he pointed, Naisi saw the face of the King's shield-bearer

peering in; and he caught up a golden chessman from the board and flung it at him, and it caught him in the face and struck out his left eye.

The man loosed his hold on the window-ledge with a sobbing cry and dropped to the ground, and ran and stumbled back to King Conor with his bloody face in his hands.

'The woman in the Red Branch Guest House is the fairest that ever I have seen. And if Naisi Son of Usna had not seen me and put out my eye with the fling of a golden chess piece, it is in my heart that I would have been clinging to the window-ledge and gazing at her still.'

Then Conor Mac Nessa in a black fury came out into his great hall and shouted to his warriors that were feasting there to be out and bring the three sons of Usna before him, he cared not whether alive or dead, or if they must pull down the Red Branch Hostel timber by timber and turf by turf to do it; for they were traitors that had done him foul wrong in the matter of the woman Deirdre.

The warriors sprang from the benches and snatched up their weapons and ran out, shouting, tossing the war-cry to and fro among them, and some in passing the fires, pulled out flaming branches and whirled them above their heads as they ran, and so Naisi and the rest within the Hostel saw the red flicker of the firebrands through the high windows, and heard the shouting. And Deirdre cried out, wild as a storm-driven bird, 'Treachery! Naisi, Naisi, I told you that I feared evil, but you would not listen to me!'

And in the same moment Naisi himself had leapt to drop the mighty bar across the floor.

'Look to the windows! The windows, my brothers, and you sons of Fergus who came here with us in his stead!'

And each catching up their weapons, they ran to their places, and for a breath of time there was stillness in the hall. Then the great voice of Celthair Son of Uthica cried to them from before the door. 'Out with you, thieves and rievers! Come out to us now, and bring with you the woman you stole from the King!'

And standing within the door Naisi shouted back, 'Neither thieves nor rievers are we, for the woman came to me for love and of her own wish; and with me and with my brothers she shall remain, though every champion of the Red Branch comes against us!'

But it was not long that they could hold the Hostel, for someone shouted, 'Burn them out, then, we have the firebrands!' And the shouting rose to a roar, and the warriors thrust their blazing branches under the thatch. And Deirdre cried out at the sight of the red flame running among the rafters, and the hall began to fill with smoke.

Then Naisi said, 'It is time to unbar the door, for it is better to die by the cold blade than the choking reek of fire!'

So they heaved up the bar and flung wide the door, and leapt to meet the King's warriors who were ready for them like terriers at the mouth of a rat hole. A great fight there was, about the threshold of the Red Branch Guest House, and many of the warriors of Ulster fell before the blades of the sons of Usna and the sons of Fergus Mac Roy. And in the fighting Illan the Fair got his death, but to Buinne the Red a worse thing befell, for the King contrived to have him surrounded and brought living out of the fight, and bought him with the promise of much land.

Then with the Red Branch Hostel roaring up in flames behind them, Naisi and his brothers linked their three shields together and set Deirdre in the midst of them and so made a great charge to break through the press of Conor's warriors. And spent and wounded as they were they might yet have won clear, but that Conor Mac Nessa, seeing how it was, bade certain of his Druids to make a strong magic against them, and the Druids made the seeming of a dark wild sea that rose and rose around the island of linked shields, so that the sons of Usna were fighting against the waves of it more than the warriors of the King's Guard. And Naisi, feeling the cold buffeting of the sea rise higher about him and seeing the white hissing break of the waves against their linked shields, caught Deirdre up on to his shoulder to save her from the sea. And they were choking and half drowned, while all the while, to all men save themselves, the King's forecourt was dry as summer drought in the red glare of the burning Hostel.

So at last their strength failed them and the Red Branch Warriors closed about them and struck the swords from their hands, and took and bound them and dragged them before King Conor where he stood looking on.

Then Conor Mac Nessa called for man after man to come forward and slay him the three, but it seemed that none of them heard him, neither Conall of the Victories, nor Cethern Son of Findtan, nor Dubthach the Beetle of Ulster, nor Cuchulain himself, who was but that moment come upon the scene, until at last Owen Prince of Ferney stepped forward and took up Naisi's own sword from the ground where it lay.

'Let you strike the heads from all three of us at one blow,' said Naisi then. 'The blade has skill enough for that; and so we shall all be away on the same breath.' And as they stood there side by side, and their arms bound behind them, the Prince of Ferney shored off their three proud heads at the one stroke. And all the Red Branch Warriors let out three heavy shouts above them. And Deirdre broke free of the men who held her, and she tore her bright hair and cast herself upon the three headless bodies and cried out to them as though they could still hear her. 'Long will be the days without you, O sons of Usna, the days that were never wearisome in your company. The High King of Ulster, my first betrothed, I forsook for the love of Naisi, and sorrow is to me and those what loved me. Make keening for the heroes that were killed by treachery at their coming back to Ulster. The sons of Usna fell in the fight like three branches that were growing straight and strong; their birth was beautiful and their blossoming, and now they are cut down.

'Oh, young men, digging the new grave, do not make it narrow, leave space there for me that follow after, for I am Dierdre without gladness, and my life is at its end!'

And as they would have dragged her away from Naisi's body, she snatched a little sharp knife from the belt of one of the men who held her, and with a last desolate cry, drove the blade home into her breast, and the life of her was gone from between their hands like a bird from its broken cage.

They buried Deirdre and Naisi not far apart, at the spot where in later times rose the great church of Armagh, and out of her grave and out of Naisi's there grew two tall yew trees, whose tops, when they were full grown, met above the church roof, mingling their dark branches so that no man might part them more. And when the sea wind hushed through the boughs, the people said, 'Listen, Dierdre and Naisi are singing together.' And when in summer the small red berries burned like jewels among the furred darkness of the boughs, they said, 'See, Deirdre and Naisi are decked for their wedding.'

Cuchulain is the Hound of Ulster, warrior-hero of the Tain. *If the* Tain *may be compared to the* Iliad, *Cuchulain is Achilles.*

In the rather sophisticated construction of the saga, Cuchulain's life story is told in a series of what might be called flashbacks. We learn of his boyhood deeds (as a lad he slew a blacksmith's fierce watchdog and volunteered to take its place—hence his name, Cu, "the Hound"), his training in arms (in the land of Alban—England) his courtship and marriage . . . and the tale of how he came to kill his only son.

The "original" is to be found in The Yellow Book of Lecan, *a ninth-century manuscript. Ths version is based on translations and adaptations by Jeremiah Curtin, Lady Gregory, Kuno Meyer, Frank O'Connor, and Thomas Kinsella.*

THE DEATH OF CONNLA

Cuchulain learned his battle skills in the land of Alban, from the warrior-woman Skatha. When it was time for him to return to Ireland, she made him the gift of a magic spear. She had taught its use to no other. There was a young woman there, a princess of Alban, and as he was leaving she told Cuchulain that she was pregnant with his child.

She would bear a son, he told her. "His name will be Connla," said he, and he gave the woman a gold ring from his hand. "On the day when this ring fits the boy," he told her, "let him come wearing it, to Ulster. Let no man stand in his way, and let him tell his name to no one until I ask it of him."

After the boy was born, word came to his mother that Cuchulain had married Emer, and her heart was struck burning cold with jealousy. But as soon as her son was old enough to understand, she would have him try on the ring, and swear to her that he would tell no man his name, and turn from combat with no one, ever. And she put him to school with the warrior-woman.

Seven years to the day Cuchulain left Alban, Conor Mac Nessa and the host of Ulster were gathered on the high cliffs that look down on the Strand of the Mark when they saw a boy in a boat of bronze coming toward them across the sea.

There was a heap of stones with him in the boat. He would put a stone in his sling and send it flying at a sea bird so it would stun the bird only, and bring it down alive into his hands. He would release it into the air, and then he would cup his hands to his mouth, and give out a cry, so the bird would return into his hands again.

"Well now," said Conor, watching that. "I pity the country that lad's bound for. Whatever people he comes from, their grown men would crush us to dust, if their boys can do such things as that!"

And he sent Condere the Sweet Spoken down to the shore, to ask the boy's name, and why he had come to Ulster. Condere met the boy just as his boat was touching the beach.

"Well met, young hero," Condere said to him. "It is the king's desire to know your name, and the name of your people."

"I give my name to no one," the boy answered him.

"But you may not land on these shores until we know your name," said Condere.

"I will go where I am going," said the boy, and made to pass by.

"Lad," said Condere, "you would do well to obey the king's commands here in Ulster. It is in Conor Mac Nessa's power to welcome you among the company of champions, or to take your life from you."

"Let these champions come down to me," said Connla, "and I'll fight them, singly or together."

From the cliff above, where Conor was, Conall the Victorious saw and heard all that. He clutched the hilt of his sword. "That is the honor of Ulster the boy is mocking," he said, and he began climbing down the cliffside to the shore.

"Enough of your games, boy!" he shouted.

"Here's a game for you," said Connla. He fitted a stone to his sling and sent it through the air, roaring like thunder, at Conall the Victorious. The hero fell, landing flat on his back, and before he could rise, the boy had his arms bound up in his own shield-strap!

"Someone else to him!" yelled Conall, but the whole army of Ulster stood shamefaced, and the boy laughed at them.

Then Conor sent word to where Cuchulain was, that a young boy had come over the sea, had humbled Conall the Victorious in battle, and was making sport of the host of Ulster.

But when Cuchulain's wife Emer heard that, she was afraid, and she threw her arms around his neck. "Don't go down to him," she said.

"It's only a boy, and no older than a son of your own might be."

"If it were my own son there," said Cuchulain, "I would kill him for the honor of Ulster." And he set out.

"Those were pretty games, boy," he said when he came up to Connla. "But if you would not have my hand against you, you will give me your name now, and be done."

Connla thought he had met no man he would sooner tell his name to than this, were he not sworn. But he said, "I have prettier games than those, if you try me," and drew his sword.

And so they fought together, blade on blade, until Connla lept behind Cuchulain, and with a swift sweeping stroke, cut off a lock of his hair.

"Enough games," said Cuchulain. "We'll wrestle now."

The boy laughed at that. "I can't reach up to your belt," he said, and he climbed up on two standing stones. They grappled together, the boy standing his ground until his feet sank into the stones up to the ankles. And it's the prints of Connla's feet left in those stones that gave the place its name—the Strand of the Mark.

Then they went down into the sea, to drown each other, and twice the boy got the better of him, and ducked him, so that his rage came upon Cuchulain, the light of it blazing about his head, and he called out to the shore for the spear that Skatha had given him.

He caught it, turned, and threw it in one motion, to send it skimming along the top of the waves until it struck Connla in the side and passed through his body. The water was red with his blood.

"That is something Skatha never taught," Connla said, and it was when he fell that Cuchulain saw the gold ring that was in his hand.

Cuculain took the boy up in both his arms, and carried him to the beach, and laid him down there. To the king and all the host standing above, he said, "Men of Ulster, here is my son for you."

Now Conor, looking on this sight, thought to himself, "If Cuchulain were to come up against us now, in his grief and rage, he would make an end to us all." He turned to his Druid, and bade him cast spells on the hero, to give him three days and nights fighting against the waves of the sea.

Cuchulain turned, and drew his sword, and walked into the sea; and he fought with the waves three days and three nights, till he fell from hunger and weakness, and the waves went over him.

*The "Ossianic controversy" raged in English literary circles for the
last half of the eighteenth century. Thomas Gray and David Hume,
Dr. Johnson and William Blake— everybody entertained strong opin-
ions upon the worth, and indeed upon the authenticity, of* Fingal, an
Ancient Epic Poem, *published by one James MacPherson, and pur-
portedly translated from the Gaelic of Ossian, the son of Finn
McCool. (Today, the Irish spell his name* Oisin; *it is, and was, pronounced* Oh-sheen).*

*Although MacPherson was a genuine student of Gaelic, and col-
lector of tales and manuscripts, his* Fingal *was, alas, a fraud and a
forgery. But its influence was great—the misty, doom-laden Celtic
twilight mood of his poem permeated the atmosphere of the young
romantic movement; in France and especially Germany his work was
treasured and imitated; Mendelssohn composed* Fingal's Cave *under
the poem's inspiration. MacPherson became a writer of political prop-
aganda.*

*Oisin himself was the minstrel of the Fianna, and, as we shall
see, its last survivor. Here is the story of his birth, as told by Eithne
Carbery.*

THE BIRTH OF OISIN

O ne day as Finn and his companions and dogs were returning from
the chase to their Dun on the Hill of Allen, a beautiful fawn started
up on their path and the chase swept after her, she taking the way
which led to their home. Soon, all the pursuers were left far behind save
only Finn himself and his two hounds Bran and Sceolaun. Of all the
hounds in Ireland they were the best, and Finn loved them much, so
that it was said he wept but twice in his life, and once was for the death
of Bran.

At last, as the chase went on down a valley side, Finn saw the fawn
stop and lie down, while the two hounds began to play round her and
lick her face and limbs. So he gave commandment that none should
hurt her, and she followed them to the Dun of Allen, playing with the
hounds as she went.

The same night Finn awoke and saw standing by his bed the fairest woman his eyes had ever beheld. 'I am Saba, O Finn,' she said,
'and I was the fawn ye chased today. Because I would not give my love

to the Druid of the Fairy Folk, who is named the Dark, he put the shape upon me by his sorceries, and I have borne it these three years. But a slave of his, pitying me, once revealed to me that if I could win to thy great Dun of Allen, O Finn, I should be safe from all enchantments and my natural shape would come to me again. But I feared to be torn in pieces by thy dogs, or wounded by thy hunters, till at last I let myself be overtaken by thee alone and by Bran and Sceolaun, who have the nature of man and would do me no hurt.' 'Have no fear, maiden,' said Finn, 'we, the Fianna, are free and out guest-friends are free; there is none who shall put compulsion on you here.'

So Saba dwelt with Finn, and he made her his wife; and so deep was his love for her that neither the battle nor the chase had any delight for him, and for months he never left her side. She also loved him as deeply, and their joy in each other was like that of the Immortals in the Land of Youth. But at last word came to Finn that the warships of the Northmen were in the bay of Dublin, and he summoned his heroes to the fight, 'for,' said he to Saba, 'the men of Erinn gave us tribute and hospitality to defend them from the foreigner, and it were shame to take it from them and not give that to which we, on our side, are pledged.' And he called to mind that great saying of Goll Mac Morna when they were once sore bested by a mighty host—'Man,' said Goll, 'lives after his life but not after his honour.'

Seven days was Finn absent, and he drove the Northmen from the shores of Erinn. But on the eighth day he returned, and when he entered his Dun he saw trouble in the eyes of his men and of their fair womenfolk, and Saba was not on the rampart expecting his return. So he bade them tell him what had chanced, and they said—

'Whilst thou, our father and lord, wert afar off smiting the foreigner, and Saba looking ever down the pass for thy return, we saw one day as it were the likeness of thee approaching, and Bran and Sceolaun at thy heels. And we seemed also to hear the notes of the Fian hunting call blown on the wind. Then Saba hastened to the great gate, and we could not stay here, so eager was she to rush to the phantom. But when she came near, she halted and gave a loud and bitter cry, and the shape of thee smote her with a hazel wand, and lo, there was no woman there any more, but a deer. Then those hounds chased it, and ever as it strove to reach again the gate of the Dun they turned it back. We all now seized what arms we could and ran out to drive away the enchanter, but when we reached the place there was nothing to be seen, only still we heard the rushing of flying feet and the baying of dogs, and one thought it came from here, and another from there, till at last the uproar died away and all was still. What we could do, O Finn, we did; Saba is gone.'

Finn then struck his hand on his breast but spoke no word, and he went to his own chamber. No man saw him for the rest of that day, nor for the day after. Then he came forth, and ordered the matters of the Fianna as of old, but for seven years thereafter he went searching for Saba through every remote glen and dark forest and cavern of Ireland, and he would take no hounds with him save Bran and Sceolaun. But at last he renounced all hope of finding her again, and went hunting as of old. One day as he was following the chase on Ben Gulban in Sligo, he heard the musical bay of the dogs change of a sudden to a fierce growling and yelping as though they were in combat with some beast, and running hastily up he and his men beheld, under a great tree, a naked boy with long hair, and around him the hounds struggling to seize him, but Bran and Sceolaun fighting with them and keeping them off. And the lad was tall and shapely, and as the heroes gathered round he gazed undauntedly on them, never heeding the rout of dogs at his feet. The Fians beat off the dogs and brought the lad home with them, and Finn was very silent and continually searched the lad's countenance with his eyes. In time the use of speech came to him, and the story that he told was this—

He had known no father, and no mother save a gentle hind with whom he lived in a most green and pleasant valley shut in on every side by towering cliffs that could not be scaled, or by deep chasms in the earth. In the summer he lived on fruits and such-like, and in the winter, store of provisions was laid for him in a cave. And there came to them sometimes a tall dark-visaged man, who spoke to his mother, now tenderly, and now in a loud menace, but she always shrunk away in fear, and the man departed in anger. At last there came a day when the Dark Man spoke very long with his mother in all tones of entreaty and of tenderness and of rage, but she would still keep aloof and give no sign save of fear and abhorrence. Then at length the Dark Man drew near and smote her with a hazel wand; and with that he turned and went his way, but she, this time, followed him, still looking back at her son and piteously complaining. And he, when he strove to follow, found himself unable to move a limb; and crying out with rage and desolation he fell to the earth and his senses left him. When he came to himself he remained some days, searching for that green and hidden valley, which he never found again. And after a while the dogs found him; but of the hind his mother and of the Dark Druid, there is no man knows the end.

Finn called his name Oisin, and he became a warrior of fame, but far more famous for the songs and tales that he made; so that of all things to this day that are told of the Fianna of Erinn, men are wont to say, 'So sang the bard, Oisin, son of Finn.'

In the 1870s the New York Sun, *a "penny paper," was in fierce competition with two rival tabloids, the* Herald *and the* Tribune, *for human-interest stories. Because New York had an enormous Irish-immigrant population, the publisher of the* Sun *decided to appeal to them with a series of Irish folktales and legends.*

Jeremiah Curtin, a young writer with a flair for languages, was dispatched to Ireland to learn Gaelic and transcribe folktales for the paper to publish.

Scholars have questioned Curtin's mastery of the language, but not the importance of his work, for he was the first to collect tales not from English-speaking sources but from the real shanachies, *the Gaelic storytellers, and from the people of "the West."*

Curtin discovered nine tales of Finn McCool (he wrote his name "Fin MacCumhail"); among them was this Paul Bunyan-ish adventure.

FINN McCOOL AND THE FENIANS OF ERIN IN THE CASTLE OF FEAR DUBH

It was the custom with Finn McCool and the Fenians of Erin, when a stranger from any part of the world came to their castle, not to ask him a question for a year and a day.

On a time, a champion came to Finn and his men, and remained with them. He was not at all pleasant or agreeable.

At last Finn and his men took counsel together; they were much annoyed because their guest was so dull and morose, never saying a word, always silent.

While discussing what kind of man he was, Diarmuid Duivne offered to try him; so one evening when they were eating together, Diarmuid came and snatched from his mouth the hind-quarter of a bullock, which he was picking.

Diarmuid pulled at one part of the quarter—pulled with all his strength, but only took the part that he seized, while the other kept the part he held. All laughed; the stranger laughed too, as heartily as any. It was the first laugh they had heard from him.

The strange champion saw all their feats of arms and practiced with them, till the year and a day were over. Then he said to Finn and his men:

"I have spent a pleasant year in your company; you gave me good treatment, and the least I can do now is to give you a feast at my own castle."

No one had asked what his name was up to that time. Finn now asked his name. He answered: "My name is Fear Dubh, of Alban."

Finn accepted the invitation; and they appointed the day for the feast, which was to be in Erin, since Fear Dubh did not wish to trouble them to go to Alban. He took leave of his host and started for home.

When the day for the feast came, Finn and the chief men of the Fenians of Erin set out for the castle of Fear Dubh.

They went, a glen at a step, a hill at a leap, and thirty-two miles at a running leap, till they came to the grand castle where the feast was to be given.

They went in; everything was ready, seats at the table, and every man's name at his seat in the same order as at Finn's castle. Diarmuid, who was always very sportive—fond of hunting, and paying court to women—was not with them; he had gone to the mountains with his dogs.

All sat down, except Conan Maol MacMorna (never a man spoke well of him); no seat was ready for him, for he used to lie on the flat of his back on the floor, at Finn's castle.

When all were seated the door of the castle closed of itself. Finn then asked the man nearest the door to rise and open it. The man tried to rise; he pulled this way and that, over and hither, but he couldn't get up. Then the next man tried, and the next, and so on, till the turn came to Finn himself, who tried in vain.

Now, whenever Finn and his men were in trouble and great danger it was their custom to raise a cry of distress (a voice of howling), heard all over Erin. Then all men knew that they were in peril of death; for they never raised this cry except in the last extremity.

Finn's son, Fialan, who was three years old and in the cradle, heard the cry, was roused, and jumped up.

"Get me a sword!" said he to the nurse. "My father and his men are in distress; I must go to aid them."

"What could you do, poor little child?"

Fialan looked around, saw an old rusty swordblade laid aside for ages. He took it down, gave it a snap; it sprang up so as to hit his arm, and all the rust dropped off; the blade was pure as shining silver.

"This will do," said he; and then he set out towards the place where he heard the cry, going a glen at a step, a hill at a leap, and thirty-two miles at a running leap, till he came to the door of the castle, and cried out.

Finn answered from inside, "Is that you, my child?"

"It is," said Fialan.

"Why did you come?"

"I heard your cry, and how could I stay at home, hearing the cry of my father and the Fenians of Erin!"

"Oh, my child, you cannot help us much."

Fialan struck the door powerfully with his sword, but no use. Then, one of the men inside asked Finn to chew his thumb, to know what was keeping them in, and why they were bound.

Finn chewed his thumb, from skin to blood, from blood to bone, from bone to marrow, and discovered that Fear Dubh had built the castle by magic, and that he was coming himself with a great force to cut the head off each one of them. (These men from Alban had always a grudge against the champions of Erin.)

Said Finn to Fialan: "Do you go now, and stand at the ford near the castle, and meet Fear Dubh."

Fialan went and stood in the middle of the ford. He wasn't long there when he saw Fear Dubh coming with a great army.

"Leave the ford, my child," said Fear Dubh, who knew him at once. "I heve not come to harm your father. I spent a pleasant year at his castle. I've only come to show him honor."

"I know why you have come," answered Fialan. "You've come to destroy my father and all his men, and I'll not leave this ford while I can hold it."

"Leave the ford; I don't want to harm your father, I want to do him honor. If you don't let us pass my men will kill you," said Fear Dubh.

"I will not let you pass so long as I'm alive before you," said Fialan.

The men faced him; and if they did, Fialan kept his place, and a battle commenced, the like of which was never seen before that day.

Fialan went through the army as a hawk through a flock of sparrows on a March morning, till he killed every man except Fear Dubh. Fear Dubh told him again to leave the ford; he didn't want to harm his father.

"Oh!" said Fialan. "I know well what you want."

"If you don't leave that place, I'll make you leave it!" said Fear Dubh. Then they closed in combat; and such a combat was never seen before between any two warriors. They made springs to rise through the centre of hard grey rocks, cows to cast their calves whether they had them or not. All the horses of the country were racing about and neighing in dread and fear, and all created things were terrified at the sound and clamor of the fight, till the weapons of Fear Dubh went to pieces in the struggle, and Fialan made two halves of his own sword.

Now they closed in wrestling. In the first round Fialan put Fear Dubh to his knees in the hard bottom of the river; the second round he put him to his hips, and the third, to his shoulders.

"Now," said he, "I have you," giving him a stroke of the half of his sword, which cut the head off him.

Then Fialan went to the door of the castle and told his father what he had done.

Finn chewed his thumb again, and knew what other danger was coming. "My son," said he to Fialan, "Fear Dubh has a younger brother more powerful than he was; that brother is coming against us now with greater forces than those which you have destroyed."

As soon as Fialan heard these words he hurried to the ford, and waited till the second army came up. He destroyed this army as he had the other, and closed with the second brother in a fight fiercer and more terrible than the first; but at last he thrust him to his armpits in the hard bottom of the river and cut off his head.

Then he went to the castle, and told his father what he had done. A third time Finn chewed his thumb, and said: "My son, a third army more to be dreaded than the other two is coming now to destroy us, and at the head of it is the youngest brother of Fear Dubh, the most desperate and powerful of the three."

Again Fialan rushed off to the ford; and, though the work was greater than before, he left not a man of the army alive. Then he closed with the youngest brother of Fear Dubh, and if the first and second

80

battles were terrible, this was more terrible by far; but at last he planted the youngest brother up to his armpits in the hard bottom of the river, and swept the head off him.

Now, after the heat and struggle of combat Fialan was in such a rage that he lost his mind from fury, not having any one to fight against; and if the whole world had been there before him he would have gone through it and conquered it all.

But having no one to face him, he rushed along the river-bank, tearing the flesh from his own body. Never had such madness been seen in any created being before that day.

Diarmuid came now and knocked at the door of the castle, having the dog Bran with him, and asked Finn what had caused him to raise the cry of distress.

"Oh, Diarmuid," said Finn, "we are all fastened in here to be killed. Fialan has destroyed three armies, and Fear Dubh with his two brothers. He is raging now along the bank of the river; you must not go near him, for he would tear you limb from limb. At this moment he wouldn't spare me, his own father; but after a while he will cease from raging and die down; then you can go. The mother of Fear Dubh is coming, and will soon be at the ford. She is more violent, more venomous, more to be dreaded, a greater warrior than her sons. The chief weapon she has are the nails on her fingers; each nail is seven perches long, of the hardest steel on earth. She is coming in the air at this moment with the speed of a hawk, and she has a kuran [a small vessel], with liquor in it, which has such power that if she puts three drops of it on the mouths of her sons they will rise up as well as ever; and if she brings them to life there is nothing to save us.

"Go to the ford; she will be hovering over the corpses of the three armies to know can she find her sons, and soon as she sees them she will dart down and give them the liquor. You must rise with a mighty bound upon her, dash the kuran out of her hand, and spill the liquor.

"If you can kill her, save her blood, for nothing in the world can free us from this place and open the door of the castle but the blood of the old hag. I'm in dread you'll not succeed, for she is far more terrible than all her sons together. Go now; Fialan is dying away, and the old woman is coming; make no delay."

Diarmuid hurried to the ford, stood watching a while; then he saw high in the air something no larger than a hawk. As it came nearer and nearer he saw it was the old woman. She hovered high in the air over the ford. At last she saw her sons, and was swooping down, when Diarmuid rose with a bound into the air and struck the vial a league out of her hand.

The old hag gave a shriek that was heard to the eastern world, and screamed: "Who has dared to interfere with me or my sons?"

"I," answered Diarmuid; "and you'll not go further till I do to you what has been done to your sons."

The fight began; and if there ever was a fight before or since, it could not be more terrible than this one; but great as was the power of Diarmuid he never could have conquered but for Bran the dog.

The old woman with her nails stripped the skin and flesh from Diarmuid almost to the vitals. But Bran tore the skin and flesh off the old woman's back from her head to her heels.

From the dint of blood-loss and fighting, Diarmuid was growing faint. Despair came on him, and he was on the point of giving way, when a little robin flew near to him, and sitting on a bush, spoke, saying:

"Oh, Diarmuid, take strength; rise and sweep the head off the old hag, or Finn and the Fenians of Erin are no more."

Diarmuid took courage, and with his last strength made one great effort, swept the head off the old hag, and caught her blood in a vessel. He rubbed some on his own wounds—they were cured; then he cured Bran.

Straightway he took the blood to the castle, rubbed drops of it on the door, which opened, and he went in.

All laughed with joy at the rescue. He freed Finn and his men by rubbing the blood on the chairs; but when he came as far as Conan Maol the blood gave out.

All were going away. "Why should you leave me here after you," cried Conan Maol. "I would rather die at once than stay here for a lingering death. Why don't you, Oscar, and you, Gol MacMorna, come and tear me out of this place; anyhow, you'll be able to drag the arms out of me and kill me at once; better that than leave me to die alone."

Oscar and Gol took each a hand, braced their feet against his feet, put forth all their strength and brought him standing; but if they did, he left all the skin and much of the flesh from the back of his head to his heels on the floor behind him. He was covered with blood, and by all accounts was in a terrible condition, bleeding and wounded.

Now there were sheep grazing near the castle. The Fenians ran out, killed and skinned the largest and best of the flock, and clapped the fresh skin on Conan's back; and such was the healing power in the sheep, and the wound very fresh, that Conan's back healed, and he marched home with the rest of the men, and soon got well; and if he did, they sheared off his back wool enough every year to make a pair of stockings for each one of the Fenians of Erin, and for Finn himself.

And that was a great thing to do and useful, for wool was scarce in Erin in those days. Finn and his men lived pleasantly and joyously for some time; and if they didn't, may we.

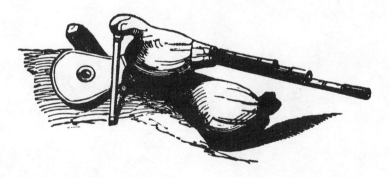

*It is the simple purpose of many folktales to explain place-names. In
Ireland, especially, it seems that every rock and tree, not to speak of
mountains and rivers, has a magical story associated with its name.
Indeed, many a tale begins: "Why is this place called———?" And
the answer comes: "That is easily told. In the days when. . . ."*

*So the tale of Finn and the giantess was offered to explain the
name of a "certain hill."*

*This unusual account of Finn actually losing a battle is told by
T.W. Rolleston, whose* Myths and Legends of the Celtic Realm *(1911)
was one of the first attempts to give order to the vast and rich and
diffuse material, oral and written, that remains of the mythology
shared by the Irish and Welsh.*

THE TALE OF FINN AND THE GIANTESS

One day Finn and Goll, Keelta and Oscar, and others of the Fianna,
were resting after the hunt on a certain hill now called the Ridge
of the Dead Woman, and their meal was being got ready, when a girl
of the kin of the giants came striding up and sat down among them.
'Didst though ever see a woman so tall?' asked Finn of Goll. 'By my
troth,' said Goll, 'never have I or any other seen a woman so big.' She
took her hand out of her bosom and on her long slender fingers there
were three gold rings each as thick as an ox's yoke. 'Let us question
her,' said Goll, and Finn said, 'If we stood up, perchance she might
hear us.'

So they all rose to their feet, but the giantess on that rose up too.
'Maiden,' said Finn, 'if thou have aught to say to us or to hear from us,
sit down and lean thine elbow on the hill-side.' So she lay down and
Finn bade her say whence she came and what was her will with them.
'Out of the World Oversea where the sun sets am I come,' she said, 'to
seek thy protection, O mighty Finn.' 'And what is thy name?' 'My
name is Vivionn of the Fair Hair, and my father Treon is called King
of the Land of Lasses, for he has but three sons and nine and sevenscore daughters, and near him is a king who hath one daughter and
eightscore sons. To one of these, Aeda, was I given in marriage sorely
against my will. Three times now have I fled from him. And this time
it was fishermen whom the wind blew to us from off this land who told
us of a mighty lord here, named Finn, son of Cumhal, who would let

none be wronged or oppressed, but he would be their friend and champion. And if thou be he, to thee am I come.' Then she laid her hand in Finn's, and he bade her to do the same with Gol MacMoma, who was second in the Fian leadership, and she did so.

Then the maiden took from her head a jewelled golden helmet, and immediately her hair flowed out in sevenscore tresses, fair, curly and golden, at the abundance of which all stood amazed; and Finn said, 'By the Immortals that we adore, but King Cormac and the poetess Ethne and the fair women-folk of the Fianna would deem it a marvel to see this girl. Tell us now, maiden, what portion wilt thou have of meat and drink? Will that of a hundred of us suffice thee?' The girl then saw Cnu, the dwarf harper of Finn, who had just been playing to them, and she said, 'Whatever thou givest to yon little man that bears the harp, be it much or little, the same, O Finn, will suffice for me.'

Then she begged a drink from them, and Finn called his gillie, Saltran, and bade him fetch the full of a certain great goblet with water from the ford; now this goblet was of wood, and it held as much as nine of the Fianna could drink. The maiden poured some of the water into her right hand and drank three sips of it, and scattered the rest over the Fianna, and she and they burst out laughing. Finn said, 'On thy conscience, girl, what ailed thee not to drink out of the goblet?' 'Never,' she replied, 'have I drunk out of any vessel but there was a rim of gold to it, or at least of silver.'

And now Keelta looking up perceived a tall youth coming swiftly towards them, who, when he approached, seemed even bigger than was the maiden. He wore a rough hairy cape over his shoulder and beneath that a green cloak fastened by a golden brooch; his tunic was of royal satin, and he bore a red shield slung over his shoulders, and a spear with a shaft as thick as a man's leg was in his hand; a gold-hilted sword hung by his side. And his face, which was smooth-shaven, was comelier than that of any of the sons of men.

When he came near, seeing among the Fians a stir of alarm at this apparition, Finn said, 'Keep every one of you his place, let neither warrior nor gillie address him. Know any of you this champion?' 'I know him,' said the maiden; 'that is even he to escape from whom I am come to thee, O Finn.' And she sat down between Finn and Goll. But the stranger drew near, and spoke never a word, but before any one could tell what he would be at he thrust fiercely and suddenly with his spear at the girl, and the shaft stood out a hand's breadth at her back. And she fell gasping, but the young man drew his weapon out and passed rapidly through the crowd and away.

Then Finn cried, red with wrath. 'Ye have seen! Avenge this wicked deed, or none of you aspire to Fianship again.' And the whole company sprang to their feet and gave chase to that murderer, save only Finn and Goll, who stayed by the dying maiden. And they ran him by hill and plain to the great Bay of Tralee and down to the Tribut Point, where the traders from oversea were wont to pay their dues, and there he set his face to the West and took to the water. By this time four of the Fianna had outstripped the rest, namely, Keelta, and Dermot, and Glas, and Oscar, son of Oisin. Of these Keelta was first, and just as the giant was mid-leg in the waves he hurled his spear and it severed the thong of the giant's shield so that it fell off in the water. And as the giant paused, Keelta seized his spear and tore it from him. But the giant waded on, and soon the Fians were floundering in deep water while the huge form, thigh deep, was seen striding towards the setting sun. And a great ship seemed to draw near, and it received him, and then departed into the light, but the Fians returned in the grey evening, bearing the spear and the great shield to Finn. There they found the maiden at point of death, and they laid the weapons before her. 'Goodly indeed are these arms,' she said, 'for that is the Thunder Spear of the King Oversea and the shield is the Red Branch Shield,' for it was covered with red arabesques. Then she bestowed her bracelets on Finn's three harpers, the dwarf Cnu, and Blanit his wife, and the harper Daira. And she bade Finn care for her burial, that it should be done becomingly, 'for under thy honour and protection I got my death, and it was to thee I came into Ireland.' So they buried her and lamented her, and made a great far-seen mound over her grave, which is called the Ridge of the Dead Woman, and set up a pillar stone upon it with her name and lineage carved in Ogham script.

In the first century of the Christian era (though Christianity had not yet come to Ireland), the Fir Bolgs, a conquered people in bondage to the Gaels, rose up in revolution, and slaughtered the nobility of their oppressors at Magh Cro (the Bloody Plain) in Galway.

After a period of anarchy, the High Kingship was returned to the Gaels, in the person of Feredach the Righteous, a child whose royal mother had escaped the massacre.

His reign, according to the old chronicles, was a troubled one; but such is the lot of any and all—however righteous—who come over the seas to rule in Ireland.

The chief god of the Gaels was Manannan Mac Lir, the sea god who had brought them to Ireland's shores; the fairies fed upon his herds of swine, and were clothed in the wool of his sheep.

This tale of Feredach's kingship is told by Eithne Carbery, who was the wife of the greatest of modern Irish storytellers, Seamus MacManus. Her manner of story telling was more "literary" than her husband's, but none the less Irish—lovely—for that.

THE SHEARING OF THE FAIRY FLEECES

The King had listened day after day to the rambling tales that were brought him by the mountain people and the people of the valley, and while he watched the fear that lurked behind their wide-open eyes his own narrowed in thought as to how this panic that had seized upon his subjects could be assuaged. That there was in truth some serious cause for their misery of mind he could not doubt. He had hearkened with them to the bleating of the phantom sheep echoing clear from the high-peaked summits far above; and gazing from the doorway of his royal *dun* he had seen the snow-white flocks moving hither and thither over the heather where the mountain folk had their homes in the mist-wreathed caves. His Druids had sought knowledge from the stars in their night vigils, and returned with awed faces to tell the futility of their research.

"It is not for us to probe, O King, the designs of the Immortals. The hand of Manannan Mac Lir is visible in the heavens, and these are his fairy flocks that appear before the eyes of men but rarely in the passing of the ages. Whether it be for good or evil that he hath shown

88

them to us now we know not, save that it were unwise to meddle with the manifestations of the Gods."

"Alas! my people are withering away before mine eyes," said the King, "and the sick are groaning on their couches while the white fear clutches at their heart-strings. Can nought be done to appease the anger of the Sea-god, or can ye discover wherefore his wrath is turned against us?"

"We shall go back to our vigils, O Monarch, and in the dawning bring thee whatever tidings may be vouchsafed to us," they answered humbly, wending forth from the royal presence; weary because of their long night watches, yet eager to fathom the mystery of the dread apparition that had caused such woe to the people of Sorcha.

Then the King bent his thoughtful gaze on the kneeling throng, looking longest at the shaggy mountaineers clad in their barbaric garments of fur and hard-tanned leather. Their hair and beards grew in wild profusion, and on their hunting-spear handles were traces of newly dried blood. They began to talk hurriedly, and in uncouth speech, lifting up hands of supplication.

"What is it that ye have seen, and what do ye dread?" said the King to them in soothing wise, and like the roar of a tumbling torrent came the clamour of their words.

"We have heard round our homes at twilight in the high secret places of the hills, O King, the bleating from a great sheep-fold, and when we followed whither it led, we became enveloped in clouds of mist so that many of our number, slipping from the narrow pathways, were dashed to pieces on the rocks below. The bleating and trampling of feet still came to us out of the mist as if a multitude were behind, and when we stretched our arms into it, it broke apart and floated upwards like huge flakes of snow. Now the sound is heard all over the mountains, so that our people are frozen in the horror of a great fear, and dare not venture forth to kill the wild animals that give them food. Our flocks have fled down into the valley, even as we have done, in terror. The hunger is on us, and the sickness hath caught our women and little ones. And the *demnaeoir* [the demons of the air] are shrieking round us in the winds, and the *geinte glindi* [the wild people of the glens] are treading in our footsteps everywhere, until we know not where to go, and for very horror pray the Gods to give us death."

"And we," said the dwellers of the valley, "also live in the shadow of this great fear, O King, for our eyes are ever turned upward towards the mountains, while our fields are left untilled and our work undone because of this cruel fascination that is on us. The *bean-sidhe*'s wail is heard from end to end of the valley, chasing sleep from us in the night hours, and the dogs shrink shuddering with bristling hair, when our women would drive them from the hearthstones into the open day."

The King moaned wearily, rocking from side to side on his gilded throne. His heart was warm for even the least of his subjects, and his wise ruling had kept peace in the land for many years. This disaster was none of his bringing, nor did one of those fear-drawn faces look at him with eyes of blame.

"When the next dawn breaks," he said to them in tender tones, "I shall climb to the summit of those high hills with ye, my children, and if the Gods be kind mayhap Manannan Mac Lir will grant speech to me. Moreover, my druids shall offer gifts in propitiation—gold and silver and precious stones—aye holocausts of cattle from my pastures that this curse may be taken off me and mine."

And kissing the hem of his royal robe they left the hall of audience, hushed into silence by the sorrow in the voice of the King.

The territory of Sorcha lay within a long high chain of mountains which guarded it on east and north and west, but sloped to the south, where the sea broke on a white sandy beach in the shelter of great protecting cliffs. There the King's royal house stood like a sentinel, and from his watch-tower, the vast horizon was visible so that no encroachment of hostile ships could come unseen within reach of the land; nor could one single stranger cross the outer boundary unknown to the captains of the army, so closely and minutely was the territory kept secure from foreign invasion. It was through his exceeding care for his people and their lands, that King Feredach had gained his title of the Generous, and wide-spread renown had haloed his name as with a glory.

Now his soul had grown sick within him at the trouble overshadowing his kingdom. He still sat, after the last suppliant had left the hall, brooding over the inexplicable panic that bade fair to turn his beautiful fertile country into waste of loneliness and want. As he leaned forward, his grey beard sweeping his breast, and his eyes glaring glassily downwards, a stranger, entering the wide doorway, came up the rush-strewn floor and bent in salutation before him.

"Hail, O King Feredach," he said. "I would have speech with thee."

The King lifted his eyes and saw a man clad in wonderful garments of colour like the changing skin of the sea-snake, and round his waist a golden snake was coiled for girdle, while over all a mantle of green, with the shifting shining hues of the sea in moonlight, was thrown, which trailed behind him on the floor. His hair was a bright ruddy golden, and on it lay a crown of wondrous sea-weeds still sparkling with the salt-moisture of the deep. His face was young and fair, and open, with clear quick-flashing eyes; and his height was beyond that of any man in Sorcha. In his hand he held a pair of immense glittering sharp shears.

"Who art thou?" said Feredach, "and how comest thou to pass my guards below, for no man enters my presence unannounced?"

"Not one of thy guards saw me, O King, for they are hiding their faces from the sun, and their ears were deaf to my footfalls. I have travelled far to take from they people the panic that hath fallen on them."

"Thy name?"

"My name is but the name of a wanderer, O King, a rover of the sea; a vendor of marvellous silks and curios from many lands. Wherever such are to be found I follow in pursuit; and having heard how thy kingdom is distressed with signs and tokens of the enmity of the Gods, I, who know no fear, have come to find the fairy flock and shear their fleeces so that thy misery may be ended."

" 'Twill be death to thee," said the King, "since no man can discover them."

"Yet shall *I* find their hiding-places," spoke the sea-stranger, "and do thou bide here on thy throne until I return."

At the command in his voice the King sat moveless, nor did the guards ranged down the audience-hall seem to see or hear.

And while the King waited, sitting erect as a statue of stone, morn gave place to noon, and noon glided gently towards the arms of sunset. Then when the vast portals of the West were opened for the passing of the Day God, the stranger re-entered the palace-hall in the radiance of the fading splendour. In his arms he held, piled high, white masses of finest silky wool, such as had never been seen before in Sorcha, so soft it was, so great in length, so snowy in colour.

91

He held the fleeces out before the King. "The blight hath gone from thy people, O Feredach, nor shall the bleating of the flocks molest them more. Thy valleys shall grow green again, and the wild boar return to thy mountains. For me, I go to the Land of Eirinn—to the looms of the de Danaans in the heart of a lonely hill, that an invisible cloak may be woven out of these fleeces for my foster-son, the young Champion of Uladh, Cuchulain. It shall protect him in battle from wounds, and in peace from sickness; nor shall aught have power over it save the people of the Sea. It has been shorn from the Sheep of Manannan, that roam invisible over many mountains of the world, and whose appearance before the eyes of men is attended with great disaster— through no ill-will of the Gods. Fare thee well, O King, my task is finished."

"Stay, thou wise stranger," cried Feredach, grasping at the sea-green cloak, but his hand closed upon the empty air, and instead of a footfall there was but faintly heard a placid murmur as of waves breaking upon a pebbly strand.

o   o   o   o   o

"It was Manannan Mac Lir, himself," said the Druids, blanched with awe. "It was the Deity of the Waters, for as we looked from the watch-tower we saw a long white narrow wave creep up the shore even to the door of thy *dun*, O King, and on the crest of it rose and fell a silver sea-chariot, with four white swift-footed horses yoked thereto, into which he stepped bearing the fleeces, and while we strained our eyes the white waves subsided into the ocean with a high-splashing of reddened foam as the Sun went through the Golden Gates."

"Praise to the Gods," said Feredach.

"Praise. And to thee, O King," chanted the Druids.

Aside from the epic tales of the High Deeds of Finn McCool, there are tall tales—jokes, really—in which the legendary hero is treated as something of a blustering fool, despite his enormous strength.

In this story, sometimes called "A Legend of Knockmany," Finn goes up against Cucullin, an even earlier hero of Irish myth now likewise diminished to the status of a giant "faction fighter."

The tale is told as you might hear it—whether you wanted to, or not—from a garrulous stranger in an Irish pub.

FINN AND THE GIANT CUCULLIN

Speaking of Finn McCool, have you heard about himself, his wife Oona, and the giant Cucullin? You haven't?

Well, listen.

They say this Cucullin was a terrific size, at least three times the height of Finn, which would have put his head up about forty feet above the ground, can you believe it?

Me neither.

But the truth of it is, Cucullin must have been big enough, and strong enough, for it's well known that he carried a thunderbolt around in his pocket. He'd flattened the thing out one time with just a blow of his fist. Bam!—like that. Just showing off, he was, which will give you some idea of his character, as well.

For a long time, Cucullin had been bragging and noising it about that he wanted to flatten your man McCool, as well, Finn being the only giant in Ireland he hadn't already fought and beaten.

But Finn kept out of Cucullin's way. As a matter of fact, he and his wife Oona moved their house up to the top of windy and waterless Knockmany, the highest hill in the kingdom, so as to keep a sharp lookout against the coming of Cucullin, the better for Finn to stay out of his way.

Not that Finn McCool was afraid. It was only that he had no wish to go and spoil another fellow's perfect record.

Now, of course, the secret of Finn's great gifts and of his power lay in his thumb; the one he'd scorched as a lad on the Salmon of Wisdom while he was cooking that fairy fish for the wizard's breakfast. From that time on, Finn had only to suck his thumb to become clever and farseeing. But everyone knows that old tale.

Anyway, the day came when Oona found Finn with his thumb stuck in his mouth, and a worried look to him.

"He's coming," said Finn. "I can see him for sure."

"Who's coming, Finn darling?" asked Oona, as if she didn't know.

"Cucullin," said he, and the way he spoke Oona knew that her poor hero of a husband had no idea what to do about it, at all.

"If I fight him, I'm sure to lose," Finn was thinking, "and if I run away, I'll be disgraced in the sight of my people, and me the best man among them. . . ."

"When will he be here?" she asked.

"Tomorrow, at two o'clock," Finn said.

"You just do as I tell you, Finn, my love, and leave this Cucullin to me," said his wife. "For haven't I always been the one to get you out of your troubles?"

"You have," said Finn, and he almost gave up his worried shivering and shaking, remembering that his wife, like most women, was well-connected among the fairy folk, and could be counted upon for a clever trick or two in time of need.

Then what did she do but make a high smoke on the hilltop, and give out three loud whistles, so Cucullin would know he was invited up, for that was the way the Irish of those days would give a sign to strangers that they were welcome to share a meal, don't you know.

And no sooner had she done that, than she was off, round to the neighbors at the foot of the mountain, borrowing from them no less than one-and-twenty iron griddles! You know the things I mean. Gridirons, skillets, fry pans, whatever you call them.

When she brought those back up to the house, she went and baked up twenty-four flat cakes, and inside twenty-one of them—listen, now—she put one of those hard iron pans!

Then she put them all aside on a shelf to cool, very neatly, so she'd remember which was which.

Just before two o'clock, as Finn's magic thumb had foretold, here comes Cucullin, marching up Knockmany mountain. At the sight of the great bulk of him, Finn nearly commenced his quaking again. But Oona, calm as a sheep, hands her husband a bonnet and a blanket, and points·to the cradle she'd brought out, and says, "Now you must pass for your own child, my darling. So lie down there snug, and suck your thumb if you like, and not a word out of you."

As you may imagine, many a brave and angry thought roared round Finn's brain as she tucked him in.

Now here comes Cucullin, stooping low to pass through the door of the house.

"Good day," he says, bold as brass. "Would you be the wife of the great Finn McCool?"

"I am, and proud of it," says she.

"And is himself at home now?" asks the giant.

"He isn't," answers Oona. "Not five minutes ago, he got word that some pitiful wretch of a giant named Cucullin was in the neighborhood, and off he ran in a terrible rage to beat the poor creature to a pulp."

"I am Cucullin," says he, proud as punch.

"Are you now?" says Oona, and begins to laugh to herself, as if to say, "You poor little handful of a man."

"Did you ever see Finn?" she says, changing her manner all at once.

"How could I?" says the giant. "He's never given me the chance."

"Well, it's your bad luck you'll have your chance soon enough," says Oona, "but in the meantime, that's a terrible wind rattling the front door there, and I was wondering if you'd be so kind as to go out for a minute and turn the house around? That's what my Finn always does, when he's at home."

Now, that was a stunner, even for Cucullin. But up he got, and went out of the house. Then he did the strangest thing. Listen to this, now. He pulled the middle finger of his right hand till it cracked three times. Then doesn't he wrap his arms about the house and turn it altogether around, as he'd been asked.

When Finn saw that, he trembled in his cradle, and pulled the blanket up to his eyes. But Oona only smiled.

"My thanks to you," she says, "and if you've a mind to do me another little favor, it's this. After this stretch of dry weather we've been having, we're badly off up here for want of water. Finn tells me there's a fine spring-well under the rocks behind the hill, but before he could tear them apart, this day, he heard of your coming, and off he ran in his fury. I'd take it as a kindness if you were to find it," says she, still smiling her sweet girlish smile.

And she showed Cucullin the spot, there on the mountainside, which was one great piece of solid rock, don't you know. Well, he looks at it a while, and then he cracks his right middle finger no less than nine times, mind you, and doesn't he tear a cleft in the rock about four hundred feet deep and a quarter of a mile in length. And then, of course, the water comes gushing out.

Lumford's Glen, they call that place now. But perhaps you've seen it yourself? Well, you should.

Anyway, by now, Finn's shaking and sweating in his cradle. But then Oona leans over to him, like a mother, and she whispers, "Did you see that business he does with the middle finger of his right hand, darling? It's there that's the secret of this bully-boy's power, and no mistake!"

"Hush, now, little one," she says, for the giant's benefit, who'd just come back in with a pitcher of water. "Sit you down, Cucullin," she turns to him and says, "and eat a bite, won't you? Have one of these little cakes here, while I put the bacon on to boil."

Just like your typical giant, Cucullin was a great greedy guts. So what does he do but stuff a whole one of those cakes—the ones with the iron griddles in them, remember—into his mouth! He takes a huge bite. AAAARRGH!

I'm sorry, did I frighten you? But that's the noise he made, you know.

"What's the matter?" says Oona, cool as the well-known cucumber.

"What class of bread is this at all?" shouts the other. "There's two of my best teeth gone!"

"Why," says she, "that's Finn's bread. Indeed, it's the only bread he'll eat when he's home. And he feeds it to this little fellow in the crib, here, in the hopes that he'll grow up to be a fine figure of a man like his dad. Here," she says kindly, "try another piece. You'll be needing some nourishment if you're to try a bout of strength with the likes of Finn McCool, after he gets back."

Cucullin was pretty well ravenous, after turning houses round and splitting rocks and whatnot, so he thought he'd have another try. Down he bites on a second cake, and AAAARRGH! again!

I didn't scare you that time, did I? You were expecting it. Aren't you the clever one, though?

"Keep the noise down, man!" says Oona. "And don't be waking the baby! Hush!" Finn must have had his thumb in his mouth that very minute, for he knew just what to do then. He sets up a terrible roaring and howling that must have made Cucullin wonder what manner of child this was altogether. "Ma! Ma!" Finn was screaming. "Gimme cake!"

Quick as a wink, Oona runs over to the cradle and hands Finn one of those cakes—you remember—that had no griddle in it! And just as quick, the things disappears down Finn's throat!

By now, Cucullin was starting to wonder, as well, about the size and strength of a man whose child could easily eat such bread as that. He began to entertain thoughts of leaving in a hurry.

"I think I'll be going now," says he, standing up. "I haven't all day to wait," he says, slowly making his way toward the door.

There in the cradle lay Finn, fairly glowing with delight that Cucullin was taking his leave without discovering the tricks that had been played on him.

"It's well for you that you go," says Oona, "before Finn gets back to make mincemeat of you. But you'll not leave, surely, without having a better look at the little fellow in the cradle there?"

"I would like a good glimpse of him," Cuciullin admits, "if only to see the class of teeth he has to eat cakes like those ones."

"Please yourself," says she, "but his cutest little grinders are far back in his head, so you'd best put your finger a good way in to appreciate them."

"I will," says Cucullin, and imagine his surprise when he brings his hand back out of Finn's mouth, and discovers that he's left behind him the very finger upon which his whole strength depended!

That was fine with Finn, who leapt from the cradle, and commenced flinging griddle-cakes at the weak and foolish Cucullin, who took to his heels, and was never seen again in the length and breadth of Ireland.

After that time, people still talked of the great strength of men, and the little strength of women. But they didn't talk that way in front of Finn McCool.

It was two (or, some say, three) centuries after the death of Finn that Saint Patrick came to Ireland. And, as the legend has it, the great missionary happened one day upon an old man, who claimed to be none other than Oisin, the son of Finn!

He it was who told (or rather sang) to the Saint most of the High Deeds of the Fianna, until it became clear to the Saint that the ancient warrior was about to die. Patrick offered to baptize Oisin and send him to heaven. But when the last of the Fianna was sorrowfully assured by the Saint that neither his great father nor his companions in arms nor any of the old heroes would be in heaven to greet him, Oisin refused, with his last breath, to be saved—preferring to go and take his chances wherever Finn McCool was spending his eternity.

The Saint had, naturally, been curious as to how Oisin had lived so long after his time; and the warrior-bard explained to him the magical adventure that had befallen him after the battle of Gavra, the last conflict in a civil war between Finn and the High King, and a fight in which Oisin's own son, Oscar, was slain.

This version of Oisin's story was translated by the scholar P. W. Joyce, from a twelfth-century manuscript.

OISIN IN TIR NA NOG
OR THE LAST OF THE FENA

A short time after the fatal battle of Gavra, where so many of our heroes fell, we were hunting on a dewy morning near the brink of Loch Lein, where the trees and hedges around us were all fragrant with blossoms, and the little birds sang melodious music on the branches. We soon roused the deer from the thickets, and as they bounded over the plain, our hounds in full cry followed after them.

We were not long so engaged, when we saw a rider coming swiftly towards us from the west; and we soon perceived that it was a maiden on a white steed. We all ceased from the chase on seeing the lady, who reined in as she approached. And Finn and the Fianna were greatly surprised, for they had never before seen so lovely a maiden. A slender golden diadem encircled her head. She wore a brown robe of silk, spangled with stars of red gold, which was fastened in front by a golden brooch, and fell from her shoulders till it swept the ground. Her yellow hair flowed far down over her robe in bright, golden ringlets. Her blue eyes were as clear as the drops of dew on the grass and while her small, white hand held the bridle and curbed her steed with a golden bit, she sat more gracefully than a swan on Loch Lein.

The white steed was covered with a smooth, flowing mantle. He was shod with four shoes of pure yellow gold, and in all Erin a better or more beautiful steed could not be found.

As she came slowly to the presence of Finn, he addressed her courteously: "Who art thou, O lovely youthful princess? Tell us thy name and the name of thy country, and relate to us the cause of thy coming."

She answered in a sweet and gentle voice: "Noble King of the Fena, I have had a long journey this day, for my country lies far off in the Western Sea. I am the daughter of the King of Tir na nOg, and my name is Niamh of the Golden Hair."

"And what is it that has caused thee to come so far across the sea? Has thy husband forsaken thee? Or what other evil has befallen thee?"

"My husband has not forsaken me, for I have never been married, or betrothed to any man. But I love thy noble son, Oisin, and this is what has brought me to Erin. It is not without reason that I have given him my love, and that I have undertaken this long journey. For I have often heard of his bravery, his gentleness, and the nobleness of his person. Many princes and high chiefs have sought me in marriage, but I was quite indifferent to all men and never consented to wed, till my heart was moved with love for they gentle son, Oisin."

When I heard these words, and when I looked on the lovely maiden with her glossy, golden hair, I was all over in love with her. I came near, and, taking her small hand in mine, I told her she was a mild star of brightness and beauty, and that I preferred her to all the princesses in the world for my wife.

"Then," said she, "I place you under 'geasa,' which true heroes never break through, to come with me on my white steed to Tir na nOg, the land of never-ending youth. It is the most delightful and the most renowned country under the sun. There is abundance of gold and silver and jewels, of honey and wine; and the trees bear fruit and blossoms and green leaves together all the year round.

"You will get a hundred swords and a hundred robes of silk and satin, a hundred swift steeds, and a hundred slender, keen-scenting hounds. You will get herds of cows without number, flocks of sheep with fleeces of gold, a coat of mail that cannot be pierced, and a sword that never missed a stroke and from which no one ever escaped alive.

"There are feasting and harmless pastimes each day. A hundred warriors fully armed shall always await you at call, and harpers shall delight you with their sweet music. You will wear the diadem of the King of Tir na nOg, which he never yet gave to anyone under the sun, and which will guard you day and night, in tumult and battle and danger of every kind.

"Lapse of time shall bring neither decay nor death, and you shall be for ever young, and gifted with unfading beauty and strength. All these delights you shall enjoy, and many others that I do not mention; and I myself will be your wife if you come with me to Tir na nOg."

I replied that she was my choice above all the maidens in the world, and that I would willingly go with her to the Land of Youth.

When my father, Finn, and the Fena heard me say this, and knew that I was going from them, they raised three shouts of grief and lamentation. And Finn came up to me and took my hand in his, saying sadly: "Woe is me, my son, that you are going away from me, for I do not expect that you will ever return to me."

The manly beauty of his countenance became quite dimmed with sorrow, and though I promised to return after a little time, and fully believed that I should see him again, I could not check my tears as I gently kissed my father's cheek.

I then bade farewell to my dear companions, and mounted the white steed, while the lady kept her seat before me. She gave the signal, and the steed galloped swiftly and smoothly towards the west, till he reached the strand; and when his gold-shod hooves touched the waves, he shook himself and neighed three times. He made no delay, but plunged forward at once, moving over the face of the sea with the speed of a cloud-shadow on a March day. The wind overtook the waves and we overtook the wind, so that we straightway lost sight of land; and we saw nothing but billows tumbling before us and billows tumbling behind us.

Other shores came into view, and we saw many wonderful things on our journey—islands and cities, lime-white mansions, bright grianans [summer houses] and lofty palaces. A hornless fawn once crossed our course, bounding nimbly along from the crest of one wave to the crest of another; and close after in full chase, a white hound with red ears. We saw also a lovely young maiden on a brown steed, with a golden apple in her hand; and as she passed swiftly by, a young warrior on a white steed plunged after her, wearing a long, flowing mantle of yellow silk, and holding a gold-hilted sword in his hand.

I knew naught of these things, and marvelling much, I asked the princess what they meant.

"Heed not what you see here, Oisin," she said, "for all these wonders are as nothing compared with what you shall see in Tir na nOg."

At last we saw at a great distance, rising over the waves on the very verge of the sea, a palace more splendid than all the others; and, as we drew near, its front glittered like the morning sun. I asked the lady what royal house this was, and who was the prince that ruled over it.

"This country is the Land of Virtues," she replied. "Its King is the giant, Fomor of the Blows, and its Queen the daughter of the King of the Land of Life. This Fomor brought the lady away by force from her own country, and keeps her in his palace. But she has put him under 'geasa' that he cannot break through, never to ask her to marry him till she can find a champion to fight him in single combat. Yet she still remains in bondage, for no hero has yet come hither who has the courage to meet the giant."

"A blessing on you, golden-haired Niamh," Oisin replied. "I have never heard music sweeter than your voice and although I feel pity for this princess, yet your story is pleasant to hear. Of a certainty I will go to the palace, and try whether I cannot kill this Fomor, and free the lady."

So we came to land, and as we drew nigh to the palace the lovely princess met us and bade us welcome. She led us in and placed us on chairs of gold. After which choice food was placed before us, and drinking-horns filled with mead, and golden goblets of sweet wine.

When we had eaten and drunk, the mild young princess told us her story, while tears streamed from her soft blue eyes. She ended by saying: "I shall never return to my own country and to my father's house, so long as this great and cruel giant is alive."

When I heard her sad voice, and saw her tears falling, I was moved with pity. Telling her to cease from her grief, I gave her my hand as a pledge that I would meet the giant, and either slay him or fall myself in her defense.

While we were yet speaking, we saw the giant coming towards the palace, large of body and ugly and hateful in appearance, carrying a load of deerskins on his back and holding a great iron club in his hand. He threw down his load when he saw us, turned a surly look on the princess, and, without greeting us, or showing the least mark of courtesy, he forthwith challenged me to battle in a loud, rough voice.

It was not my wont to be dismayed by a call to battle, or to be terrified at the sight of an enemy, and I went forth at once without the least fear in my heart. But though I had fought many battles in Erin against wild boars and enchanters and foreign invaders, never before did I find it so hard to preserve my life. We fought for three days and three nights without food or drink or sleep, for the giant did not give me a moment for rest and neither did I give him. At length, when I looked at the two princesses weeping in great fear, and when I called to mind my father's deeds in battle, the fury of my valour arose. With a sudden onset I felled the giant to the earth and instantly, before he could recover himself, I cut off his head.

When the maidens saw the monster lying on the ground dead, they uttered three cries of joy and they came to me, and led me into the palace. For I was indeed bruised all over, and covered with gory wounds, and a sudden dizziness of brain and feebleness of body seized me. But the daughter of the King of the Land of Life applied precious balsam and healing herbs to my wounds and in a short time I was healed, and my cheerfulness of mind returned.

Then I buried the giant in a deep and wide grave and I raised a great carn over him, and placed on it a stone with his name graved in Ogham.

We rested that night, and at the dawn of the next morning, Niamh said to me that it was time for us to resume our journey to Tir na nOg. So we took leave of the daughter of the King of the Land of Life; and though her heart was joyful after her release, she wept at our departure, and we were not less sorry at parting from her. When we had mounted the white steed, he galloped towards the strand. As soon as his hooves touched the wave, he shook himself and neighed three times. We plunged forward over the clear, green sea with the speed of a march wind on a hillside. Soon we saw nothing but billows tumbling before us and billows tumbling behind us. We saw again the fawn chased by the white hound with red ears, and the maiden with the golden apple passed swiftly by, followed by the young warrior in yellow silk on his white steed. And again we passed many strange islands and cities and white palaces.

The sky now darkened, so that the sun was hidden from our view. A storm arose, and the sea was lighted up with constant flashes. But though the wind blew from every point of the heavens, and the waves rose up and roared around us, the white steed kept his course straight on, moving as calmly and swiftly as before, through the foam and blinding spray, without being delayed or disturbed in the least, and without turning either to the right or to the left.

At length the storm abated, and after a time the sun again shone brightly. When I looked up, I saw a country near at hand, all green and full of flowers, with beautiful smooth plains, blue hills, and bright lakes and waterfalls. Not far from the shore stood a palace of surpassing beauty and splendour. It was covered all over with gold and with gems of every colour—blue, green, crimson, and yellow. On each side were grianans shining with precious stones, built by artists the most skillful that could be found.

I asked Niamh the name of that delightful country, and she replied: "This is my native country, Tir na nOg. And there is nothing I have promised you that you will not find in it."

As soon as we reached the shore, we dismounted; and now we saw advancing from the palace a troop of noble-looking warriors, all clad in bright garments, who came forward to meet and welcome us. Following these we saw a stately glittering host, with the King at their head wearing a robe of bright yellow satin covered with gems, and a crown that sparkled with gold and diamonds. The Queen came after, attended by a hundred lovely young maidens; and as they advanced towards us, it seemed to me that this King and Queen exceeded all the kings and queens of the world in beauty and gracefulness and majesty.

After they had kissed their daughter, the King took my hand, and said aloud in the hearing of the host: "This is Oisin, son of Finn, for whom my daughter, Niamh, travelled over the sea to Erin. This is Oisin, who is to be the husband of Niamh, of the Golden Hair. We give you a hundred thousand welcomes, brave Oisin. You will be forever young in this land. All kinds of delights and innocent pleasures are awaiting you, and my daughter, the gentle, golden-haired Niamh, shall be your wife, for I am King of Tir na nOg."

I gave thanks to the King, and I bowed low to the Queen; after which we went into the palace, where we found a banquet prepared. The feasting and rejoicing lasted for ten days, and on the last day I was wedded to the gentle Niamh of the Golden Hair.

I lived in the Land of Youth more than three hundred years, but it appeared to me that only three years had pased since the day I parted from my friends. At the end of that time, I began to have a longing desire to see my father, Finn, and all my old friends, and I asked leave of Niamh and of the King to visit Erin.

The King gave permission, and Niamh said: "I will give consent, though I feel sorrow in my heart, for I fear much you will never return to me."

I replied that I would surely return, and that she need not feel any doubt or dread, for that the white steed knew the way and would bring me back in safety. Then she addressed me in these words, which seemed very strange to me.

"I will not refuse this request, though your journey afflicts me with great grief and fear. Erin is not now as it was when you left it. The great King Finn and his Fena are all gone. You will find, instead of them, a holy father and hosts of priests and saints. Now, think well on what I say to you, and keep my words in your mind. If once you alight from the white steed, you will never come back to me. Again I warn you, if you place your feet on the green sod in Erin, you will never return to this lovely land. A third time, O Oisin, my beloved husband, a third time I say to you, if you alight from the white steed, you will never see me again."

I promised that I would faithfully attend to her words, and that I would not alight from the white steed. Then, as I looked into her gentle face and marked her grief, my heart was weighed down with sadness, and my tears flowed plentifully. But even so, my mind was bent on coming back to Erin.

When I had mounted the white steed, he galloped straight towards the shore. We moved as swiftly as before over the clear sea. The wind overtook the waves and we overtook the wind, so that we straightway left the Land of Youth behind. We passed by many islands and cities, till at length we landed on the green shores of Erin.

As I travelled on through the country, I looked closely around me, but I scarcely knew the old places, for everything seemed strangely altered. I saw no sign of Finn and his host, and I began to dread that Niamh's saying was coming true. At length, I espied at a distance a company of little men and women, all mounted on horses as small as themselves; and when I came near, they greeted me kindly and courteously. They looked at me with wonder and curiosity, and they marvelled much at my great size, and at the beauty and majesty of my person.

I asked them about Finn and the Fena—whether they were still living, or if any sudden disaster had swept them away. And one replied: "We have heard of the hero Finn, who ruled the Fena of Erin in times of old, and who never had an equal for bravery and wisdom. The poets of Gael have written many books concerning his deeds and the deeds of the Fena, which we cannot now relate, but they are gone long since, for they lived many ages ago. We have heard also, and we have seen it written in very old books, that Finn had a son named Oisin. Now this Oisin went with a young fairy maiden to Tir na nOg, and his father and friends sorrowed greatly after him, and sought him long; but he was never seen again."

When I heard all this, I was filled with amazement, and my heart grew heavy with sorrow. I silently turned my steed from the wondering people, and set forward straightway for Allen of the mighty deeds, on the broad, green plains of Leinster. It was a miserable journey to me; and though my mind, being full of sadness at all I saw and heard, forecasted further sorrows, I was grieved more than ever when I reached Allen. For there, indeed, I found the hill deserted and lonely, and my father's palace all in ruins and overgrown with grass and weeds.

I turned slowly away, and afterwards fared through the land in every direction in search of my friends. But I met only crowds of little people, all strangers, who gazed at me with wonder, and none knew me. I visited every place throughout the country where I knew the Fena had lived, but I found their houses all like Allen, solitary and in ruins and overgrown with grass and weeds.

At length I came to Glenasmole, where many a time I had hunted in days of old with the Fena, and there I saw a crowd of people in the glen.

As soon as they saw me, one of them came forward and said: "Come to us, thou mighty hero, and help us out of our strait, for thou art a man of vast strength."

I went to them, and found a number of men trying in vain to raise a large, flat stone. It was half-lifted from the ground, but those who were under it were not strong enough either to raise it further or to free themselves from its weight. And they were in great distress, and on the point of being crushed to death.

I thought it a shameful thing that so many men should be unable to lift this stone, which Oscar, if he were alive, would take in his right hand and fling over the heads of the feeble crowd. After I had looked a little while, I stooped forward and seized the flag with one hand; and, putting forth my strength, I flung it seven perches from its place, and relieved the little men. But with the great strain the golden saddle-girth broke, and bounding forward to keep myself from falling, I suddenly came to the ground on my two feet.

The moment the white steed felt himself free, he shook himself and neighed. Then, starting off with the speed of a cloud-shadow on a March day, he left me standing helpless and sorrowful. Instantly, a woeful change came over me; the sight of my eyes began to fade, the ruddy beauty of my face fled, I lost all my strength, and I fell to the earth, a poor, withered old man, blind, and wrinkled and feeble.

The white steed was never seen again. I never recovered my sight, my youth, or my strength; and I have lived in this manner, sorrowing without ceasing for my gentle, golden-haired wife, Niamh, and think ever of my father, Finn, and of the lost companions of my youth.

Like Robin Hood, and Paul Bunyan, and many a movie and comic-book hero, Finn was fortunate in his companions—in his case, a group not always, even, drawn from among his own troops, the Fianna, but invariably endowed with exactly the skills and qualities necessary to save the hero and the day against a horrible adversary.

In this tale (from Kennedy's Legendary Fictions), *Finn is accompanied on his mission by a trio of young men he happens upon while playing Irish field hockey (hurling), a game at which he, like every single Irish hero before or since, is the best that ever was.*

It is perfectly proper to squirm, gasp, writhe, and even giggle as the teller of this tale lays on the gory details. Kennedy entitled the tale "Beanriogain na Sciana Breaca," which he tells us might mean either "Queen with the Speckled Dagger" or "Queen of the Many-Colored Bed-Chamber." A curious ambiguity.

BEANRIOGAIN NA SCIANA BREACA

Fion son of Cumhail was one day separated from his knights as they were engaged at the chase, and came out on a wide grassy plain that stretched along the sea strand. There he saw the twelve sons of Bawr Sculloge playing at *coman* (hurling), and wonderful were the strokes they gave the ball, and fleeter than the wind their racing after it. As Fion approached they ceased their sport, and all coming forward hailed him as the protector of the wronged, and the defender of the island against the white strangers. "If you like to amuse yourself, Fion son of Cumhail," said the chief of one party, "take my coman, and pull down the vanity of our opponents." "I would do your party no honour with this toy," said Fion, taking the coman between his finger and thumb. "Let that not disturb you," said the hurling chief. So he pulled up a *neanthog* (nettle), and muttering a charm over it, and changing it thrice from one hand to the other, it became a weapon fitting for the hand of the son of Cumhail. It was worth a year of idle life to see the blows struck by the chief, and hear the terrible heavy sound as the coman met the ball, and drove it out of sight. And there was Cosh Lua (fleet foot) to pursue the flying globe and bring it back. "My hand to you," said the eldest boy, "I never saw hurling till now." Fion's party won the first game, and while they were resting for the second a boat neared the land. and a man sprang out and approached the party.

"Hail, very noble and courageous chief!" said he, addressing Fion. "My lady, the Queen of Sciana Breaca, lays on you geasa, that you come forthwith to visit her in her island. She is persecuted by the powerful witch Cluas Haistig (flat ear), and she has been advised to call on you for help." "Perhaps in vain," said Fion. "I can find out from the gift of the Salmon of Wisdom what is passing in any part of the island, but I am unprovided with charms against witchcraft." "Let not that be a hindrance," said the eldest boy of Bawr Sculloge, Grunne Ceanavaltha (young bearded man); "my two brothers Bechunah (thief) and Cluas Guilin (Guilin's ears) and myself will go with you. We were not born yesterday."

He took two hazel twigs in his hand; and when they came to the edge of the water, one became a boat and the other a mast. He steered; one brother managed the sail, the other bailed out the water, and so they sailed till they came to the harbour of the island.

They visited the Queen, and were hospitably treated, and after they were refreshed with the best of food and liquor she explained her trouble. "I had two fair children, and when each was a year old it fell sick, and on the third night was carried away by the wicked sorceress Cluas Haistig. My youngest, now a twelve-month-old, has spent two sick nights. This night she will surely carry him away unless you or your young friends prevent her."

When the darkness came, Fion and the three brothers took their station in the room of the sick child; Grunne and Bechunah played at chess, Cluas Guilin watched, and Fion reclined on a couch. Vessels full of Spanish wine, Greek honey (mead), and Danish beer were laid on the table. The two chess players were intent on their game, the watcher kept his senses on the strain, and a druidic sleep seized on the son of Cumhail. Three times he made mighty efforts to keep awake, and thrice he was overcome by powerful weariness. The brothers smiled at his defeat, but left him to repose. Soon the watcher felt a chill shiver run over him, and the infant began to moan. A feeling of horror seized on the three boys, and a thin, long, hairy arm was seen stealing down the opening above the fire. Though the teeth of Cluas Guilin were chattering with terror, he sprang forward, seized the hand, and held it firm. A violent effort was made by the powerful witch sprawling on the roof to draw it away, but in vain. Another, and then another, and down

110

it came across the body of Cluas Guilin. A deadly faintness came over him, the chess players ran to his aid, and when his senses returned neither child nor arm was to be seen. They looked at each other in dismay, but in a moment Cluas cried, "Grunne, take your arrows, you Bechunah, your cord, and let us pursue the cursed Druidess." In a few minutes they were at the mooring post, and away in their boat they went as fleet as the driving gale till the enchanted tower of the witch came in sight. It seemed built with strong upright bars of iron with the spaces between them filled by iron plates. A pale blue flame went out from it on every side, and it kept turning, turning, and never stood at rest. As soon as the boat approached, Cluas began to mutter charms in verse, and to raise and sink his arms with the palms downwards. He called on his gods to bring a mighty sleep on the evil dweller within, and cause the tower to cease its motion. It was done according to his incantation, and Bechunah taking his cord ladder and giving it an accurate and very powerful heave, it caught on the pike of the steep circular roof, and up he sprung fleeter than the wild cat of the woods. Looking in through the opening, he beheld the dread woman lying on the floor weighed down with the magic sleep, the floor stained with the blood which was still flowing from her torn shoulder, and the three children crying, and striving to keep their feet out of it. Descending into the room he soothed them, and one by one he conveyed them through the opening, down the knotted cords, and so into the boat. The power of the spell ceasing as soon as the boat began to shoot homewards, the tower began again to whirl, and the witch's shriek came over the waves. It was so terrible that if Cluas had not covered the heads of the children with a thick mantle, their souls would have left their bodies with terror. A dark form was seen gliding down the building, and the dash of an oar was heard from the witch's corrach, which was soon in swift pursuit. "Draw your bowstring to your ear, O Grunne," said Cluas, "and preserve your renown." He waved his arms and said his spells, and light proceeding from his finger-ends illumined the rough, dark, foam-crested waves for many a fathom behind them. The hellish woman and her corrach were coming fleet as thought behind, but the light had not rested on the fearful figure and face a second moment when were heard the shrill twang of the bowstring, and the dull stroke of the arrow in her breast. Corrach and rower sunk in the waters; the magic light from Cluas's hands vanished, but a purple-red flame played over the spot where the witch had gone down till the boat was miles ahead.

As they approached the harbour, the landing-place and all around were lighted up with numberless torches held in the hands of the anxious people; the sight of the three children and their three deliverers made the sky ring with cheers of gladness.

At the entrance of the fort they met the mother and her attendants, and the joy the sight of the recovered children gave them is not to be told. Fion had awakened at the moment of the witch's destruction, and was found walking to and fro in high resentment against himself. He knew by his druidic knowledge that the children were safe on their return, and cheered the Queen with the glad news, and thus the people had been waiting at the mooring point.

Three months did Fion and the three boys remain with the Queen of Sciana Breaca, and every year a boat laden with gold, and silver, and precious stones, and well-wrought helmets, shields, and loricas, and chess tables, and rich cloaks, arrived for the sons of ⌐awr Sculloge at the point of the shore where the Queen's messenger had laid geasa on the famous son of Cumhail.

Ireland is the country of small horses and big dogs. Not that there aren't tall thoroughbreds and little beagles enough for the hunt—but a uniquely Irish sight is a four-foot-high Irish wolfhound passing a four-foot-high Connemara pony on the road. It might have given Jonathan Swift ideas. . . .

The Irish wolfhound is the world's tallest dog, swift, keen-sighted, and powerful, bred thousands of years ago to hunt the (now extinct) elk and wolves of Erin.

It was doubtless after such a great beast that Cuchulain (the Hound of Culain) was named; and Finn McCool's hounds, Bran and Sceolan, accompanied him on many an adventure.

Wolfhounds remain favorites today for their dignity, strength, and stature, and for their notorious gentleness with young children.

HOW FINN GOT HIS HOUNDS

They say Finn McCool was only seen to shed tears twice in his life. Once was when his own grandson Oscar was killed in battle, and the other time was when Bran died. Bran was Finn's hound.

The way the animal died was strange enough—he'd scented out a doe on a mountainside and was chasing after her, when Finn thought he recognized the creature as an old love of his own, under some sort of enchantment, most like. The dog Bran was just that moment sprinting through Finn's legs and for the doe's throat. Without thinking, Finn squeezed his knees together, and that way the dog died.

But that story's nothing compared to the one of how Bran came to be born.

They say one time Finn's mother came to visit him, and brought along her young and beautiful sister, Tuiren, that was Finn's aunt. Well, there was an Ulsterman staying there at Finn's house, a chief by the name of Iollan, that took a fancy to Tuiren, and asked Finn could he marry her. "Well and good," said Finn, and he gave his consent, but he warned the man to look after his aunt well, or he'd answer to himself. So they were married, the two of them.

But for a long while before all that, your man Iollan had a sweetheart among the people of the Sidhe, and those ones are well known for their jealousy. So this Sidhe woman swore revenge against Tuiren, and she went to her disguised as one of Finn's servant women, and bade her come along to a feast Finn was having.

Tuiren went with her, but not to any feast of Finn's. The woman of the Sidhe led her out into the wild woods, and then took a wand out from underneath her cloak, and struck her with it. And didn't the mortal woman turn into a hound bitch that minute? Of course, she was the most beautiful ever seen in Ireland, but a dog all the same.

And that woman of the Sidhe wasn't finished with her yet. There was a king out west in those times called Fergus, that was famous for hating dogs. He wouldn't let one of them under his roof with him. It was to Fergus that the woman of the Sidhe took Finn's poor aunt, and gave her to him. "Finn wishes you long life and health, and makes you a present of this hound, to treat as you will," she said.

Then she went away content, and Fergus was puzzled, for wasn't he well known for hating dogs? It was a queer gift from his friend Finn, he thought.

But when he came to try the hound bitch in the field, she was the best he ever saw. There wasn't a wild creature she couldn't run down and take in the hunt, so fierce was she; but at home by the hearth she was gentle and quiet and sweet, so that in the end Fergus took a great liking to her, and to dogs in general.

And when her time came, Fergus kept her out of the hunt awhile, and she gave birth to two whelps.

Now, word came to Finn that his aunt was no longer living in the house of Iollan, and that made him angry. He sent for the man. Iollan begged Finn for the time he'd need to find out where Tuiren was, and Finn gave him a night and a day, or he'd answer for it with his life.

The poor man must have had some idea there was Sidhe mischief in it all the while, for he went straight out to call on his old sweetheart, and told her the way things were with him.

"Give me your pledge," said she, "that you will be mine and I will be yours till the end of your life, and I will save you from the anger of Finn."

So he promised her that, and she went to the fort where Fergus was, and brought Tuiren away with her own shape on her again, and returned her to Finn.

And as to the two whelps, the names Finn gave them were Bran and Sceolan, and they stayed with him always, the finest dogs for tracking and fighting and loyalty in all Ireland—for weren't they the cousins of Finn McCool?

114

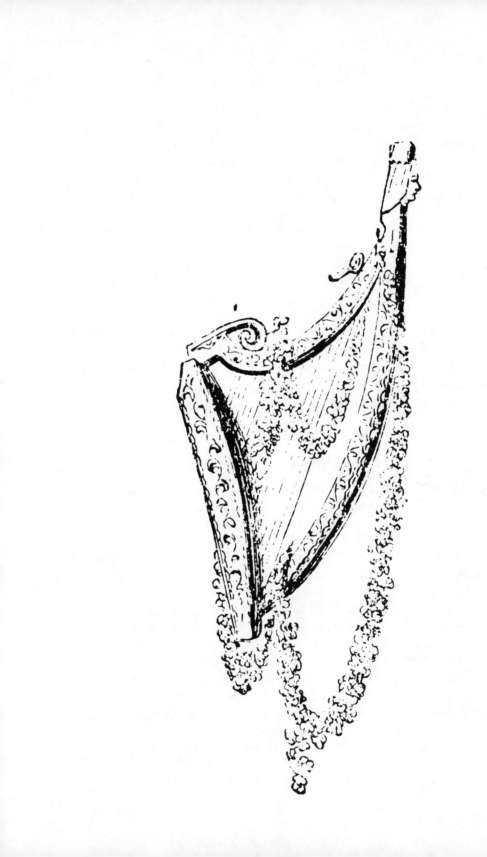

At the heart of the saga of King Arthur is a love story—a tale of
passion and loyalty, jealousy and revenge. And thus it is with Ireland's cycle of the adventures of Finn McCool.

Like Arthur, Finn, when almost an old man, takes a young wife.
Like Guinevere, Finn's bride Grainne falls in love with the most beau-
tiful and trusted of her husband's followers and runs away with him.
The Lancelot of this tale is named Diarmaid, or Dermot.

This tragic love triangle (think of Deirdre, King Conor and
Naisi . . . Iseult, King Mark, and Tristan . . . or indeed of Arthur and
Guinevere, who were Welsh, and Lancelot of Brittany) appears to
have a central place in the Celtic imagination.

"The Pursuit of Diarmaid and Grainne" is the subject of many
long tellings, by Lady Gregory, Rolleston, and others. Here is a version recorded in 1954 in Donegal, where, as throughout Ireland, the
many ancient "dolmens" (which are two standing stones with another flat stone laid across them) are still known as Leapacha Dhiarmada
agus Ghrainne; the Beds of Diarmaid and Grainne, where the lovers
are said to have rested during their flight. The tale is taken from Sean
O'Sullivan's book The Folklore of Ireland.

DIARMAID AND GRAINNE

The Fianna in tradition were bands of roving warriors and hunters,
who were under the command of their leader Finn mac Cool
(Fionn mac Cumhail), and were called upon by the King of Ireland to
defend the country when danger threatened from outside. Hundreds of
tales, in prose and verse, about their exploits and adventures, were
more popular than the tales of the Ulster Cycle. The characteristic
qualities of the Fianna were summarised in the saying 'cleanliness of
heart, strength of arm and fulfilment of promises.' Tales of the Fianna
were well-known in Gaelic-speaking Scotland, as in Ireland.

Like the preceding tale of the Fate of the Sons of Uisneach, the
main theme is centered on the desertion by the heroine of her elderly
suitor for a younger lover, the pursuit of the eloping lovers and the
death of the hero, Diarmaid. The tale of Diarmaid and Grainne was
mentioned in a saga-list of the tenth century, and the earliest full manuscript version dates from the fourteenth century.

Many dolmens throughout Ireland were popularly known as Lea-

pacha Dhiarmada agus Ghrainne (Beds of Diarmaid and Grainne)
where the lovers were said to have rested during their flight.

One day when the Fianna were hunting on the mountains of Ireland,
they arrived at the palace of King Cormac Airt. He had a daughter
named Grainne, and it was said that she was as beautiful a woman as
was to be found in Ireland at that time. Finn mac Cool was a widower
just then, and his one wish in the world was to get Grainne as his
wife.

As the Fianna were crossing the ford towards the king's palace, a
fairy appeared before them and said:

> "Go back, go back, Finn mac Cool!
> Don't go to mac Airt's house!
> If you get Grainne, the king's young daughter,
> It won't be for your benefit!"

This didn't discourage Finn or his men. They went on to the palace and Finn told Cormac why he had come. Cormac heartily consented to give him his daughter. At that time, Finn was well known all
over Ireland, and both high and low had great esteem for him.

A night was fixed for the betrothal and a day for the marriage.
Cormac invited all his own court, and Finn and his Fianna also came
for the festivities. On the night of the betrothal, when all had arrived at
the palace, Cormac went out and locked all the gates around it. It was
as fine a night of celebration as had ever been held in Ireland. Around
midnight, Grainne got to her feet and said that she had not yet handed
out a drink, and it was time now to do so. She ordered a servant to go
out to the room where the whiskey was stored and to bring in a certain
keg. The servant did so and when he had brought in the keg, Grainne
took up a goblet and filled it with whiskey. She gave it to drink to the
man who sat at Diarmaid O Duibhne's right hand and passed it around
the circle until it came back, empty, to Diarmaid.

"Diarmaid," said she, "it looks as if I did not wish to give you
anything to drink!"

"I wouldn't hold that against you, Grainne," said Diarmaid. "I
have had plenty to drink already."

"Well, there's more where that drink came from," said Grainne.

117

She took the goblet and went out to the whiskey-room. She delayed there for a while, and when she returned, everybody in the room had fallen fast asleep, except Diarmaid O Duibhne.

"Gentle Diarmaid of the brown hair," said Grainne,
"Most comely of body from head to feet,
Come away with me to the edge of the waves!
You, not Finn, are my choice."

"I assure you, Grainne," said Diarmaid, "that I would be glad to have you as wife in honour of the king. Many's the fine day I hunted with him over moors and mountains, enjoying ourselves. But Finn mac Cool is the great leader of the Fianna, and we'll never hear the end of it, if you and I elope together!"

"That's the way it will have to be, Diarmaid," said she.

"Don't say any more," said Diarmaid.

They left the palace and found all the gates closed.

"There's a secret way out," said Grainne.

"If I get out of here," said Diarmaid, "I'll go as a warrior would, and if I can't do that, I'll stay here."

He went to the main gate in front of the palace. He then stepped back a few paces, jumped and went clear out across the gate. Grainne did the same. They went to a stable that was outside the walls, harnessed two horses to a coach and drove off till they came to the edge of a river. Grainne said that they could go no further. They untied the horses, and Diarmaid led one of them through the river and left it grazing at the other side. They walked up a small, nice hillock, and sat down to talk about the times that had gone and what lay ahead of them. Then they both fell asleep.

When the Fianna awoke in Cormac's palace and found Diarmaid and Grainne missing, Finn chewed his thumb of knowledge and learned that they were asleep on the hill. He ordered his men to get up and go in pursuit of them immediately. They set out, Finn at their head, and went straight to where the pair were asleep. When they came within shouting distance of them, Finn said that they had never yet killed a bird or a beast, let alone a person, without giving them a chance of escaping or defending themselves.

"Diarmaid and Grainne must get that chance too," said Finn.

He shouted loudly to the pair to defend themselves. They woke up and found that they were in danger. Grainne saw that they were in trouble and she began to cry.

"Sit up here on my arm!" said Diarmaid.

He drew his sword from its scabbard and faced for where the Fianna were thickest. He hewed a passage through them and hid on the other side—it was said of Diarmaid that he was as swift as a hare in a mountain glen! The Fianna had to return home empty-handed. Diarmaid and Grainne knew that they would be pursued again the next night. When night came, they made their bed on the mountain lying on sand from the sea-shore. Finn chewed his thumb again and learned that the fugitives were asleep on the sand of the sea-shore. He ordered his men to search the sea-shore, but he did not accompany them. The Fianna searched the shore, but returned home without finding anything. Diarmaid and Grainne knew that they would be pursued again the next night. They took heather from the mountain and made a bed of it on the sand-hills at the shore. Finn chewed his thumb again and learned that they were asleep on the heather of the mountain. He ordered his men to search the mountain, but it was all in vain; they came home as they had left, empty-handed.

Finn suspected that his men were deceiving him, so he sent a request to the King of Scotland to send his best men to Ireland to capture one of the Fianna, Diarmaid O Duibhne. No sooner had Finn sent this message to Scotland than Diarmaid and Grainne learned about it. The Fianna spent some time watching the harbours and coast of Ireland, waiting for the Scotsmen to land, but when they were slow in coming, the Fianna went inland.

Dairmaid and Grainne were sitting one day on a mountain-side in County Down, when they saw a sailing-ship approaching. They knew that it was carrying the Scotsmen. When the ship came to the shore, Diarmaid and Grainne went down to meet it, and the captain asked them did they know where Finn mac Cool lived. Diarmaid said that they did, and that Finn had sent him to meet them and to teach them some feats of prowess, without which they would never be able to capture the man they were after.

"Tis too late to start teaching you today," said Diarmaid. "Be ready tomorrow morning, and I'll be here!"

When Diarmaid arrived at the ship next morning, the Scotsmen were ready. He brought them to a field near the shore, at the top of which was a small wood. He cut two poles in the wood and stood them near each other in the field. He then placed his sword, with its edge upwards, on top of the poles. He drew back a few paces and jumped clear over the sword.

"I would like to know now," said Diarmaid, "which man of you can imitate that."

The first Scotsman that tried the jump came down on the sword and was cut in two. The same thing happened to the second and so on until the bodies of thirty of them were lying in a heap beyond the sword.

"Enough of you have died today," said Diarmaid, "without being able to do what I did! We'll try another trick tomorrow."

The Scotsmen returned to their ship that night, and Diarmaid and Grainne slept soundly. Next morning, Diarmaid went to the ship again, and the Scotsmen were waiting for him. There was an empty barrel lying beside the quay, and Diarmaid took it on his shoulders to the top of a small, green hill. There he filled the barrel with stones and let it roll down the slope, while he himself danced on top of the barrel all the way to the shore. He then emptied the barrel of stones and took it to the top of the hill again. He filled it with stones once more, and asked the Scotsmen to do the trick. When one of them attempted to dance on the barrel as it rolled downhill, it turned and he was killed. And so it went on until thirty-four of them lost their lives in the same way.

"I see," said Diarmaid, "that not a man among you is able to imitate me. I am the man ye came to Ireland to capture. Now I am ready to fight ye or to allow ye to return home as quickly as ye came."

"I think we had better go back home," said the captain.

"Very well," said Diarmaid.

The Scotsmen went back to the ship, hoisted the sails and set out for their own country. Diarmaid and Grainne spent a season in every part of Ireland. It was a hard, uncomfortable life for both of them: the king's daughter who had been reared in a palace, with girls and women attending on her with the best of food, and one of the Fianna, who also had got the best of food and had thrown the worst of it over his shoulder. Still, they were satisfied with the way things were. One day when they were seated on a mountain-side in Sligo, they heard the baying of hounds approaching.

"They sound very much like the hounds of Finn," said Diarmaid.

He went to the top of the mountain and saw an enraged boar coming towards him, pursued by a pack of eager hounds.

"If I were with Finn mac Cool today," said Diarmaid, "that boar wouldn't go very far."

He ran down the side of the mountain and faced the boar. He jumped on its back and slowed it down. When the boar heard the hounds baying at its heels, it turned its head and took a full bite out of Diarmaid's thigh. Blood poured from the gash; Diarmaid grew dizzy and fell to the ground. Grainne ran to him, but could do nothing, only look at him. At least the Fianna came up. Finn ordered one of his men to fetch a plaster for the wound, but when he brought it, Diarmaid was already dead. They waked and buried him, and when the last of the clay was thrown on the grave, Finn said:

"Well, Grainne," said he, "you left me and went off with Diarmaid. You have now lost him. Are you willing to have me as your husband?"

Grainne agreed. The two of them got married, but, if they did, they spent an unhappy life till they too went to the grave.

III. FIRESIDE TALES

Fireside Tales

And still around the fires of peat
Live on the ancient days;
There still do living lips repeat
The old and deathless lays. . . .

from *An Anthology of Irish Verse*
Padraic Colum, editor

Imagine, if you will, a scene that might be from your grandparents' time—or a hundred centuries before.

The night is pitch black, and cold, and (this being Ireland) probably wet as well. The cottages of the fisherfolk along the coast, or the farmers inland, are few and far apart. But there, around a bend in the road, or over the crest of a hill, is a small, flickering light—like a star in the mist.

You find a little, low, thatched dwelling, only one room, really, with a bedroom off to one end . . . but in the room's center, the heart of the home—the hearth, where a slow, sweet-smelling peat fire burns. Around the fire stools, chairs, and perhaps a long, low bench are gathered, and you are welcomed in, with a blessing and a cup of tea or maybe something stronger.

A place of honor—nearest the hearth—is given you. And after the Rosary is said, and gossip exchanged, and the weather marvelled at, it's time for the tales to be told.

The oldest man or woman of the house may well be a sha-nachie—a gatherer and teller of tales.

"Tis a lee and a long time now since . . ." or "Once upon a time, when pigs were swine . . ." the story begins. There is no other sound but the sea hushing, or maybe the cry of a curlew out in the dark. The baby sleeps on mother's breast, and the older children listen, wide-eyed. Dad puffs his pipe. And, in the corner, the English folklorist squints in the little light and scribbles furiously in his notepad.

The world's folklore abounds with stories of poor people outwitting the rich and powerful. In such tales the trickster-hero often plays the fool and traps his enemies in a net woven of their own greed and cruelty. Consider Br'er Rabbit.

"Hudden and Dudden and Donal O'Neary" is a tale from Donegal, in the north—and in some versions has sectarian overtones, with Donal cast as the native Irish tenant farmer, and Hudden and Dudden representing the transplanted Presbyterian "landed gentry."

Joseph Jacobs presented a version in his Celtic Fairy Tales, *but was careful to expurgate the marvelously casual matricide episode.*

HUDDEN AND DUDDEN
AND DONAL O'NEARY

There were two rich farmers lived in the North one time. Their names were Hudden and Dudden. They had big herds of fat black cattle, the pair of them, and Hudden and Dudden were such good friends as rich men can be.

They had a neighbor, a poor farmer named Donal O'Neary, who put the one skinny cow that was all he possessed out to pasture on the wee strip of land between their two big fields.

Hudden and Dudden were jealous of Donal O'Neary's little field, and always on the look-out for a way to take it away from him. Because poor as he was, Donal O'Neary was a happy, smiling class of person, always singing and joking, and they thought he lowered the tone of the place, you see.

One night they decided they'd poison his cow, and that way Donal would have no reason to stay. So they did that. And, come morning, Donal O'Neary found the poor old beast stretched out on the ground.

But he was the sort of man who'd always try to make the best of a bad lot, so after shedding a tear and saying a prayer for the animal, didn't he set to work skinning the hide off it? Hudden and Dudden watched over their hedges while Donal headed down the road to town, with the hide over his shoulder. The man was whistling! They ground their teeth at the sound of it.

There was a river ran through the town, and a bridge over the river, and a pub beside the bridge. Donal O'Neary stopped in front of

the pub, and he did a funny thing. He took out his pocket knife and
made little cuts, about the size of button holes, in the cow's hide; and he
took the few pennies he had left in the world, and he slipped them into
the holes.

Then as bold as a crow he strode into the pub, hung the cowhide
up on a nail in the wall, and ordered a pint. Well, the publican drew
the pint all right, but all the while he was giving Donal O'Neary, and
his ragged old coat, a squinty kind of once-over look.

"Is it that I can't pay for me drink you're after thinking?" Donal
O'Neary asked the publican. "No fear of that, man!" he said, and with
his stick he gave a whack to the hide on the wall. Out popped a penny,
and fell onto the bar with a clatter.

The publican stood, with the glass in his hand, and his eyes half out
of his head with wonder.

"And if it's no trouble to you, I think I'll take a ball of malt to go
with me stout," said Donal, and he gave the hide another thump, so
another penny came flying out. He snatched the coin out of the air,
casual-like, and laid it down on the mahogany, beside the first.

The publican served Donal his stout and his whiskey with a smile
and a wink. "No charge," said he. "They're on the house."

Donal drank to his health.

"That bit of hide is a wonderful thing, and no mistake," said the
publican now.

"Isn't it, though?" said Donal. "It's kept me and mine for many a
year, I tell you."

"What would you take for it?" asked the publican.

Donal wouldn't hear of selling it, of course, but he'd taken a liking
to the publican, who he could see was a generous class of man
. . . and, in the end, he went whistling out of the pub without his
cowhide, but with ten gold guineas in his pocket.

When Donal O'Neary got to his gate, who did he see there but
Hudden and Dudden. "Sorry about your cow," says the one. "You must
be in a desperate state now," says the other.

"Not a bit of it," said Donal O'Neary. "The whole affair was a
blessing in disguise, as the man says. Have a look here at this." And he
showed them his ten gold guineas.

"How'd the like of you come by a sum of money the like of
that?"

"Would you believe it now," said Donal, "but whoever killed me old cow did me the best turn of me life? It seems the king and queen of France have started a fashion for dressing in cowhide, and it's all the rage with the gentry. Your tanners and tailors can't get enough of the things. Sure, there's dealers in town paying ten guineas a hide for them, and more."

Donal O'Neary walked into his house, the guineas clinking in his pockets, and Hudden and Dudden ran off to their fields, to slaughter their herds.

There wasn't a beast grazing the next morning, as they set off for town in a cart piled high with hides. It was all the team of horses could do to pull it.

In the town square they jumped down and began calling out, "Cowhides here! Hides for sale! Ten gold guineas apiece for the finest cowhides in the county!" They drew quite a crowd, as you can imagine. There's nothing like a pair of madmen for drawing a crowd. Even the pub keeper who'd struck yesterday's bargain with Donal O'Neary came out to see them, and he took it into his head that Hudden and Dudden were members of the gang that had made a fool of him.

"Get out of it with your ten-guinea hides!" he shouted, and he threw a convenient cobblestone in their direction. As you know, inside every crowd, there's a mob, waiting to hatch. "Ten-guinea cowhides yourself!" someone shouted, and tossed up another brick. Soon the air was filled with shouts and stones, and Hudden and Dudden shook the reins and started the cart rolling across the bridge. Now, the bridge was steady enough, but the load wasn't, and half way across it slipped, and tipped, and into the water tumbled the hundreds of hides, and the river swept them away to the sea.

It as at that moment, with the jeers and the laughter of the townspeople in their ears, that Hudden and Dudden resolved to murder Donal O'Neary.

Now, Donal himself had an old mother, who wasn't up to much. It was in his mind that Hudden and Dudden mightn't be too pleased with the turn he'd served them, so that very night, what did he do but tuck his old mother into his own bed, while he went to sleep in hers.

An hour after the moon went down, Hudden and Dudden came creeping through the window of Donal O'Neary's room, made short work of the figure in the bed there, and went back to their homes content with a good night's work.

When Donal O'Neary found his poor old mother dead and murdered in the morning, he said a prayer for her, and hitched up the wagon to haul her remains to the graveyard.

Beside the graveyard was another pub, and outside it was a well. Donal O'Neary got busy then.

He jumped down off the cart, he took the mortal remains of his old mother, and he leaned her up against the well, as if she was looking down into it, so. Then into the pub he went whistling, and ordered up a couple of drinks. The landlord's daughter was in it, and Donal says to her, "Me old mother is out by the well, there. Woud you be so kind as to fetch her inside for a drink of something better than water?"

"I will, sir," says she.

"But mind," says Donal, "the old one's a bit deaf, don't you know, so if she doesn't heed you, just give her a good shake, that's a girl."

Donal O'Neary stood sipping his whiskey in a thoughtful sort of way, and gave a great leap of surprise when the landlord's daughter came banging back into the room, howling like a banshee.

"Oh, what have I done? What have I done, at all?"

She was bawling away into the chest of the landlord, her father. "I called the old woman, but she never moved. So I went to give her a little shake, like himself said I was to do, and down she went into the well, and drownded for certain!"

At this news, Donal himself shed a tear, and the landlord as well. "She was the only mother I had," said Donal. "It's an orphan I'll be now till the end of me days!" And to the girl he said, "It's easy for you. You'll be hanged for the murder and not suffer long at all."

At this point the landlord joined the conversation, with a few heartfelt words about not wishing to trouble the authorities in a personal matter like this one; and drinks were poured, and tears were shed, and sentiments exchanged; so that in the end the poor orphan Donal went home with another ten gold guineas in his pocket.

And who should he meet at the gate of his house but his neighbors, Hudden and Dudden.

"We thought you were dead," said they.

"That's me old mother," said Donal O'Neary. "Cruelly murdered in the night, by persons unkown. But look here," he said to them, and showed them his pocketful of gold, "it's an ill wind, as the man says. On my way to the graveyard, I came across a fellow who's paying ten gold guineas a crack for the bones of old mothers!"

"Don't be talking," said Hudden and Dudden.

"It's the truth, I tell you," said Donal. "There's some class of war going on between the Hungarians and the Germans, and there's nothing makes gunpowder like the bones of old mothers! But they're mighty scarce, boys. It's a seller's market!" And into his house he went, the coins ringing in his pockets.

Hudden and Dudden had old mothers living at home, the both of them, but not for long. Soon the two rich farmers were standing again in the town square, but today they were shouting different wares. "Old mothers for sale! Old mothers for gunpowder! Ten guineas each, and cheap at the price!" Then began the angry words, and the downpour of bricks and stones, until they had to dump their old mothers over the bridge and make a run for it. Back home they came, more battered and bruised, and swearing a terible revenge on Donal O'Neary.

Their plan was to catch him in a sack, tie it up, and sink him in the deepest part of the river, and the morning of the morrow, when Donal came whistling out of his house, they were waiting for him. Into the sack with him, and off to town, to drop him off the bridge.

Donal O'Neary kicked and punched and thrashed around a good bit inside the sack, and it was hot hard work for the two of them carrying him. When they got to town, they were in need of a drink, so they hung the sack up in a tree, and went in for a quick one, at the pub by the bridge.

Donal O'Neary peeped out through a pinhole in the sack, and what did he see but a farmer coming down the road with a drove of cattle? Then he began to shout and moan: "I won't have her! I tell you, I won't have her at all!"

The drover was passing him by, and paying him no heed, so Donal howled the louder:

"I won't have her! Forget about it entirely! I won't have her, that's all! And the devil with all her jewels!"

At that, the farmer came over to the sack in the tree. "You won't have who?" says he.

"The king's own daughter," says Donal O'Neary.

"What jewels?" sayd the farmer.

"She's covered in jewels from head to toe, being a princess and all," says Donal O'Neary. "But that's all one to me. I won't have her!"

"Wisha!" says the farmer. "I'd give me eye-teeth to be in your shoes, man!"

"I don't want your old teeth," says Donal, "but you can take my place any time you like. They tied me up, so I couldn't get away from her, beautiful as she is."

The farmer undid the sack, and in he crept, as Donal crept out. "Good luck to you," said Donal to him. "I'll take along these cattle of yours you won't be needing from this out."

"Right enough," said the happy farmer from inside the sack, "and welcome to them." And Donal O'Neary was at their tails, driving them home, when he heard behind him on the road a voice crying out, "I'll have her now! I'll have her!" and then a terrific splash.

When Hudden and Dudden got back to their place, there was Donal O'Neary, standing at his gate; and the green meadows behind him were black with fat cattle, and the bull calves kicking their heels and butting their heads together.

"Is it you, Donal?" they asked him. "And aren't we just after throwing you into the river?"

"So it was you did it," said Donal. "My thanks to the both of you for that! You're the best neighbors a man ever had!

"Have you ever seen the bottom of that river? It's sweet grass and clover, from bank to bank, and a herd of big black cattle stretching to the sea! This bunch I brought out with me," he said, pointing to the meadow, "are the little skinny ones I could take away easily. I'll go back tomorrow for the good ones. . . ."

Hudden and Dudden were off on the dead run, for the town, and the bridge, and the river bottom.

And whatever became of them, Donal O'Neary lived long and well, with land and cattle to his heart's content, from that day forward.

There's "The Twelve Days of Christmas" and "The Old Lady Who Swallowed the Fly." In Mother Goose, there's "The House that Jack Built." In American folk song, there's "A Hole in the Bucket, Dear Liza." There's one of these memory-testing, tongue-twisting, child-delighting, adult-maddening jingles in every culture. In Ireland, it's "Munachar and Manachar."

Now, this version (taken from Joseph Jacob's Celtic Fairy Tales) *isn't pure Irish. It's based on a Gaelic version collected by Douglas Hyde, but in the Irish, ax, rod, dog, cow, and all greet one another with "God save you" and "God and Mary save you" rather than "What news to-day?"*

And Jacobs has added bits and details from several Scottish variations, including the punch line—which really must be shouted to evoke the appropriate fit of giggles among the children round the fire.

MUNACHAR AND MANACHAR

There once lived a Munachar and a Manachar, a long time ago, and it is a long time since it was, and if they were alive now they would not be alive then. They went out together to pick raspberries, and as many as Munachar used to pick Manachar used to eat. Munachar said he must go look for a rod to make a gad to hang Manachar, who ate his raspberries every one; and he came to the rod. "What news to-day?" said the rod. "It is my own news that I'm seeking. Going looking for a rod, a rod to make a gad, a gad to hang Manachar, who ate my raspberries every one."

"You will not get me," said the rod, "until you get an axe to cut me." He came to the axe. "What news to-day?" said the axe. "It's my own news I'm seeking. Going looking for an axe, an axe to cut a rod, a rod to make a gad, a gad to hang Manachar, who ate my raspberries every one."

"You will not get me," said the axe, "until you get a flag to edge me." He came to the flag. "What news to-day?" said the flag. "It's my own news I'm seeking. Going looking for a flag, flag to edge axe, axe to cut a rod, a rod to make a gad, a gad to hang Manachar, who ate my raspberries every one."

"You will not get me," said the flag, "till you get water to wet me." He came to the water. "What news to-day?" said the water. "It's my own news I'm seeking. Going looking for water, water to wet flag, flag to edge axe, axe to cut a rod, a rod to make a gad, a gad to hang Manachar, who ate my raspberries every one."

"You will not get me," said the water, "until you get a deer who will swim me." He came to the deer. "What news to-day?" said the deer. "It's my own news I'm seeking. Going looking for a deer, deer to swim water, water to wet flag, flag to edge axe, axe to cut a rod, a rod to make a gad, a gad to hang Manachar, who ate my raspberries every one."

"You will not get me," said the deer, "until you get a hound who will hunt me." He came to the hound. "What news to-day?" said the hound. "It's my own news I'm seeking. Going looking for a hound, hound to hunt deer, deer to swim water, water to wet flag, flag to edge axe, axe to cut a rod, a rod to make a gad, a gad to hang Manachar, who ate my raspberries every one."

"You will not get me," said the hound, "until you get a bit of butter to put in my claw." He came to the butter. "What news to-day?" said the butter. "It's my own news I'm seeking. Going looking for butter, butter to go in claw of hound, hound to hunt deer, deer to swim water, water to wet flag, flag to edge axe, axe to cut a rod, a rod to make a gad, a gad to hang Manachar, who ate my raspberries every one."

"You will not get me," said the butter, "until you get a cat who shall scrape me." He came to the cat. "What news to-day?" said the cat. "It's my own news I'm seeking. Going looking for a cat, cat to scrape butter, butter to go in claw of hound, hound to hunt deer, deer to swim water, water to wet flag, flag to edge axe, axe to cut a rod, a rod to make a gad, a gad to hang Manachar, who ate my raspberries every one."

"You will not get me," said the cat, "until you get milk which you will give me." He came to the cow. "What news to-day?" said the cow. "It's my own news I'm seeking. Going looking for a cow, cow to give me milk, milk I will give to the cat, cat to scrape butter, butter to go in claw of hound, hound to hunt deer, deer to swim water, water to wet flag, flag to edge axe, axe to cut a rod, a rod to make a gad, a gad to hang Manachar, who ate my raspberries every one."

"You will not get any milk from me," said the cow, "until you bring me a wisp of straw from those threshers yonder." He came to the threshers. "What news to-day?" said the threshers. "It's my own news I'm seeking. Going looking for a wisp of straw from ye to give to the cow, the cow to give me milk, milk I will give to the cat, cat to scrape butter, butter to go in claw of hound, hound to hunt deer, deer to swim water, water to wet flag, flag to edge axe, axe to cut a rod, a rod to make a gad, a gad to hang Manachar, who ate my raspberries every one."

"You will not get any wisp of straw from us," said the threshers, "until you bring us the makings of a cake from the miller over yonder." He came to the miller. "What news to-day?" said the miller. "It's my own news I'm seeking. Going looking for the makings of a cake which I will give to the threshers, the threshers to give me a wisp of straw, the wisp of straw I will give to the cow, the cow to give me milk, milk I will give to the cat, cat to scrape butter, butter to go in claw of hound, hound to hunt deer, deer to swim water, water to wet flag, flag to edge axe, axe to cut a rod, a rod to make a gad, a gad to hang Manachar, who ate my raspberries every one."

"You will not get any makings of a cake from me," said the miller, "till you bring me the full of that sieve of water from the river over there."

He took the sieve in his hand and went over to the river, but as often as ever he would stoop and fill it with water, the moment he raised it the water would run out of it again, and sure, if he had been there from that day till this, he never could have filled it. A crow went flying by him, over his head. "Daub! Daub!" said the crow. "My blessings on ye, then," said Munachar, "but it's the good advice you have," and he took the red clay and the daub that was by the brink, and he rubbed it to the bottom of the sieve, until all the holes were filled, and then the sieve held the water, and he brought the water to the miller, and the miller gave him the makings of a cake, and he gave the makings of the cake to the threshers, and the threshers gave him a wisp of straw, and he gave the wisp of straw to the cow, and the cow gave him milk, the milk he gave to the cat, the cat scraped the butter, the butter went into the claw of the hound, the hound hunted the deer, the deer swam the water, the water wet the flag, the flag sharpened the axe, the axe cut the rod, and the rod made a gad, and when he had it ready to hang Manachar he found that Manachar had BURST.

134

"Typical Irish" is an expression used to priaise and ridicule. Typical Irish was Edmund Leamy, who, in a country with a vast treasure hoard of fairy tales, undertook to write his own originals!

But Leamy was so steeped in the old lore that his stories sound and feel like ancient fireside tales. Details, characters, incidents are borrowed from age-old sagas, ballads, and tales, and, in the eighty years since he first offered the world his Irish Fairy Tales, *such stories as "The Little White Cat" have become a living part of the Irish tradition.*

THE LITTLE WHITE CAT

A long, long time ago, in a valley far away, the giant Trencoss lived in a great castle, surrounded by trees that were always green. The castle had a hundred doors, and every door was guarded by a huge, shaggy hound, with tongue of fire and claws of iron, who tore to pieces anyone who went to the castle without the giant's leave. Trencoss had made war on the King of the Torrents, and, having killed the king, and slain his people, and burned his palace, he carried off his only daughter, the princess Eileen, to the castle in the valley. Here he provided her with beautiful rooms, and appointed a hundred dwarfs, dressed in blue and yellow satin, to wait upon her, and harpers to play sweet music for her, and he gave her diamonds without number, brighter than the sun; but he would not allow her to go outside the castle, and told her if she went one step beyond its doors, the hounds, with tongues of fire and claws of iron, would tear her to pieces. A week after her arrival, war broke out between the giant and the King of the Islands, and before he set out for battle, the giant sent for the princess, and informed her that on his return he would make her his wife. When the princess heard this she began to cry, for she would rather die than marry the giant who had slain her father.

'Crying will only spoil your bright eyes, my little princess,' said Trencoss, 'and you will have to marry me whether you like it or no.'

He then bade her go back to her room, and he ordered the dwarfs to give her everything she asked for while he was away, and the harpers to play the sweetest music for her. When the princess gained her room she cried as if her heart would break. The long day passed slowly, and

136

the night came, but brought no sleep to Eileen, and in the grey light of the morning she rose and opened the window, and looked about in every direction to see if there were any chance of escape. But the window was ever so high and above the ground, and below were the hungry and ever watchful hounds. With a heavy heart she was about to close the window when she thought she saw the branches of the tree that was nearest to it moving. She looked again, and she saw a little white cat creeping along one of the branches.

'Mew!' cried the cat.

'Poor little pussy,' said the princess. 'Come to me, pussy.'

'Stand back from the window,' said the cat, 'and I will.'

The princess stepped back, and the little white cat jumped into the room. The princess took the little cat on her lap and stroked him with her hand, and the cat raised its back and began to purr.

'Where do you come from, and what is your name?' asked the princess.

'No matter where I come from or what's my name,' said the cat. 'I am a friend of yours, and I come to help you.'

'I never wanted help worse,' said the princess.

'I know that,' said the cat; 'and now listen to me. When the giant comes back from battle and asks you to marry him, say to him you will marry him.'

'But I will never marry him' said the princess.

'Do what I tell you,' said the cat. "When he asks you to marry him, say to him you will if his dwarfs will wind for you three balls from the fairy dew that lies on the bushes on a misty morning as big as these,' said the cat, putting his right forefoot into his ear and taking out three balls—one yellow, one red, and one blue.

'They are very small,' said the princess. 'They are not much bigger than peas, and the dwarfs will not be long at their work.'

'Won't they,' said the cat. 'It will take them a month and a day to make one, so that it will take three months and three days before the balls are wound; but the giant, like you, will think they can be made in a few days, and so he will readily promise to do what you ask. He will soon find out his mistake, but he will keep his word, and will not press you to marry him until the balls are wound.'

'When will the giant come back?' asked Eileen.

'He will return tomorrow afternoon,' said the cat.

137

'Will you stay with me until then?' said the princess. 'I am very lonely.'

'I cannot stay,' said the cat. "I have to go away to my palace on the island on which no man ever placed his foot, and where no man but one shall ever come.'

'And where is that island?' asked the princess, 'and who is the man?'

'The island is in the far-off seas where vessel never sailed; the man you will see before many days are over; and if all goes well, he will one day slay the giant Trencoss, and free you from his power.'

'Ah!' sighed the princess, 'that can never be, for no weapon can wound the hundred hounds that guard the castle, and no sword can kill the giant Trencoss.'

'There is a sword that will kill him,' said the cat; 'but I must go now. Remember what you are to say to the giant when he comes home, and every morning watch the tree on which you saw me, and if you see in the branches anyone you like better than yourself,' said the cat, winking at the princess, 'throw him these three balls and leave the rest to me; but take care not to speak a single word to him, for if you do all will be lost.'

'Shall I ever see you again?' asked the princess.

'Time will tell,' answered the cat, and, without saying so much as good-bye, he jumped through the window onto the tree, and in a second was out of sight.

The morrow afternoon came, and the giant Trencoss returned from battle. Eileen knew of his coming by the furious barking of the hounds, and her heart sank, for she knew that in a few moments she would be summoned to his presence. Indeed, he had hardly entered the castle when he sent for her, and told her to get ready for the wedding. The princess tried to look cheerful, as she answered:

'I will be ready as soon as you wish; but you must first promise me something.'

'Ask anything you like, little princess,' said Trencoss.

'Well, then,' said Eileen, 'before I marry you, you must make your dwarfs wind three balls as big as these from the fairy dew that lies on the bushes on a misty morning in summer.'

'Is that all?' said Trencoss, laughing. 'I shall give the dwarfs orders at once, and by this time tomorrow the balls will be wound, and our wedding can take place in the evening.'

'And will you leave me to myself until then?'

'I will,' said Trencoss.

'On your honour as a giant?' said Eileen.

'On my honour as a giant,' replied Trencoss.

The princess returned to her rooms, and the giant summoned all his dwarfs, and he ordered them to go forth in the dawning of the morn and to gather all the fairy dew lying on the bushes, and to wind three balls—one yellow, one red, and one blue. The next morning, and the next, and the next, the dwarfs went out into the fields and searched all the hedgerows, but they could gather only as much fairy dew as would make a thread as long as a wee girl's eyelash; and so they had to go out morning after morning, and the giant fumed and threatened, but all to no purpose. He was very angry with the princess, and he was vexed with himself that she was so much cleverer than he was, and, moreover, he saw now that the wedding could not take place as soon as he expected.

When the little white cat went away from the castle he ran as fast as he could up hill and down dale, and never stopped until he came to the Prince of the Silver River. The prince was alone, and very sad and sorrowful he was, for he was thinking of the princess Eileen, and wondering where she could be.

'Mew,' said the cat, as he sprang softly into the room; but the prince did not heed him. 'Mew,' again said the cat; but again the prince did not heed him. 'Mew,' said the cat the third time, and he jumped up on the prince's knee.

'Where do you come from, and what do you want?' asked the prince.

'I come from where you would like to be,' said the cat.

'And where is that?' said the prince.

'Oh, where is that, indeed! As if I didn't know what you are thinking of, and of whom you are thinking,' said the cat; 'and it would be far better for you to try and save her.'

'I would give my life a thousand times over for her,' said the prince.

'For whom?' said the cat, with a wink. 'I named no name, your highness,' said he.

'You know very well who she is,' said the prince, 'if you knew what I was thinking of; but do you know where she is?'

'She is in danger,' said the cat. 'She is in the castle of the giant Trencoss, in the valley beyong the mountains.'

'I will set out there at once,' said the prince, 'and I will challenge the giant to battle, and will slay him.'

'Easier said than done,' said the cat. 'There is no sword made by the hands of man can kill him, and even if you could kill him, his hundred hounds, with tongues of fire and claws of iron, would tear you to pieces.'

'Then, what am I to do?' asked the prince.

'Be said by me,' said the cat. 'Go to the wood that surrounds the giant's castle, and climb the high tree that's the nearest to the window that looks towards the sunset, and shake the branches, and you will see what you will see. Then hold out your hat with the silver plumes, and three balls—one yellow, one red, and one blue—will be thrown into it. And then come back here as fast as you can but speak no word, for if you utter a single word the hounds will hear you, and you shall be torn to pieces.'

Well, the prince set off at once, and after two days' journey he came to the wood around the castle, and he climbed the tree that was nearest to the window that looked towards the sunset, and he shook the branches. As soon as he did so, the window opened and he saw the princess Eileen, looking lovelier than ever. He was going to call out her name, but she placed her fingers on her lips, and he remembered what the cat had told him, that he was to speak no word. In silence he held out the hat with the silver plumes, and the princess threw into it the three balls, one after another, and, blowing him a kiss, she shut the window. And well it was she did so, for at that very moment she heard the voice of the giant, who was coming back from hunting.

The prince waited until the giant had entered the castle before he descended the tree. He set off as fast as he could. He went up hill and down dale, and never stopped until he arrived at his own palace, and there waiting for him was the little white cat.

'Have you brought the three balls?' said he.

'I have,' said the prince.

'Then follow me,' said the cat.

On they went until they left the palace far behind and came to the edge of the sea.

'Now,' said the cat, 'unravel a thread of the red ball, hold the thread in your right hand, drop the ball into the water, and you shall see what you shall see.'

The prince did as he was told, and the ball floated out to sea, unravelling as it went, and it went on until it was out of sight.

'Pull now,' said the cat.

The prince pulled, and, as he did, he saw far away something on the sea shining like silver. It came nearer and nearer, and he saw it was little silver boat. At last it touched the sand.

'Now,' said the cat, 'step into this boat and it will bear you to the palace on the island on which no man has ever placed his foot—the island in the unknown seas that were never sailed by vessels made of human hands. In that palace there is a sword with a diamond hilt, and by that sword alone the giant Trencoss can be killed. There also are a hundred cakes, and it is only on eating these the hundred hounds can die. But mind what I say to you: if you eat or drink until you reach the palace of the little cat in the island in the unknown seas, you will forget the princess Eileen.'

'I will forget myself first,' said the prince, as he stepped into the silver boat, which floated away so quickly that it was soon out of sight of land.

The day passed and the night fell, and the stars shone down upon the waters, but the boat never stopped. On she went for two whole days and nights, and on the third morning the prince saw an island in the distance, and very glad he was; for he thought it was his journey's end, and he was almost fainting with thirst and hunger. But the day passed and the island was still before him.

At long last, on the following day, he saw by the first light of the morning that he was quite close to it, and that trees laden with fruit of every kind were bending down over the water. The boat sailed round and round the island, going closer every round, until, at last, the drooping branches almost touched it. The sight of the fruit within his reach made the prince hungrier and thirstier than he was before, and forgetting his promise to the little cat—not to eat anything until he entered the palace in the unknown seas—he caught one of the branches, and, in a moment, was in the tree eating the delicious fruit. While he was doing so the boat floated out to sea and soon was lost to sight; but the prince, having eaten, forgot all about it, and, worse still, forgot all about the princess in the giant's castle. When he had eaten enough he

141

descended the tree, and, turning his back on the sea, set out straight before him. He had not gone far when he heard the sound of music, and soon after he saw a number of maidens playing on silver harps coming towards him. When they saw him they ceased playing, and cried out:

'Welcome! Welcome! Prince of the Silver River, welcome to the island of fruits and flowers. Our king and queen saw you coming over the sea, and they sent us to bring you to the palace.'

The prince went with them, and at the palace gates the king and queen and their daughter Kathleen received him, and gave him welcome. He hardly saw the king and queen, for his eyes were fixed on the princess Kathleen, who looked more beautiful than a flower. He thought he had never seen anyone so lovely, for, of course, he had forgotten all about poor Eileen pining away in her castle prison in the lonely valley. When the king and queen had given welcome to the prince a great feast was spread, and all the lords and ladies of the court sat down to it, and the prince sat between the queen and the princess Kathleen, and long before the feast was finished he was over head and ears in love with her. When the feast was ended the queen ordered the ballroom to be made ready, and when night fell the dancing began, and was kept up until the morning star, and the prince danced all night with the princess, falling deeper and deeper in love with her every minute. Between dancing by night and feasting by day weeks went by. All the time poor Eileen in the giant's castle was counting the hours, and all this time the dwarfs were winding the balls, and a ball and a half were already wound. At last the prince asked the king and queen for their daughter in marriage, and they were delighted to be able to say yes, and the day was fixed for the wedding. But on the evening before the day on which it was to take place the prince was in his room, getting ready for a dance, when he felt something rubbing against his leg, and, looking down, who should he see but the little white cat. At the sight of him the prince remembered everything, and sad and sorry he was when he thought of Eileen watching and waiting and counting the days until he returned to save her. But he was very fond of the princess Kathleen, and so he did not know what to do.

'You can't do anything tonight,' said the cat, for he knew what the prince was thinking of, 'but when morning comes go down to the sea, and look not to the right or the left, and let no living thing touch you, for if you do you shall never leave the island. Drop the second ball into the water, as you did the first, and when the boat comes step in at once. Then you may look behind you, and you shall see what you shall see, and you'll know which you love best, the princess Eileen or the princess Kathleen, and you can either go or stay.'

The prince didn't sleep a wink that night, and at the first glimpse of the morning he stole from the palace. When he reached the sea he threw out the ball, and when it had floated out of sight, he saw the little boat sparkling on the horizon like a newly risen star. The prince had scarcely passed through the palace doors when he was missed, and the king and queen and the princess, and all the lords and the ladies of the court, went in search of him, taking the quickest way to the sea. While the maidens with the silver harps played the sweetest music, the princess, whose voice was sweeter than any music, called on the prince by his name, and so moved his heart that he was about to look behind, when he remembered how the cat had told him that he should not do so until he was in the boat. Just as it touched the shore the princess put out her hand and almost caught the prince's arm, but he stepped into the boat in time to save himself, and it sped away like a receding wave. A loud scream caused the prince to look round suddenly, and when he did he saw no sign of king or queen, or princess, or lords or ladies, but only big green serpents, with red eyes and tongues, that hissed out fire and poison as they writhed in a hundred horrible coils.

The prince, having escaped from the enchanted island, sailed away for three days and three nights, and every night he hoped the coming morning would show him the island he was in search of. He was faint with hunger and beginning to despair, when on the fourth morning he saw in the distance an island that, in the first rays of the sun, gleamed like fire. On coming closer to it he saw that it was clad with trees, so covered with bright red berries that hardly a leaf was to be seen. Soon the boat was almost within a stone's cast of the island, and it began to sail round and round until it was well under the bending branches. The scent of the berries was so sweet that it sharpened the prince's hunger, and he longed to pluck them; but, remembering what had happened to him on the enchanted island, he was afraid to touch them. But the boat kept on sailing round and round, and at last a great wind rose from the sea and shook the branches, and the bright, sweet berries fell into the boat unil it was filled with them, and they fell upon

143

the prince's hands, and he took up some to look at them, and as he looked the desire to eat them grew stronger, and he said to himself it would be no harm to taste one; but when he tasted it the flavour was so delicious he swallowed it, and, of course, at once he forgot all about Eileen, and the boat drifted away from him and left him standing in the water.

He climbed onto the island, and having eaten enough of the berries, he set out to see what might be before him, and it was not long until he heard a great noise, and a huge iron ball knocked down one of the trees in front of him, and before he knew where he was a hundred giants came running after it. When they saw the prince they turned towards him, and one of them caught him up in his hand and held him up that all might see him. The prince was nearly squeezed to death, and seeing this the giant put him on the ground again.

'Who are you, my little man?' asked the giant.

'I am a prince,' replied the prince.

'Oh, you are a prince, are you?' said the giant. 'And what are you good for?' said he.

The prince did not know, for nobody had asked him the question before.

'I know what he's good for,' said an old giantess, with one eye in her forehead and one in her chin. 'I know what he's good for. He's good to eat.'

When the giants heard this they laughed so loud that the prince was frightened almost to death.

'Why,' said one, 'he wouldn't make a mouthful.'

'Oh, leave him to me,' said the giantess, 'and I'll fatten him up; and when he is cooked and dressed he will be a nice dainty dish for the king.'

The giants, on this, gave the prince into the hands of the old giantess. She took him home with her to the kitchen, and fed him on sugar and spice and all things nice, so that he should be a sweet morsel for the king of the giants when he returned to the island. The poor prince would not eat anything at first, but the giantess held him over the fire until his feet were scorched, and then he said to himself that it was better to eat than to be burnt alive.

Well, day after day passed, and the prince grew sadder and sadder, thinking that he would soon be cooked and dressed for the king;

144

but sad as the prince was, he was not half as sad as the princess Eileen in the giant's castle, watching and waiting for the prince to return and save her.

And the dwarfs had wound two balls, and were winding a third.

At last the prince heard from the old giantess that the king of the giants was to return on the following day, and she said to him:

'As this is the last night you have to live, tell me if you wish for anything, for if you do your wish will be granted.'

'I don't wish for anything,' said the prince, whose heart was dead within him.

"Well, I'll come back again,' said the giantess, and she went away.

The prince sat down in a corner, thinking and thinking, until he heard close to his ear a sound like 'purr, purr!' He looked around, and there before him was the little white cat.

'I ought not to come to you,' said the cat; 'but, indeed, it is not for your sake I come. I come for the sake of princess Eileen. Of course, you forgot all about her, and, of course, she is always thinking of you. It's always the way—

Favoured lovers may forget,
Slighted lovers never yet.

The prince blushed with shame when he heard the name of the princess.

"'Tis you that ought to blush,' said the cat; 'but listen to me now, and remember, if you don't obey my directions this time you'll never see me again, and you'll never set your eyes on the princess Eileen. When the old giantess comes back tell her your wish, when the morning comes, to go down to the sea to look at it for the last time. When you reach the sea you will know what to do. But I must go now, as I hear the giantess coming.' And the cat jumped out of the window and disappeared.

'Well,' said the giantess, when she came in, 'is there anything you wish?'

'Is it true I must die tomorrow?' asked the prince.

'It is.'

'Then,' said he, 'I should like to go down to the sea to look at it for the last time.'

145

'You may do that,' said the giantess, 'if you get up early.'

'I'll be up with the lark in the light of the morning,' said the prince.

'Very well,' said the giantess, and, saying 'good night,' she went away.

The prince thought the night would never pass, but at last it faded away before the grey light of the dawn, and he sped down to the sea. He threw out the third ball, and before long he saw the little boat coming towards him swifter than the wind. He threw himself into it the moment it touched the shore. Swifter than the wind it bore him out to sea, and before he had time to look behind him the island of the giantess was like a faint red speck in the distance. The day passed and the night fell, and the stars looked down, and the boat sailed on, and just as the sun rose above the sea it pushed its silver prow on the golden strand of an island greener than the leaves in summer. The prince jumped out, and went on and on until he entered a pleasant valley, at the head of which he saw a palace white as snow.

As he approached the central door it opened for him. On entering the hall he passed into several rooms without meeting anyone; but, when he reached the principal apartment, he found himself in a circular room, in which were a thousand pillars, and every pillar was of marble, and on every pillar save one, which stood in the centre of the room, was a little white cat with black eyes. Ranged round the wall, from one door-jamb to the other, were three rows of precious jewels. The first was a row of brooches of gold and silver, with their pins fixed in the wall and their heads outwards; the second a row of torques of gold and silver; and the third a row of great swords, with hilts of gold and silver. And on many tables was food of all kinds, and drinking horns filled with foaming ale.

While the prince was looking about him the cats kept on jumping from pillar to pillar; but seeing that none of them jumped on to the pillar in the centre of the room, he began to wonder why this was so, when, all of a sudden, and before he could guess how it came about, there right before him on the centre pillar was the little white cat.

'Don't you know me?' said he.

'I do,' said the prince.

'Ah, but you don't know who I am. This is the palace of the Little

White Cat, and I am the King of the Cats. But you must be hungry, and the feast is spread.'

Well, when the feast was ended, the king of the cats called for the sword that would kill the giant Trencoss, and the hundred cakes for the hundred watch-dogs.

The cats brought the sword and the cakes and laid them before the king.

'Now,' said the king, 'take these; you have no time to lose. Tomorrow the dwarfs will wind the last ball, and tomorrow the giant will claim the princess for his bride. So you should go at once; but before you go take this from me to your little girl.'

And the king gave him a brooch lovelier than any on the palace walls.

The king and the prince, followed by the cats, went down to the strand, and when the prince stepped into the boat all the cats 'mewed' three times for good luck, and the prince waved his hat three times, and the little boat sped over the waters all through the night as brightly and as swiftly as a shooting star. In the first flush of morning it touched the strand. The prince jumped out and went on and on, up hill and down dale, until he came to the giant's castle. When the hounds saw him they barked furiously, and bounded towards him to tear him to pieces. The prince flung the cakes to them, and as each hound swallowed his cake he fell dead. The prince then struck his shield three times with the sword which he had brought from the palace of the little white cat.

When the giant heard the sound he cried out:

'Who comes to challenge me on my wedding-day?'

The dwarfs went out to see, and, returning, told him it was a prince who challenged him to battle.

The giant, foaming with rage, seized his heaviest iron club, and rushed out to the fight. The fight lasted the whole day, and when the sun went down the giant said:

'We have had enough of fighting for the day. We can begin at sunrise tomorrow.'

'Not so,' said the prince. 'Now or never; win or die.'

'Then take this,' cried the giant, as he aimed a blow with all his force at the prince's head; but the prince, darting forward like a flash of lightning, drove his sword into the giant's heart, and, with a groan, he fell over the bodies of the poisoned hounds.

When the dwarfs saw the giant dead they began to cry and tear their hair. But the prince told them they had nothing to fear, and he bade them go and tell the princess Eileen he wished to speak with her. But the princess had watched the battle from her window, and when she saw the giant fall she rushed out to greet the prince, and that very night he and she and all the dwarfs and harpers set out for the Palace of the Silver River, which they reached the next morning, and from that day to this there never has been a gayer wedding than the wedding of the Prince of the Silver River and the princess Eileen, and though she had diamonds and pearls to spare, the only jewel she wore on her wedding-day was the brooch which the prince had brought her from the Palace of the Little White Cat in the far-off seas.

The wonderful story of the red pony was told, in Gaelic, by Pat Mina-
han of Glencolumkill to William Larmine, who translated it for his
West Irish Folk Tales, published in 1893.

Larmine was the first to seek tales among the native Irish speak-
ers, and the style in which his tales are told is stark and beautiful as
standing stones—quite a contrast to the flamboyant and self-con-
scious wordplay of the Anglicized storytellers of the eastern Pale.

West Irish Folk Tales is long out of print; but maybe John Stein-
beck came across a copy of "The Red Pony" before writing his own
lovely story of the same name. . . .

THE RED PONY

There was a poor man there. He had a great family of sons. He had no means to put them forward. He had them at school. One day, when they were coming from school, he thought that whichever of them was last at the door he would keep him out. It was the youngest of the family was last at the door. He would not let him in. The boy went weeping. He would not let him in till night came. The father said he would never let him in; that he had boys enough.

The lad went away. He was walking all night. He came to a house on the rugged side of a hill on a height, one feather giving it shelter and support. He went in. He got a place till morning. When he made his breakfast in the morning, he was going. The man of the house made him a present of a red pony, a saddle, and a bridle. He went riding on the pony. He went away with himself.

"Now," said the pony, "whatever thing you may see before you, don't touch it."

They went on with themselves. He saw a light before him on the high-road. When he came as far as the light, there was an open box on the road, and a light coming out of it. He took up the box. There was a lock of hair in it.

"Are you going to take up the box?" said the pony.

"I am. I cannot go past it."

"It's better for you to leave it," said the pony.

He took up the box. He put it in his pocket. He was going with himself. A gentleman met him.

"Pretty is your little beast. Where are you going?"

149

"I am looking for service."

"I am in want of one like you, among the stable boys."

He hired the lad. The lad said he must get room for the little beast in the stable. The gentleman said he would get it. They went home then. He had eleven boys. When they were going out into the stable at ten o'clock, each of them took a light but he. He took no candle at all with him.

Each of them went to his own stable. When he went into his stable he opened the box. He left it in a hole in the wall. The light was great. It was twice as much as in the other stables. There was wonder on the boys what was the reason of the light being so great, and he without a candle with him at all. They told the master they did not know what was the cause of the light with the last boy. They had given him no candle and he had twice as much light as they had.

"Watch tomorrow night what kind of light he has," said the master.

They watched the night of the morrow. They saw the box in the hole that was in the wall, and the light coming out of the box. They told the master. When the boys came to the house, the king asked him what was the reason why he did not take a candle to the stable, as well as the other boys. The lad said he had a candle. The king said he had not. He asked him how he got the box from which the light came. He said he had no box. The king said he had, and that he must give it to him; that he would not keep him unless he gave him the box. The boy gave it to him. The king opened it. He drew out the lock of hair, in which was the light.

"You must go," said the king, "and bring me the woman to whom the hair belongs."

The lad was troubled. He went out. He told the red pony.

"I told you not to take up the box. You will get more than that on account of the box. When you have made your breakfast tomorrow, put the saddle and bridle on me."

When he made his breakfast on the morning of the morrow, he put saddle and bridle on the pony. He went until they came to three miles of sea.

"Keep a good hold now. I am going to give a jump over the sea. When I arrive yonder there is a fair on the strand. Everyone will be coming up to ask you for a ride, because I am such a pretty little beast.

150

Give no one a ride. You will see a beautiful woman drawing near you, her in whose hair was the wonderful light. She will come up to you. She will ask you to let her ride for a while. Say you will and welcome. When she comes riding, I will be off."

When she came to the sea, she cleared three miles at a jump. She came upon the land opposite, and everyone was asking for a ride on the beast, she was that pretty. He was giving a ride to no one. He saw that woman in the midst of the people. She was drawing near. She asked him would he give her a little riding. He said he would give it, and a hundred welcomes. She went riding. When the pony came to the sea, she made the three-mile jump again, the beautiful woman along with her. She took her home to the king. There was great joy on the king to see her. He took her into the parlour. She said to him, she would not marry anyone until he would get the bottle of healing water that was in the eastern world. The king said to the lad he must go and bring the bottle of healing water that was in the eastern world to the lady. The lad was troubled. He went to the pony. He told the pony he must go to the eastern world for the bottle of healing water there was in it, and bring it to the lady.

"My advice was good," said the pony, "on the day you took the box up. Put saddle and bridle on me."

He went riding on her. They were going till they came to the sea. She stood then.

"You must kill me," said the pony; "that, or I must kill you."

"It is hard to me to kill you," said the boy. "If I kill you there will be no way to myself."

He cut her belly down. He opened it up. She was not long opened when there came two black ravens and one small one. The two ravens went into the body. They drank their fill of the blood. When they came out the little raven went in. He closed the belly of the pony. He would not let the little bird come out till he got the bottle of healing water was in the eastern world. The ravens were very troubled. They were begging him to let the little bird out. He said he would not let it out till they brought him the bottle. They went to seek the bottle. They came back and there was no bottle with them. They were entreating him to let the bird out to them. He would not let the bird out till he got the bottle. They went away again for the bottle. They came at evening. They were tossed and scorched, and they had the bottle. They came to the place where the pony was. They gave the bottle to the boy. He rubbed the healing water to every place where they were burned. Then he let out the little bird. There was great joy on them to see him. He rubbed some of the healing water to the place where he cut the pony. He spilt a drop into her ear. She arose as well as she ever was. He had a little bottle in his pocket. He put some of the healing water in it. They went home.

When the king perceived the pony coming he rose out. He took hold of her with his two hands. He took her in. He smothered her with kisses and he drowned her with tears: he dried her with finest cloths of silk and satin.

This is what the lady was doing while they were away. She boiled pitch and filled a barrel, and that boiling. Now she went beside it, and stripped herself. She rubbed the healing water to herself. She came out; she went to the barrel, naked. She gave a jump in and out of the barrel. Three times she went in and out. She said she would never marry anyone who could not do the same. The young king came. He stripped himself. He went to the barrel. He fell half in, half out.

He was all boiled and burned. Another gentleman came. He stripped himself. He gave a jump into the barrel. He came not out till he died. After that there was no one going in or out. The barrel was there, and no one at all was going near it. The lad went up to it and stripped himself. He rubbed the healing water on himself. He came to the barrel. He jumped in and out three times. He was watching her. She came out. She said she would never marry anyone but him.

Came the priest of the patterns, and the clerk of the bells. The pair were married. The wedding lasted three days and three nights. When it was over, the lad went to look at the place where the pony was. He never remembered to go and see the pony during the wedding. He found nothing but a heap of bones. There were two champions and two young girls playing cards. The lad went crying when he saw the bones of the pony. One of the girls asked what was the matter with him. He said it was all one to her; she cared nothing for his troubles.

"I would like to get knowledge of the cause why you are crying."

"It is my pony who was here. I never remembered to see her during the wedding. I have nothing but her bones. I don't know what I shall do after her. It was she who did all that I accomplished."

The girl went laughing. "Would you know your pony if you saw her?"

"I would know," said he.

She laid aside the cards. She stood up.

"Isn't that your pony?" said she.

"It is," he said.

"I was the pony," said the girl, "and the two ravens who went in to drink my blood my brothers. When the ravens came out, a little bird went in. You closed the pony. You would not let the little bird out till they brought the bottle of healing water that was in the eastern world. They brought the bottle to you. The little bird was my sister. It was my brothers were the ravens. We were all under enchantments. It is my sister who is married to you. The enchantments are gone from us since she was married."

William Carleton (1798–1869) has been called "the prose Burns of Ireland," for like the great Scottish poet, he was peasant born and rose to sudden fame as a writer and spokesman for his oppressed people's ways and beliefs.

Carleton received his education in the "hedge schools" conducted in secrecy in the countryside (for English law forbade Irish Catholics to learn or be taught, to buy, sell, or own, to vote, to speak their language, or to worship their God).

It was understood that the best of the "hedge scholars" would be sent abroad, to study for the priesthood, but young Carleton, however much Latin they beat into him, was not that way inclined.

He made his way to Dublin, and wrote his Traits and Stories of the Irish Peasantry, *which was published in the belief that it would expose the awful, primitive superstition in which the native Irish lived. On the contrary, it is a celebration of indomitable wit, whimsy, and courage, and the work served as a great inspiration to the nationalist Young Ireland Movement.*

Like his counterpart, Burns, William Carleton had a weakness for liquor. ("A good man's failing," they say in Ireland.) Between sprees, he wrote voluminously—thrillers, tracts, essays, and an autobiography—but he died, as he had lived, in poverty.

"The Bewitched Pudden" is taken from his Traits and Stories. *It is, according to Carleton, a typical "Wake Amusement," and, hearing it, we are to imagine that we "are sitting in the chimney corner, at an Irish wake, and that some droll Senachie, his face lit up into an expression of broad farcical humour, is proceeding somewhat as follows:"*

THE BEWITCHED PUDDEN

"Moll Roe Rafferty was the son—daughter I mane—of ould Jack Rafferty, who was remarkable for a habit he had of always wearing his head under his hat; but indeed the same family was a quare one, as everybody knew that was acquainted wid them. It was said of them—but whether it was thrue or not I won't undhertake to say, for 'fraid I'd tell a lie—that whenever they didn't wear shoes or boots, they always went barefooted; but I hard afthterwards that this was disputed, so rather than say anything to injure their caracther, I'll let that pass.

155

Now, ould Jack Rafferty had two sons, Paddy and Molly—hut! what are you all laughing at?—I mane a son and daughter, and it was generally believed among the neighbours, that they were brother and sisther, which you know might be thrue or it might not; but that's a thing that, wid the help o' goodness, we have nothing to say to. Throth there was many ugly things put out on them that I don't wish to repate, such as that neither Jack nor his son Paddy ever walked a perch widout puttin' one foot afore the other, like a salmon; an' I know that it was whispered abot, that whenever Moll Roe slep', she had an out of the way custom of keepin' her eyes shut. If she did, however, God forgive her—the loss was her own; for sure we all know that when one comes to shut their eyes they can't see as far before them as another.

"Moll Roe was a fine young bouncin' girl, large and lavish, wid a purty head o' hair on her like scarlet, that bein' one of the raisons why she was called Roe or Red; her arms an' cheeks were much the colour of the hair, an' her saddle nose was the purtiest thing of its kind that ever was on a face. Her fists—for, thank goodness, she was well sarved wid them too—had a strong simularity to two thumpin' turnips, reddened by the sun; an' to keep all right and tight, she had a temper as fiery as her head—for, indeed, it was well known that all the Rafferties were *warm*-hearted. Howandiver, it appears that God gives nothing in vain, and of course the same fists, big and red as they were, if all that is said about them is thrue, were not so much given to her for ornament as use. At laist, takin' them in connexion wid her lively temper, we have it upon good authority, that there was no danger of their getting blue-moulded for want of practice. She had a twist, too, in one of her eyes that was very becomin' in its way, and made her poor husband, when she got him, take it into his head that she could see round a corner. She found him out in many quare things, widout doubt; but whether it was owin' to that or not I wouldn't undertake to say, *for fraid I'd tell a lie*.

"Well, begad, anyhow, it was Moll Roe that was the *dilsy;* and as they say that marriages does be *sometimes* made in heaven, so did it happen that there was a nate vagabone in the neighbourhood, just as much overburdened wid beauty as herself, and he was named Gusty Gillespie. Gusty, the Lord guard us, was what they call a blackmouth Prosbytarian, and wouldn't keep Christmas day, the blagard, except what they call 'ould style.' Gusty was rather good-lookin' when seen in

156

the dark, as well as Moll herself; and indeed it was purty well known that—accordin' as the talk went—it was in nightly meetings that they had an opportunity of becomin' detached to one another. The quensequence was, that in due time both families began to talk very seriously as to what was to be done. Moll's brother, Pawdien O'Rafferty, gave Gusty the best of two choices. What they were it's not worth spaikin' about; but att any rate *one* of them was a poser, an' as Gusty knew his man, he soon came to his senses. Accordingly everything was deranged for their marriage, and it was appointed that they should be spliced by the Reverend Samuel M'Shuttle, the Prosbytarian parson, on the following Sunday.

"Now this was the first marriage that had happened for a long time in the neighbourhood betune a blackmouth an' a Catholic, an' of coorse there was strong objections on both sides against it; an' begad, only for one thing it would never a tuck place at all. At any rate, faix, there was one of the bride's uncles, ould Harry Connolly, a fairy man, who could cure all complaints wid a secret he had, and as he didn't wish to see his niece marrid upon such a fellow, he fought bittherly against the match. All Moll's friends, however, stood up for the marriage barrin' him, an' of coorse the Sunday was appointed, as I said, that they were to be dove-tailed together.

"Well, the day arrived, and Moll as became her went to mass, and Gusty to meeting, afther which they were to join one another in Jack Rafferty's, where the priest, Father M'Sorley, was to slip up afther mass, to take his dinner wid them, and to keep Misther M'Shuttle, who was to marry them, company. Nobody remained at home but ould Jack Rafferty an' his wife, who stopped to dress the dinner, for to tell the truth it was to be a great let out entirely. Maybe, if all was known, too, that Father M'Sorley was to give them a cast of his office over an' above the Ministher, inregard that Moll's friends weren't altogether satisfied at the kind of marriage which M'Shuttle could give them. The sorrow may care about that—splice here—splice there—all I can say is, that when Mrs. Rafferty was goin' to tie up a big bag pudden, in walks Harry Connolly, the fairy-man, in a rage, and shouts out—'Blood and blunderbushes, what are yez here for?'

" 'Arra why, Harry? Why avick?'

" 'Why, the sun's in the suds and the moon in the high Horicks; there's a clipstick comin; an, an; there you're both as unconsarned as if it was about to rain mether. Go out and cross yourselves three times in the name o' the four Mandromarvins, for as prophecy says: Fill the pot, Eddy supernaculum—a blazing star's a rare spectaculum. Go out both of your and look at the sun, I say, an' ye'll see the condition he's in— off!'

"Begad, sure enough, Jack gave a bounce to the door, an' his wife leaped like a two year ould, till they were both got on a stile beside the house to see what was wrong in the sky.

" 'Arra, what is it, Jack,' said she, 'can you see anything?'

" 'No,' says he, 'sorra the full o' my eye of anything I can spy, barrin' the sun himself, that's not visible in regard of the clouds. God guard us! I doubt there's something to happen.'

" 'If there wasn't, Jack, what 'ud put Harry that knows so much in the state he's in?'

" 'I doubt it's this marriage,' said Jack, 'betune ourselves, it's not over and above religious for Moll to marry a blackmouth, an' only for————, but it can't be helped now, though you see, the divil a taste o' the sun is willin' to show his face upon it.'

" 'As to that,' says the wife, winkin' wid both her eyes, 'if Gusty's satisfied with Moll, it's enough. I know who'll carry the whip hand, any how; but in the mane time let us ax Harry 'ithin what ails the sun.'

" 'Well, they accordingly went in an' put the question to him.

" 'Harry, what's wrong, ahagur? What is it now, for if anybody alive knows, 'tis yourself?'

" 'Ah!' said Harry, screwin' his mouth with a kind of a dhry smile, 'the sun has a hard twist o' the cholic; but never mind that, I tell you you'll have a merrier weddin' than you think, that's all'; and havin' said this he put on his hat and left the house.

"Now Harry's answer relieved them very much, and so, afther calling to him to be back for the dinner, Jack sat down to take a shough o' the pipe, and the wife lost no time in tying up the pudden and puttin' it in the pot to be boiled.

"In this way things went on well enough for a while, Jack smokin' away, an' the wife cookin' an' dhressin' at the rate of a hunt. At last Jack, while sittin', as I said, contentedly at the fire, thought he could persave an odd dancin' kind of motion in the pot, that puzzled him a good deal.

" 'Katty,' said he, 'what the dickens is in this pot on the fire?'

" 'Nerra thing but the big pudden. Why do you ax?' says she.

" 'Why,' said he, 'if ever a pot took it into its head to dance a jig, and this did. Thunder and sparables, look at it!'

"Begad, it was true enough; there was the pot bobbin' up an' down and from side to side, jiggin' it away as merry as a grig; an' it was quite aisy to see that it wasn't the pot itself, but what was inside of it, that brought about the hornpipe.

" 'Be the hole o' my coat,' shouted Jack, 'there's something alive in it, or it would never cut such capers!'

" 'Be the vestment, there is, Jack; something strange entirely has got into it. Wirra, man alive, what's to be done?'

"Jist as she spoke, the pot seemed to cut the buckle in prime style, and afther a spring that 'ud shame a dancin'-masther, off flew the lid, and out bounced the pudden itself, hoppin', as nimble as a pea on a drum-head, about the floor. Jack blessed himself, and Katty crossed herself. Jack shouted, and Katty screamed. 'In the name of the nine Evangils,' said he, 'keep your distance, no one here injured you!'

"The pudden, however, made a set at him, and Jack lepped first on a chair and then on the kitchen table to avoid it. It then danced towards Katty who was now repatin' her pather an' avys at the top of her voice, while the cunnin' thief of pudden was hoppin' and jiggen it round her, as if it was amused at her distress.

"If I could get the pitchfork,' said Jack, 'I'd dale wid it—by goxty I'd thry its mettle.'

" 'No, no,' shouted Katty thinkin' there was a fairy in it, 'let us spake it fair. Who knows what harm it might do?' 'Aisy now,' said she to the pudden, 'aisy, dear; don't harm honest people that never meant to offend you. It wasn't us—no, in throth, it was ould Harry Connolly that bewitched you; pursue *him* if you wish, but spare a woman like me; for, whisper, dear, I'm not in a condition to be frightened—throth I'm not.'

"The pudden, bedad, seemed to take her at her word, and danced away from her towards Jack, who, like the wife, believin' there was a fairy in it, an' that spakin' it fair was the best plan, thought he would give it a soft word as well as her.

" 'Please your honour,' said Jack, 'she only spaiks the truth. You don't know what harm you might do her; an', upon my voracity, we both feels much oblaiged to your honour for your quietness. Faith, it's quite clear that if you weren't a gentlemanly pudden all out, you'd act otherwise. Ould Harry, the dam' rogue, is your mark; he's jist gone down the road there, and if you go fast you'll overtake him. Be me song, your dancin'-masther did his duty any how. Thank your honour! God speed you, an' may you never meet wid a priest, parson, or alderman in your thravels!'

" 'Jist as Jack spoke the pudden appeared to take the hint, for it quietly hopped out, and as the house was directly on the road side, turned down towards the bridge, the very way that ould Harry went. It was very natural of coorse that Jack and Katty should go out to see how it intended to thravel: and, as the day was Sunday, it was but natural, too, that a greater number of people than usual were passin' the road. This was a fact. And when Jack and his wife were seen followin' the pudden, the whole neighbourhood was soon up and afther it.

" 'Jack Rafferty, what is it? Katty, ahagur, will you tell us what it manes?'

" 'Why,' replied Katty, 'be the vestments, it's my big pudden that's bewitched, an' it's now hot-foot pursuin—,' here she stopped, not wishin' to mention her brother's name,—'*some one* or other that surely put *pistrogues* an it.'

"This was enough; Jack now seein' that he had assistance, found his courage comin' back to him, so says he to Katty, 'Go home,' says he, 'an' lose no time in makin' another pudden as good, an' here's Paddy Scanlan's wife, Bridget, says she'll let you boil it on her fire, as you'll want our own to dress the rest o' the dinner; and Paddy himself will lend me a pitchfork, for divle resave the morsel of the same pudden will escape till I let the wind out of it, now that I've the neighbours to back an' support me,' says Jack.

"This was agreed to, and Katty went back to prepare a fresh pudden, while Jack an' half the townland pursued the other wid spades, graips, pitchforks, scythes, flails, and all possible description of instruments. On the pudden went, however, at the rate of about six Irish miles an hour, an' divle sich a chase ever was seen. Catholics, Prodestans, an' Prosbytarians were all afther it, armed as I said, an' bad end to the thing but its own activity could save it. Here it made a hop, and there was a prod was made at it; but off it went, an' some one as aiger to get a slice at it on the other side, got the prod instead of the pudden. Big Frank Farrell, the miller of Ballyboulteen, got a prod backwards that brought a hullabaloo out of him you might hear at the other end of the parish. One got a slice of a scythe, another a whack of a flail, a third a rap of a spade that made him look nine ways at wanst.

" 'Where is it going'?' asked one.

" 'It's goin' to mass,' replied a second. 'Then it's a Catholic pudden,' exclaimed a third—'down wid it.' 'No,' said a fourth, 'it's above superstition; my life for you, it's on its way to Meeting. Three cheers for it, if it turns to Carntaul.' 'Prod the sowl out of it, if it's a Prodestan,' shouted the others; 'if it turns to the left, slice it into pancakes: we'll have no Prodestan puddens here.'

"Begad, by this time the people were on the point of beginnin' to have a regular fight about it, when, very fortunately, it took a short turn down a little bye-lane that led towards the Methodist praichin'-house, an' in an instant all parties were in an uproar against it as a Methodist pudden. 'It's a Wesleyan,' shouted several voices, 'an' by this an' by that into a Methodist chapel it won't put a foot to-day, or we'll lose a fall. Let the wind out of it. Come, boys, where's your pitchforks?'

"The divle purshue the one of them, however, ever could touch the pudden, an' jist when they thought they had it up against the gavel of the Methodist chapel, bedad it gave them the slip, and hops over the left, clane into the river, and sails away before all their eyes as light as an egg-shell.

"Now, it so happened, that a little below this place, the demesne-wall of Colonel Bragshaw was built up to the very edge of the river on each side of its banks; and so findin' there was a stop put to their pursuit of it, they went home again, every man, woman, and child of them puzzled to think what the pudden was at all—whether Catholic, Prodestan, Prosbytarian, or Methodist—what it meant, or where it was goin'! Had Jack Rafferty an' his wife been willin' to let out the opinion they held about Harry Connolly bewitchin' it, there is no doubt but poor Harry might be badly trated by the crowd when their blood was up. They had sense enough, howandiver, to keep that to themselves, for Harry, bein' an' ould bachelor, was a kind friend to the Raffertys. So, of course, there was all kinds of talk about it—some guessin' this, and some guessin' that—one party sayin' pudden was on their side, another party denyin' it, an' insistin' it belonged to them, an' so on.

"In the mane time, Katty Rafferty, for 'fraid the dinner might come short, went home and made another pudden much about the same size as the one that had escaped, and bringin' it over to their next neighbour, Paddy Scanlan's, it was put into a pot and placed on the fire to boil, hopin' that it might be done in time, espishilly as they were to have the priest an' the ministher, and that both loved a warm slice of a good pudden as well as e'er a pair of gintlemen in Europe.

"Anyhow, the day passed; Moll and Gusty were made man an' wife, an' no two could be more lovin'. Their friends that had been asked to the weddin' were saunterin' about in pleasant little groups till dinner time, chattin' an' laughin', but, above all things, sthrivin' to account for the figaries of the pudden, for, to tell the truth, its adventures had now gone through the whole parish.

"Well, at any rate, dinner-time was dhrawin' near, and Paddy Scanlan was sittin' comfortably wid his wife at the fire, the pudden boilen before their eyes, when in walks Harry Connolly, in a flutter, shoutin'—'Blood and blunderbushes, what are yez here for?'

" 'Arra, why, Harry—why, avick?' said Mrs. Scanlan.

" 'Why,' said Harry, 'the sun's in the suds an' the moon in the high Horicks. Here's a clipstick comin' an, an' there you sit as unconsarned as if it was about to rain mether! Go out an' cross yourselves three times in the name of the four Mandromarvins, for, as the prophecy says: —Fill the pot, Eddy, supernaculum—a blazin' star's a rare spectaculum. Go out both of you, an' look at the sun, I say, and ye'll see the condition he's in—off!'

" 'Ay, but, Harry, what's that rowled up in the tail of your cothamore [big coat]?'

" 'Out wid yez,' said Harry; 'cross yourselves three times in the name of the four Mandromarvins, an' pray aginst the clipstick—the sky's fallin'.'

"Begad it was hard to say whether Paddy or the wife got out first, they were so much alarmed by Harry's wild thin face, an' piercin' eyes; so out they went to see what was wondherful in the sky, an' kep' lookin' an' lookin' in every direction, but divle a thing was to be seen, barrin' the sun shinin' down with great good humour, an' not a single cloud in the sky.

"Paddy an' the wife now came in laughin', to scould Harry, who, no doubt, was a great wag, in his way, when he wished. 'Musha bad scran to you, Harry—'. They had time to say no more, howandiver, for, as they were goin' into the door, they met him comin' out of it wid a reek of smoke out of his tail like a lime-kiln.

" 'Harry,' shouted Bridget, 'my sowl to glory, but the tail of your cothamore's a-fire—you'll be burned. Don't you see the smoke that's out of it?'

" 'Cross yourselves three times,' said Harry, widout stoppin', or even lookin' behind him—'cross yourselves three times in the name of the four Mandromarvins, for, as the prophecy says:—Fill the pot, Eddy—'. They could hear no more, for Harry appeared to feel like a man that carried something a great deal hotter than he wished, as any one might see by the liveliness of his motions, and the quare faces he was forced to make as he went along.

" 'What the dickens is he carryin' in the skirts of his big coat?' asked Paddy.

" 'My sowl to happiness, but maybe he has stole the pudden,' said Bridget, 'for it's known that many a sthrange thing he does.'

"They immediately examined the pot, but found that the pudden was there as safe as tuppence, an' this puzzled them the more, to think what it was he could be carryin' about wid him in the manner he did. But little they knew what he had done while they were sky gazin'.

"Well, anyhow, the day passed and the dinner was ready, an' no doubt but a fine gatherin' there was to partake of it. The priest and the Prosbytarian ministher had met the Methodist praicher—a divilish stretch of an appetite he had, in troth—on their way to Jack Rafferty's, an' as they knew they could take the liberty, why they insisted on his dinin' wid them; for afther all, begad, in thim times the clargy of all descriptions lived on the best footin' among one another, not all as one as now—but no matter. Well, they had nearly finished their dinner, when Jack Rafferty himself axed Katty for the pudden; but jist as he spoke, in it came as big as a mess-pot.

" 'Gintlemen,' said he, 'I hope none of you will refuse tastin' a bit of Katty's pudden; I don't mane the dancin' one that took to its travels to-day, but a good solid fellow that she med since.'

" 'To be sure we won't,' replied the priest; 'so, Jack, put a thrifle on them three plates at your right hand, and send them over here to the clargy, an' maybe,' he said laughin'—for he was a droll good-humoured man—'maybe, Jack, we won't set you a proper example.'

" 'Wid a heart an' a half, yer reverence an' gintlemen; in throth, it's not a bad example ever any of you set us at the likes, or ever will set us, I'll go bail. An' sure I only wish it was betther fare I had for you; but we're humble people, gintlemen, and so you can't expect to meet here what you would in higher places.'

" 'Betther a male of herbs,' said the Methodist praicher, 'where pace is—.' He had time to go no farther, however, for, much to his amazement, the priest and the ministher started up from the table jist as he was goin' to swallow the first spoonful of the pudden, and before you could say Jack Robinson, started away at a lively jig down the floor.

"At this moment a neighbour's son came runnin' in an' tould them that the parson was comin' to see the new-married couple, an' wish them all happiness; an' the words were scarcely out of his mouth when he made his appearance. What to think he knew not, when he saw the priest an' ministher footing it away at the rate of a weddin'. He had very little time, however, to think, for, before he could sit down, up starts the Methodist praicher, and clappin' his two fists in his sides, chimes in in great style along wid them.

" 'Jack Rafferty,' says he—and, by the way, Jack was his tenant—'what the dickens does all this mane?' says he; 'I'm amazed!'

" 'The divle a particle o' me can tell you,' says Jack; 'but will your reverence jist taste a morsel of' pudden merely that the young couple may boast that you ait at their weddin'; for sure if *you* wouldn't, *who* would?'

" 'Well,' says he, 'to gratify them I will; so just a morsel'. 'But, Jack, this bates Banagher,' says he again, puttin' the spoonful o' pudden into his mouth, 'has there been dhrink here?'

" 'Oh, the divle a spudh,' says Jack, 'for although there's plinty in the house, faith, it appears the gintlemen wouldn't wait for it. Unless they took it elsewhere, I can make nothin' of this.'

"He had scarcely spoken, when the parson, who was an active man, cut a caper a yard high, an' before you could bless yourself, the four clargy were hard at work dancin', as if for a wager. Begad, it would be impossible for me to tell you the state the whole meetin' was in when they seen this. Some were hoarse wid laughin'; some turned up their eyes wid wondher; many thought them mad, an' others thought they had turned up their little fingers a thrifle too often.

164

" 'Be goxty, it's a burnin' shame,' said one, 'to see four clargy in sich a state at this early hour!' 'Thunder an' ounze, what's over them all?' says others; 'why, one would think they're bewitched. Holy Moses, look at the caper the Methodist cuts! An' Father M'Sorley! Honam an dioual! Who would think he could handle his feet at such a rate! Be this an' be that, he cuts the buckle, and does the treblin step aiquil to Paddy Horaghan, the dancin'-masther himself! An' see! Bad cess to the morsel of the ministher an' the parson that's not hard at Pease upon a trencher, an' it of a Sunday too! Whirroo, gintlemen, the fun's in yez afther all—whish! more power to yez.'

"The sorra's own fun they had, an' no wondher; but judge of what they felt, when all at once they saw ould Jack Rafferty himself bouncin' in among them, an' footin' it away like the best o' them. Bedad no play could come up to it, an' nothin' could be heard but laughin', shouts of encouragement, and clappin' of hands like mad. Now the minute Jack Rafferty left the chair where he had been carvin' the pudden, ould Harry Connolly comes over and claps himself down in his place, in ordher to send it round, of coorse; an' he was scarcely sated when who should make his appearance but Barney Hartigan, the piper. Barney, by the way, had been sent for early in the day; but bein' from home when the message for him went, he couldn't come any sooner.

" 'Begorra,' said Barney, 'you're airly at the work, gintlemen! Oh, blessed Phadrig!—the clargy too! Honam an dioual, what does this mane? But, divle may care, yez shan't want the music while there's a blast in the pipes, any how!' So sayin' he gave them Jig Polthogue, an' after that Kiss My Lady, in his best style.

"In the meantime the fun went on thick an' three fold, for it must be remimbered that Harry, the ould knave, was at the pudden; an' maybe he didn't sarve it about in double quick time too. The first he helped was the bride, and, before you could say chopstick, she was at it hard an' fast before the Methodist praicher, who immediately quit Father M'Sorley and gave a jolly spring before her that threw them into convulsions. Harry liked this, and made up his mind soon to find partners for the rest; so he accordingly sent the pudden about like lightnin'; an' to make a long story short, barrin' the piper an' himself, there wasn't a pair o' heels in the house but was as busy at the dancin' as if their lives depinded on it.'

165

" 'Barney,' says Harry, 'jist taste a morsel o' this pudden, divle the sich a bully of a pudden ever you ett; here, your sowl! thry a snig of it—it's beautiful.

" 'To be sure I will,' says Barney, 'I'm not the boy to refuse a good thing; but, Harry, be quick, for you know my hands is engaged; an' it would be a thousand pities not to keep them in music, an' they so well inclined. Thank you, Harry; begad that is a famous pudden; but blood an' turnips, what's this for!'

"The word was scarcely out of his mouth when he bounced up, pipes an' all, an' dashed into the middle of them. 'Hurroo, your sowls, let us make a night of it! The Ballyboulteen boys for ever! Go it, your reverence—turn your partner—heel an' toe, ministher. Good! Well done again.—Whish! Hurroo! Here's for Ballyboulteen, an' the sky over it!'

"Bad luck to sich a set ever was seen together in this world, or will again, I suppose. The worst, however, wasn't come yet, for jist as they were in the very heat and fury of the dance, what do you think comes hoppin' in among them but another pudden, as nimble an' as merry as the first! That was enough; they all had heard of—the clergy among the rest—an' most o' them had seen, the other pudden, and knew that there must be either the divle or a fairy in it, sure enough. Well as I said, in it comes to the thick o' them; but the very appearance of it was enough. Off the four clargy danced, and off the whole weddiners danced after them, every one makin' the best of their way home; but divle a sowl of them able to break out of the step, if they were to be hanged for it. Throth it wouldn't lave a laugh in you to see the priest an' the parson dancin' down the road on their way home together, and the ministher and Methodist praicher cuttin' the buckle as they went along in the opposite direction. To make short work of it, they all danced home at last, wid scarce a puff of wind in them; the bride and bridegroom danced away to bed; an' now, boys, come an' let us dance the Horo Lheig in the barn 'idout. But you see, boys, before we go, an' in ordher that I may make every thing plain, I had as good tell you, that Harry, in crossing the bridge of Ballyboulteen, a couple of miles below Squire Bragshaw's demesne-wall, saw the pudden floatin' down the river—the truth is he was waitin' for it; but be this as it may, he took it out, for the wather had made it as clane as a new pin, and tuckin' it up in the tail of his big coat, contrived as you all guess, I suppose, to change it while

Paddy Scanlan an' the wife were examinin' the sky; an' for the other, he contrived to bewitch it in the same manner, by gettin' a fairy to go onto it, for, indeed, it was purty well known that the same Harry was hand an' glove wid the *good people*. Others will tell you that it was half a pound of quicksilver he put into it; but that doesn't stand to raison. At any rate, boys, I have tould you the adventures of the Mad Pudden of Ballyboulteen; but I don't wish to tell you many other things about it that happened—for 'fraid I'd tell a lie."

*W.Y. Evans Wentz was a great student of the mystical and myster-
ious, who introduced to the West the sacred texts of Tibetan Bud-
dhism (such as the* Book of the Dead).

*In Stanford, California (of all places), as a young student of the
new science called anthropology, he fell under the spell of the Irish
fairies, and traveled to Ireland (and Wales and Scotland and Brittany) to research his first book,* The Fairy Faith in Celtic Countries.

*It's a great bruiser of a book, full of wonders and delights, not the
least of which can be found between the lines, where we can hear the
old men and women interviewed, amused by the earnestness of the
young American scholar, telling him whatever they think he wants to
hear.*

*Owen Morgan had a cottage on the banks of the Boyne River, not
far from the fairy hill of Newgrange, the Druid tomb where Angus
Og made his home two thousand years before.*

*In the twilight of a soft 1907 summer day, Owen sat in a chair
beside his door, and lit his pipe, and told Evans Wentz this one:*

HOW THE SHOEMAKER'S DAUGHTER BECAME
THE QUEEN OF TARA

In olden times there lived a shoemaker and his wife up there near
Moat Knowth, and their first child was taken by the queen of the
fairies who lived inside the moat, and a little leprechaun left in its
place. The same exchange was made when the second child was born.
At the birth of the third child the fairy queen came again and ordered
one of her three servants to take the child; but the child could not be
moved because of a great beam of iron, too heavy to lift, which lay
across the baby's breast. The second servant and then the third failed
like the first, and the queen herself could not move the child. The
mother being short of pins had used a needle to fasten the child's
clothes, and that was what appeared to the fairies as a beam of iron, for
there was virtue in steel in those days.

So the fairy queen decided to bestow gifts upon the child and
advised each of the three servants to give, in turn, a different gift. The
first one said: "May she be the grandest lady in the world;" the second
one said, "May she be the greatest singer in the world;" and the third
one said, "May she be the best mantle-maker in the world." Then the

168

fairy queen said, "Your gifts are all very good, but I will give a gift of my own better than any of them: the first time she happens to go out of the house let her come back into it under the form of a rat." The mother heard all that the fairy women said, and so she never permitted her daughter to leave the house.

When the girl reached the age of eighteen, it happened that the young prince of Tara, in riding by on a hunt, heard her singing, and so entranced was he with the music that he stopped to listen; and, the song ended, he entered the house, and upon seeing the wonderful beauty of the singer asked her to marry him. The mother said that could not be, and taking the daughter out of the house for the first time brought her back into it in an apron under the form of a rat, that the prince might understand the refusal.

This enchantment, however, did not change the prince's love for the beautiful singer; and he explained how there was a day mentioned with his father, the king, for all the great ladies of Ireland to assemble in the Halls of Tara, and that the grandest lady and the greatest singer and the best mantle-maker would be chosen as his wife. When he added that each lady must come in a chariot, the rat spoke to him and said that he must send to her home, on the day named, four piebald cats and a pack of cards, and that she would make her appearance, provided that at the time her chariot came to the Halls of Tara no one save the prince should be allowed near it; and, she finally said to the prince, "Until the day mentioned with your father, you must carry me as a rat in your pocket."

But before the great day arrived, the rat had made everything known to one of the fairy women, and so when the four piebald cats and the pack of cards reached the girl's home, the fairies at once turned the cats into the four most splendid horses in the world; and, as the chariot was setting out from the moat for Tara, the fairy queen clapped her hands and laughed, and the enchantment over the girl was broken. so that she became, as before, the prettiest lady in the world, and she sitting in the chariot.

When the prince saw the wonderful chariot coming, he knew whose it was, and went out alone to meet it; but he could not believe his eyes on seeing the lady inside. And then she told him about the witches and fairies, and explained everything.

Hundreds of ladies had come to the Halls of Tara from all Ireland,

and every one as grand as could be. The contest began with the singing, and ended with the mantle-making, and the young girl was the last to appear; but to the amazement of all the company the king had to give in (admit) that the strange woman was the grandest lady, the greatest singer, and the best mantle-maker in Ireland; and when the old king died she became the Queen of Tara.

"The well of the World's End" (in Gaelic, "D'yeree-in-Dowan") is from Douglas Hyde's anthology Beside the Fire, *the first folktale collection in which the Irish language original and the English translation were presented on facing pages.*

More than any other man, Douglas Hyde was responsible for the revival of the native Irish language, as founder of the Gaelic League and first professor of modern Gaelic at University College, Dublin. He was both an enthusiast and a scholar.

He resigned the presidency of the Gaelic League in 1915, when it became apparent to him that it was being politicized; indeed, many members took part in the Easter Insurrection of 1916.

But Hyde himself continued to embody the spirit of Irish cultural nationalism. In 1938 he was appointed president of the new nation of Eire, a post he held until his death in 1949.

THE WELL OF THE WORLD'S END

A long time ago—before St. Patrick's time—there was an old king in Connacht, and he had three sons. The king had a sore foot for many years, and he could get no cure. One day he sent for the wise man which he had, and said to him:

"I am giving you wages this twenty years, and you can't tell me what will cure my foot."

"You never asked me that question before," said the wise man, "but I tell you now that there is nothing in the world to cure you but a bottle of water from the Well of the World's End."

In the morning, the day on the morrow, the king called his three sons, and he said to them, "My foot will never be better until I get a bottle of water from the Well of the World's End, and whichever of you will bring me that, he has my kingdom to get."

"We will go in pursuit of it tomorrow," said the three. The names of the three were Art, Nart (strength), and Cart (right).

On the morning of the day on the morrow, the king gave to each one of them a purse of gold, and they went on their way. When they came as far as the cross-roads, Art said, "Each one of us ought to go a road for himself, and if one of us is back before a year and a day, let him wait till the other two come; or else let him set up a stone as a sign that he has come back safe."

171

They parted from one another after that, and Art and Nart went to an inn and began drinking; but Cart went on by himself. He walked all that day without knowing where he was going. As the darkness of the night came on he was entering a great wood, and he was going forward in the wood, until he came to a large house. He went in and looked round him, but he saw nobody, except a large white cat sitting beside the fire. When the cat saw him she rose up and went into another room. He was tired and sat beside the fire. It was not long till the door of the chamber opened, and there came out an old hag.

"One hundred thousand welcomes before you, son of the king of Connacht," says the hag.

"How did you know me?" says the king's son.

"Oh, many's the good day I spent in your father's castle in Bweesounee, and I know you since you were born," said the hag.

Then she prepared him a fine supper, and gave it to him. When he had eaten and drunk enough, she said to him:

"You made a long journey to-day; come with me until I show you a bed."

Then she brought him to a fine chamber, showed him a bed, and the king's son fell asleep. He did not awake until the sun was coming in on the windows the next morning.

Then he rose up, dressed himself, and was going out, when the hag asked him where he was going.

"I don't know," said the king's son. "I left home to find out the Well of the World's end."

"I'm after walking a good many places," said the hag, "but I never head talk of the Well of the World's End before."

The king's son went out, and he was travelling till he came to a cross-roads between two woods. He did not know which road to take. He saw a seat under the trunk of a great tree. When he went up to it he found it written, "This is the seat of travellers."

The king's son sat down, and after a minute he saw the most lovely woman in the world coming towards him, and she dressed in red silk, and she said to him, "I often heard that it is better to go forward than back."

Then she went out of his sight as though the ground should swallow her.

172

The king's son rose up and went forward. He walked that day till the darkness of the night was coming on, and he did not know where to get lodgings. He saw a light in a wood, and he drew towards it. The light was in a little house. There was not as much as the end of a feather jutting up on the outside nor jutting down on the inside, but only one single feather that was keeping up the house. He knocked at the door, and an old hag opened it.

"God save all here," says the king's son.

"A hundred welcomes before you, son of the king of the castel of Bwee-sounee," said the hag.

"How do you know me?" said the king's son.

"It was my sister nursed you," said the hag, "and sit down till I get your supper ready."

When he ate and drank his enough, she put him to sleep till morning. When he rose up in the morning, he prayed to God to direct him on the road of his luck.

"How far will you go to-day?" said the hag.

"I don't know," said the king's son. "I'm in search of the Well of the World's End."

"I'm three hundred years here," said the hag, "and I never heard of such a place before; but I have a sister older than myself, and perhaps she may know of it. Here is a ball of silver for you, and when you will go out upon the road throw it up before you and follow it till you come to the house of my sister."

When he went out on the road he threw down the ball, and he was following it until the sun was going under the shadow of the hills. Then he went into a wood, and came to the door of a little house. When he struck the door, a hag opened it and said, "A hundred thousand welcomes before you, son of the king of the castle of Bwee-sounee, who were at my sister's house last night. You made a long journey to-day. Sit down; I have a supper ready for you."

When the king's son ate and drank his enough, the hag put him to sleep, and he did not wake up till the morning. Then the hag asked, "Where are you going?"

"I don't rightly know," said the king's son. "I left home to find out the Well of the World's end."

"I am over five hundred years of age," said the hag, "and I never heard talk of that place before; but I have a brother, and if there is any such place in the world, he'll know of it. He is living seven hundred miles from here."

"It's a long journey," said the king's son.

"You'll be there tonight," said the hag.

Then she gave him a little horse about the size of a goat.

"That little beast won't be able to carry me," said the king's son.

"Wait till you go riding on it," said the hag.

The king's son got on the horse, and out for ever with him as fast as lightning.

When the sun was going under, that evening, he came to a little house in a wood. The king's son got off the horse, went in, and it was not long till an old grey man came out, and said, "A hundred thousand welcomes to you, son of the king of the castle of Bwee-sounee. You're in search of the Well of the World's End."

"I am, indeed," said the king's son.

"Many's the good man went that way before you; but not a man of them came back alive," said the old man. "However, I'll do my best for you. Stop here to-night, and we'll have sport to-morrow."

Then he dressed a supper and gave it to the king's son, and when he ate and drank, the old man put him to sleep.

In the morning of the day on the morrow, the old man said, "I found out where the Well of the World's End is; but it is difficult to go as far as it. We must find out if there's any good in you with the tight bow."

Then he brought the king's son out into the wood, gave him the bow, and put a mark on a tree two score yards from him, and told him to strike it. He drew the loop and struck the mark.

"You'll do the business," said the old man.

They then went in, and spent the day telling stories till the darkness of the night was come.

When the darkness of the night was come, the old man gave him a loop and a sheaf of sharp stings and said, "Come with me now."

They were going until they came to a great river. Then the old man said, "Go on my back, and I'll swim across the river with you; but if you see a great bird coming, kill him, or we shall be lost."

Then the king's son got on the old man's back, and the old man

174

began swimming. When they were in the middle of the river the king's son saw a great eagle coming, and his gob [beak] open. The king's son drew the loop and wounded the eagle.

"Did you strike him?" said the old man.

"I struck him," said the king's son, "but here he comes again."

He drew the loop the second time and the eagle fell dead.

When they came to the land, the old man said, "We are on the island of the Well of the World's End. The queen is asleep, and she will not waken for a day and a year. She never goes to sleep but once in seven years. There is a lion and a monster [*uillpheist*] watching at the gate of the well, but they go to sleep at the same time with the queen, and you will have no difficulty in going to the well. Here are two bottles for you; fill one of them for yourself, and the other for me, and it will make a young man of me."

The king's son went off, and when he came as far as the castle he saw the lion and the monster sleeping on each side of the gate. Then he saw a great wheel throwing up water out of the well, and he went and filled the two bottles, and he was coming back when he saw a shining light in the castle. He looked in through the window and saw a great table. There was a loaf of bread, with a knife, a bottle, and a glass on it. He filled the glass, but he did not diminish the bottle. He observed that there was a writing on the bottle and on the loaf; and he read on the bottle, "Water for the World," and on the loaf, "Bread for the World." He cut a piece off the loaf, but it only grew bigger.

"My grief! That we haven't that loaf and that bottle at home," said the king's son, "and there'd be neither hunger nor thirst on the poor people."

Then he went into a great chamber, and he saw the queen and eleven waiting-maidens asleep, and a sword of light hung above the head of the queen. It was it that was giving light to the whole castle.

When he saw the queen, he said to himself, "It's a pity to leave that pretty mouth without kissing it." He kissed the queen, and she never awoke; and after that he did the same to the eleven maidens. Then he got the sword, the bottle, and the loaf, and came to the old man, but he never told him that he had those things.

"How did you get on?" said the old man.

"I got the thing I was in search of," said the king's son.

175

"Did you see any marvel since you left me?" said the old man.

The king's son told him that he had seen a wonderful loaf, bottle, and sword.

"You did not touch them?" said the old man. "Shun them, for they would bring trouble on you. Come on my back now till I bring you across the river."

When they went to the house of the old man, he put water out of the bottle on himself, and made a young man of himself. Then he said to the king's son, "My sisters and myself are now free from enchantment, and they are young women again."

The king's son remained there until most part of the year and day were gone. Then he began the journey home; but, my grief, he had not the little nag with him. He walked the first day until the darkness of the night was coming on. He saw a large house. He went to the door, struck it, and the man of the house came out to him.

"Can you give me lodgings?" said he.

"I can," said the man of the house, "only I have no light to light you."

"I have a light myself," said the king's son.

He went in then, drew the sword, and gave a fine light to them all, and to everybody that was in the island. They then gave him a good supper, and he went to sleep. When he was going away in the morning, the man of the house asked him for the honour of God, to leave the sword with them.

"Since you asked for it in the honour of God, you must have it," said the king's son.

He walked the second day till the darkness was coming. He went to another great house, beat the door, and it was not long till the woman of the house came to him, and he asked lodgings of her. The man of the house came and said:

"I can give you that; but I have not a drop of water to dress food for you."

"I have plenty of water myself," said the king's son.

He went in, drew out the bottle, and there was not a vessel in the house he did not fill, and still the bottle was full. Then a supper was dressed for him, and when he ate and drank his enough, he went to sleep. In the morning, when he was going, the woman asked of him, in the honour of God, to leave them the bottle.

"Since it has chanced that you ask it for the honour of God," said the king's son, "I cannot refuse you, for my mother put me under *gassa* [mystic obligations] before she died, never, if I could, to refuse anything that a person would ask of me for the honour of God."

Then he left the bottle to them.

He walked the third day until darkness was coming, and he reached a great house on the side of the road. He struck the door; the man of the house came out, and he asked lodgings of him.

"I can give you that, and welcome," said the man, "but I'm grieved that I have not a morsel of bread for you."

"I have plenty of bread myself," said the king's son.

He went in, got a knife, and began cutting the loaf, until the table was filled with pieces of bread, and yet the loaf was as big as it was when he began. Then they prepared a supper for him, and when he ate his enough, he went to sleep. When he was departing in the morning, they asked of him, for the honour of God, to leave the loaf with them, and he left it with them.

The three things were now gone from him.

He walked the fourth day until he came to a great river, and he had no way to get across it. He went upon his knees, and asked God to send him help. After half a minute, he saw the beautiful woman he saw the day he left the house of the first hag. When she came near him, she said. "Son of the king of the castle of Bwee-sounee, has it succeeded with you?"

"I got the thing I went in search of," said the king's son, "but I do not know how I shall pass over this river."

She drew out a thimble and said: "Bad is the day I would see your father's son without a boat."

Then she threw the thimble into the river, and made a splendid boat of it.

"Get into the boat now," said she, "and when you will come to the other side, there will be a steed before you to bring you as far as the cross-roads, where you left your brothers."

The king's son stepped into the boat, and it was not long until he was at the other side, and there he found a white steed before him. He went riding on it, and it went off as swiftly as the wind. At about twelve o'clock that day, he was at the cross-roads. The king's son looked round him, and he did not see his brothers, nor any stone set up, and he said to himself, 'Perhaps they are at the inn. He went there, and found Art and Nart, and they two-thirds drunk.

They asked him how he went on since he left them.

"I have found out the Well of the World's End, and I have the bottle of water," said Cart.

Nart and Art were filled with jealousy, and they said one ot the other, "It's a great shame that the youngest son should have the kingdom."

"We'll kill him, and bring the bottle of water to my father," said Nart, "and we'll say that it was ourselves who went to the Well of the World's End."

"I'm not with you there," said Art, "but we'll get him drunk, and we'll take the bottle off him. My father will believe me and you before he'll believe our brother, because he has an idea that there's nothing in him but a half *omadawn* [simpleton].

"Then," he said to Cart, "since it has happened that we have come home safe and sound we'll have a drink before we go home."

They called for a quart of whiskey, and they made Cart drink the most of it, and he fell drunk. Then they took the bottle of water from him, went home themselves, and gave it to the king. He put a drop of the water on his foot, and it made him as well as ever he was.

Then they told him that they had great trouble to get the bottle of water—that they had to fight giants, and to go through great dangers.

"Did you see Cart on your road?" said the king.

"He never went farther than the inn, since he left us," said they, "and he's in it now, blind drunk."

"There never was any good in him," said the king, "but I cannot leave him there."

Then he sent six men to the inn, and they carried Cart home. When he came to himself, the king made him into a servant to do all the dirty jobs about the castle.

When a year and a day had gone by, the queen of the Well of the World's End and her waiting-maidens woke up and the queen found a young son by her side, and the eleven maidens the same.

There was great anger on the queen, and she sent for the lion and the monster, and asked them what was become of the eagle that she left in charge of the castle.

"He must be dead, or he'd be here now, when you woke up," said
they.

"I'm destroyed, myself, and the waiting-maidens ruined," said the
queen, "and I never will stop till I find out the father of my son."

Then she got ready her enchanted coach, and two fawns under it.
She was going till she came to the first house where the king's son got
lodging, and she asked was there any stranger there lately. The man of
the house said there was.

"Yes!" said the queen, "and he left the sword of light behind him;
it is mine, and if you do not give it to me quickly I will throw your
house upside down."

They gave her the sword, and she went on till she came to the
second house, in which he had got lodging, and she asked was there any
stranger there lately. They said that there was. "Yes!" said she, "and he
left a bottle after him. Give it to me quickly, or I'll throw the house on
ye."

They gave her the bottle, and she went till she came to the third
house, and she asked was there any stranger there lately. They said
there was.

"Yes!" said she, "and he left the loaf of lasting bread after him.
That belongs to me, and if ye don't give it to me quickly I will kill ye
all."

She got the loaf, and she was going, and never stopped till she
came to the castle of Bwee-sounee. She pulled the pole of combat and
the king came out.

"Have you any son?" said the queen.

"I have," said the king.

"Send him out here till I see him," said she.

The king sent out Art, and she asked him, "Were you at the Well
of the World's End?"

"I was," said Art.

"And are you the father of my son?" said she.

"I believe I am," said Art.

"I will know that soon," said she.

Then she drew two hairs out of her head, flung them against the
wall, and they were made into a ladder that went up to the top of the
castle. Then she said to Art, "If you were at the Well of the World's
End, you can go up to the top of that ladder."

Art went up half way, then he fell, and his thigh was broken.

"You were never at the Well of the World's End," said the queen.

Then she asked the king, "Have you any other son?"

"I have," said the king.

"Bring him out," said the queen.

Nart came out, and she asked him, "Were you ever at the Well of the World's End?"

"I was," said Nart.

"If you were, go up to the top of that ladder," said the queen.

He began going up, but he had not gone far till he fell and broke his foot.

"You were not at the Well of the World's End," said the queen.

Then she asked the king if he had any other son, and the king said he had. "But," said he, "it's a half fool he is, that never left home."

"Bring him here," said the queen.

When Cart came, she asked him, "Were you at the Well of the World's End?"

"I was," said Cart, "and I saw you there."

"Go up to the top of that ladder," said the queen.

Cart went up like a cat, and when he came down she said, "You are the man who was at the Well of the World's End, and you are the father of my son."

Then Cart told of the trick his brothers played on him, and the queen was going to slay them, until Cart asked pardon for them. Then the king said that Cart must get the kingdom.

Then the father dressed him out and put a chain of gold beneath his neck, and he got into the coach along with the queen, and they departed to the Well of the World's End.

The waiting-maidens gave a great welcome to the king's son, and they all of them came to him, each one asking him to marry herself.

He remained there for one-and-twenty years, until the queen died, and then he brought back with him his twelve sons, and it is from them that the twelve tribes of Galway are descended.

"Fair, Brown, and Trembling" is the Irish version of the Cinderella story, wicked sisters, fairy godmother, Prince Charming, and all.

There is no glass slipper in it—only an ordinary shoe. As a matter of fact, the glass slipper exists only in the English version; and that's because, when Cinderella was first translated from the French, somebody confused a slipper of fur (vair) with a slipper of glass (verre).

But we do hear of the further adventures of the prince and his bride, involving a cowboy, a whale, and a silver bullet.

Actually, it's a double feature—two stories, cleverly woven together. Perhaps the old woman who told the tale to Jeremiah Curtin was so pleased at his reaction that she went and made up a sequel on the spot.

FAIR, BROWN, AND TREMBLING

King Hugh Curucha lived in Tir Conal, and he had three daughters, whose names were Fair, Brown, and Trembling.

Fair and Brown had new dresses, and went to church every Sunday. Trembling was kept at home to do the cooking and work. They would not let her go out of the house at all; for she was more beautiful than the other two, and they were in dread she might marry before themselves.

They carried on in this way for seven years. At the end of seven years the son of the King of Emania fell in love with the eldest sister.

One Sunday morning, after the other two had gone to church, the old henwife came into the kitchen to Trembling, and said, "It's at church you ought to be this day, instead of working here at home."

"How could I go?" said Trembling. "I have no clothes good enough to wear at church; and if my sisters were to see me there, they'd kill me for going out of the house."

"I'll give you," said the henwife, "a finer dress than either of them has ever seen. And now tell me what dress you will have?"

"I'll have," said Trembling, "a dress as white as snow, and green shoes for my feet."

Then the henwife put on the cloak of darkness, clipped a piece from the old clothes the young woman had on, and asked for the whitest robes in the world and the most beautiful that could be found, and a pair of green shoes.

That moment she had the robe and the shoes, and she brought them to Trembling, who put them on.

When Trembling was dressed and ready, the henwife said, "I have a honey-bird here to sit on your right shoulder, and a honey-finger to put on your left. At the door stands a milk-white mare, with a golden saddle for you to sit on, and a golden bridle to hold in your hand."

Trembling sat on the golden saddle, and when she was ready to start, the henwife said, "You must not go inside the door of the church, and the minute the people rise up at the end of Mass, do you make off, and ride home as fast as the mare will carry you."

When Trembling came to the door of the church there was no one inside who could get a glimpse of her but was striving to know who she was; and when they saw her hurrying away at the end of Mass, they ran out to overtake her. But no use in their running, she was away before any man could come near her. From the minute she left the church till she got home, she overtook the wind before her, and outstripped the wind behind.

She came down at the door, went in, and found the henwife had dinner ready. She put off the white robes, and had on her old dress in a twinkling.

When the two sisters came home the henwife asked:

"Have you any news today from the church?"

"We have great news," said they. "We saw a wonderful grand lady at the church-door. The like of the robes she had we have never seen on woman before. It's little that was thought of our dresses beside what she had on; and there wasn't a man at the church, from the king to the beggar, but was trying to look at her and know who she was."

The sisters would give no peace till they had two dresses like the robes of the strange lady, but honey-birds and honey-fingers were not to be found.

Next Sunday the two sisters went to church again, and left the youngest at home to cook the dinner.

After they had gone, the henwife came in and asked: "Will you go to church today?"

"I would go," said Trembling, "if I could get the going."

"What robe will you wear?" asked the henwife.

"The finest black satin that can be found, and red shoes for my feet."

"What colour do you want the mare to be?"

"I want her to be so black and so glossy that I can see myself in her body."

The henwife put on the cloak of darkness, and asked for the robes and the mare. That moment she had them. When Trembling was dressed, the henwife put the honey-bird on her right shoulder and the honey-finger on her left. The saddle on the mare was silver, and so was the bridle.

When Trembling sat in the saddle and was going away, the henwife ordered her strictly not to go inside the door of the church, but to rush away as soon as the people rose at the end of Mass, and hurry home on the mare before any man could stop her.

That Sunday the people were more astonished than ever, and gazed at her more than the first time; and all they were thinking of was to know who she was. But they had no chance, for the moment the people rose at the end of Mass she slipped from the church, was in the silver saddle, and home before a man could stop her or talk to her.

The henwife had the dinner ready. Trembling took off her satin robe, and had on her old clothes before her sisters got home.

"What news have you today?" asked the henwife of the sisters, when they came from the church.

"Oh, we saw the grand strange lady again! And it's little that any man could think of our dresses after looking at the robes of satin that she had on! And all at church, from high to low, had their mouths open, gazing at her, and no man was looking at us."

The two sisters gave neither rest nor peace till they got dresses as nearly like the strange lady's robes as they could find. Of course they were not so good; for the like of those robes could not be found in Erin.

When the third Sunday came, Fair and Brown went to church dressed in black satin. They left Trembling at home to work in the kitchen, and told her to be sure and have dinner ready when they came back.

After they had gone and were out of sight, the henwife came to the kitchen and said, "Well, my dear, are you for church today?"

"I would go if I had a new dress to wear."

"I'll get you any dress you ask for. What dress would you like?" asked the henwife.

"A dress red as a rose from the waist down, and white as snow from the waist up; a cape of green on my shoulders; and a hat on my head with a red, a white, and a green feather in it; and shoes for my feet with the toes red, the middle white, and the backs and heels green."

The henwife put on the cloak of darkness, wished for all these things, and had them. When Trembling was dressed, the henwife put the honey-bird on her right shoulder and the honey-finger on her left, and, placing the hat on her head, clipped a few hairs from one lock and a few from another with her scissors, and that moment the most beautiful golden hair was flowing down over the girl's shoulders. Then the henwife asked what kind of a mare she would ride. She said white, with blue- and gold-coloured diamond-shaped spots all over her body, on her back a saddle of gold, and on her head a golden bridle.

The mare stood there before the door, and a bird sitting between her ears, which began to sing as soon as Trembling was in the saddle, and never stopped till she came home from the church.

The fame of the beautiful strange lady had gone out through the world, and all the princes and great men that were in it came to church that Sunday, each one hoping that it was himself would have her home with him after Mass.

The son of the King of Emania forgot all about the eldest sister, and remained outside the church, so as to catch the strange lady before she could hurry away.

The church was more crowded than ever before, and there were three times as many outside. There was such a throng before the church that Trembling could only come inside the gate.

As soon as the people were rising at the end of Mass, the lady slipped out through the gate, was in the golden saddle in an instant, and sweeping away ahead of the wind. But if she was, the Prince of Emania was at her side, and, seizing her by the foot, he ran with the mare for thirty perches, and never let go of the beautiful lady till the shoe was pulled from her foot, and he was left behind with it in his hand. She came home as fast as the mare could carry her, and she was thinking all the time that the henwife would kill her for losing a shoe.

Seeing her so vexed and so changed in the face, the old woman asked, "What's the trouble that's on you now?"

"Oh! I've lost one of the shoes off my feet," said Trembling.

"Don't mind that; don't be vexed," said the henwife; "maybe it's the best thing that ever happened to you."

Then Trembling gave up all the things she had to the henwife, put on her old clothes, and went to work in the kitchen. When the sisters came home, the henwife asked, "Have you any news from the church?"

"We have indeed," said they, "for we saw the grandest sight to-day. The strange lady came again, in grander array than before. On herself and the horse she rode were the finest colours of the world, and between the ears of the horse was a bird which never stopped singing from the time she came till she went away. The lady herself is the most beautiful woman ever seen by man in Erin."

After Trembling had disappeared from the church, the son of the King of Emania said to the other kings' sons, "I will have that lady for my own."

They all said, "You didn't win her just by taking the shoe off her foot; you'll have to win her by the point of the sword; you'll have to fight for her with us before you can call her your own."

"Well," said the son of the King of Emania, "when I find the lady that shoe will fit, I'll fight for her, never fear, before I leave her to any of you."

Then all the kings' sons were uneasy, and anxious to know who was she that lost the shoe; and they began to travel all over Erin to know how they could find her. The Prince of Emania and all the others went in a great company together, and made the round of Erin; they went everywhere—north, south, east, and west. They visited every place where a woman was to be found, and left not a house in the kingdom they did not search, to know could they find the woman the shoe would fit, not caring whether she was rich or poor, of high or low degree.

The Prince of Emania always kept the shoe; and when the young women saw it, they had great hopes, for it was of proper size, neither large nor small, and it would beat any man to know of what material it was made. One thought it would fit her if she cut a little from her great toe; and another with too short a foot, put something in the tip of her stocking. But no use; they only spoiled their feet, and were curing them for months afterwards.

The two sisters, Fair and Brown, heard that the princes of the world were looking all over Erin for the woman that could wear the shoe, and every day they were talking of trying it on; and one day Trembling spoke up and said: "Maybe it's my foot that the shoe will fit."

"Oh, the breaking of the dog's foot on you! Why say so when you were home every Sunday?"

They were that way waiting, and scolding the younger sister till the princes were near the place. The day they were to come, the sisters put Trembling in a closet, and locked the door on her. When the company came to the house, the Prince of Emania gave the shoe to the sisters. But though they tried and tried, it would fit neither of them.

"Is there any other young woman in the house?" asked the prince.

"There is," said Trembling, speaking up in the closet. "I'm here."

"Oh! we have her for nothing but to put out the ashes," said the sisters.

But the prince and the others wouldn't leave the house till they had seen her; so the two sisters had to open the door. When Trembling came out, the shoe was given to her, and it fitted exactly.

The Prince of Emania looked at her and said, "You are the woman the shoe fits, and you are the woman I took the shoe from."

Then Trembling spoke up, and said, "Do you stay here till I return."

Then she went to the henwife's house. The old woman put on the cloak of darkness, got everything for her she had the first Sunday at church, and put her on the white mare in the same fashion. Then Trembling rode along the highway to the front of the house. All who saw her the first time said, "This is the lady we saw at church."

Then she went away a second time, and a second time came back on the black mare in the second dress which the henwife gave her. All who saw her the second Sunday said, "That is the lady we saw at church."

A third time she asked for a short absence, and soon came back on the third mare and in the third dress. All who saw her the third time said, "That is the lady we saw at church." Every man was satisfied, and knew that she was the woman.

Then all the princes and great men spoke up, and said to the son of the King of Emania, "You'll have to fight now for her before we let her go with you."

"I'm here before you, ready for combat," answered the prince.

Then the son of the King of Lochlin stepped forth. The struggle began, and a terrible struggle it was. They fought for nine hours; and then the son of the King of Lochlin stopped, gave up his claim, and left the field. Next day the son of the King of Spain fought six hours, and yielded his claim. On the third day the son of the King of Nyerfoi fought eight hours, and stopped. The fourth day the son of the King of Greece fought six hours, and stopped. On the fifth day no more strange princes wanted to fight; and all the sons of kings in Erin said they would not fight with a man of their own land, that the strangers had had their chance, and, as no others came to claim the woman, she belonged of right to the son of the King of Emania.

The marriage-day was fixed, and the invitations were sent out. The wedding lasted for a year and a day. When the wedding was over, the king's son brought home the bride, and when the time came a son was born. The young woman sent for her eldest sister, Fair, to be with her and care for her.

One day, when Trembling was well, and when her husband was away hunting, the two sisters went out to walk; and when they came to the seaside, the eldest pushed the youngest sister in. A great whale came and swallowed her.

The eldest sister came home alone, and the husband asked, "Where is your sister?"

"She has gone home to her father in Ballyshannon; now that I am well, I don't need her."

"Well," said the husband, looking at her, "I'm in dread it's my wife that has gone."

"Oh! no," siad she. "It's my sister Fair that's gone."

Since the sisters were very much alike, the prince was in doubt. That night he put his sword between them, and said, "If you are my wife, this sword will get warm; if not, it will stay cold."

In the morning when he rose up, the sword was as cold as when he put it there.

It happened, when the two sisters were walking by the seashore, that a little cowboy was down by the water minding cattle, and saw Fair push Trembling into the sea; and next day, when the tide came in, he saw the whale swim up and throw her out on the sand.

When she was on the sand she said to the cowboy, "When you go home in the evening with the cows, tell the master that my sister Fair pushed me into the sea yesterday; that a whale swallowed me, and then threw me out, but will come again and swallow me with the coming of the next tide; then he'll go out with the tide, and come again with to-morrow's tide, and throw me again on the strand. The whale will cast me out three times. I'm under the enchantment of this whale, and cannot leave the beach or escape myself. Unless my husband saves me before I'm swallowed the fourth time, I shall be lost. He must come and shoot the whale with a silver bullet when he turns on the broad of his back. Under the breast-fin of the whale is a reddish-brown spot. My husband must hit him in that spot, for it is the only place in which he can be killed."

When the cowboy got home, the eldest sister gave him a draught of oblivion, and he did not tell.

Next day he went again to the sea. The whale came and cast Trembling on shore again. She asked the boy, "Did you tell the master what I told you to tell him?"

"I did not," said he; "I forgot."

"How did you forget?" asked she.

"The woman of the house gave me a drink that made me forget."

"Well, don't forget telling him this night; and if she gives you drink, don't take it from her."

As soon as the cowboy came home, the eldest sister offered him a drink. He refused to take it till he had delivered his message and told all to the master.

The third day the prince went down with his gun and a silver bullet in it. He was not long down when the whale came and threw Trembling upon the beach as the two days before. She had no power to speak to her husband till he had killed the whale. Then the whale went out, turned over once on the broad of his back, and showed the spot for a moment only. That moment the prince fired. He had but the one chance, and a short one at that; but he took it, and hit the spot, and the whale, mad with pain, made the sea all around red with blood, and died.

That minute Trembling was able to speak, and went home with her husband, who sent word to her father what the eldest sister had done. The father came, and told him any death he chose to give her to give it. The prince told the father he would leave her life and death with himself. The father had her put out then on the sea in a barrel, with provisions in it for seven years.

In time Trembling had a second child, a daughter. The prince and she sent the cowboy to school, and trained him up as one of their own children, and said: "If the little girl that is born to us now lives, no other man in the world will get her but him."

The cowboy and the prince's daughter lived on till they were married. The mother said to her husband, "You could not have saved me from the whale but for the little cowboy: on that account I don't grudge him my daughter."

The son of the King of Emania and Trembling had fourteen children, and they lived happily till the two died in old age.

If "Fair, Brown, and Trembling" is the Irish "Cinderella," "The Widow's Daughter" is "Rumpelstiltskin," a story of a poor girl receiving supernatural help in order to accomplish a series of impossible household tasks.

Not far beneath the surface of the patriarchy of the Irish peasants, a matriarchy has remained alive and well, and having its way . . . underground, witty and powerful as the Sidhe themselves. This is the story of a power struggle involving a mother, a daughter, and a mother-in-law, in which female fairies play a part. The prince, who thinks he's the prize, is hardly even a spectator at the game.

The story is taken from a collection of Donegal folktales retold by Seamus MacManus, entitled In Chimney Corners.

THE WIDOW'S DAUGHTER

There was once a poor widow woman, living in the North of Ireland, who had one daughter named Nabla. And Nabla grew up both idle and lazy, till at length, when she had grown to be a young woman, she was both thriftless and useless, fit only to sit with her heels in the ashes and croon to the cat the day long. Her mother was annoyed with her, so that one day, when Nabla refused to do some little trifle about the house, her mother got out a good stout sallyrod and came in and thrashed her with it.

As her mother was giving Nabla the whacking she had so richly earned, who should happen to be riding past but the King's son himself. He heard the mother walloping and scolding, and Nabla crying and pleading within. So he drew rein, and at the top of his voice shouted to know what was the matter. The widow came to the door, curtseying when she saw who he was. Not wishing to give out a bad name on her daughter, she told the King's son that she had a daughter who killed herself working the leelong day and refused to rest when her mother asked her, so that she had always to be beaten before she would stop.

"What work can your daughter do?" the Prince asked.

"She can spin, weave and sew, and do every work that ever a woman did," the mother replied.

Now, it so happened that a twelvemonth before the Prince had taken a notion of marrying, and his mother, anxious he should have

191

none but the best wife, had, with his approval, sent messengers over all
Ireland to find him a woman who could perform all a woman's duties,
including the three accomplishments the widow named—spinning,
that is, weaving and sewing. But all the candidates whom the messengers had secured were found unsatisfactory on being put to trial, and
the Prince had remained unwedded. When, now, the King's son heard
this account of Nabla from her own mother he said:

"You are not fit to have the charge of such a good girl. For twelve
months, through all parts of my mother's kingdom, search was being
made for just such a young woman that she might become my wife. I'll
take Nabla with me."

Poor Nabla was rejoiced and her mother astonished. The King's
son helped Nabla to a seat behind him on the horse's back and bidding
adieu to the widow rode off.

When he had got Nabla home, he introduced her to his mother,
telling the Queen that by good fortune he had secured the very woman
they had so long sought in vain. The Queen asked what Nabla could do,
and he replied that she would spin, weave and sew, and do everything
else a woman should; and moreover, she was so eager for work that her
mother was flailing her within an inch of her life to make her rest
herself when he arrived on the scene at Nabla's own cottage. The
Queen said that was well.

She took Nabla to a large room and gave her a heap of silk and a
golden wheel, and told her she must have all the silk spun into thread in
twenty-four hours. Then she bolted her in.

Poor Nabla, in amazement, sat looking at the big heap of silk and
the golden wheel. And at length she began to cry, for she had not spun
a yard of thread in all her life. As she cried an ugly woman, having one
of her feet as big as a bolster, appeared before her.

"What are you crying for?" she asked.

Nabla told her, and the woman said, "I'll spin the silk for you if
you ask me to the wedding."

"I'll do that," Nabla said. And then the woman sat down to the
wheel, and working it with her big foot, very soon had the whole heap
spun.

When the Queen came and found all spun she said: "That is
good." Then she brought in a golden loom and told Nabla she must
have all that thread woven in twenty-four hours.

When the Queen had gone Nabla sat down and looked from the thread to the loom and from the loom to the thread, wondering, for she had not in all her life even thrown a shuttle. At length she put her face in her hands and began to cry. There now appeared to her an ugly woman with one hand as big as a pot hanging by her side. She asked Nabla why she cried. Nabla told her, and then the woman said:

"I'll weave all that for you if you'll give me the promise of your wedding."

Nabla said she would surely. So the woman sat down to the golden loom, and very soon had all the thread woven into webs.

When again the Queen came and found all woven she said: "That is good." And then she gave Nabla a golden needle and thimble and said that in twenty-four hours more she must have all the webs made into shirts for the Prince.

Again when the Queen had gone, Nabla, who had never even threaded a needle in all her life, sat for a while looking at the needle and thimble and looking at the webs of silk. And again she broke down, and began to cry heartily.

As she cried an ugly woman with a monstrously big nose came into the room and asked:

"Why do you cry?"

When Nabla had told her, the ugly woman said:

"I'll make up all those webs into shirts for the Prince if you promise me the wedding."

"I'll do that," Nabla said, "and a thousand welcomes."

So the woman with the big nose, taking the needle and thimble, sat down, and in a short time had made all the silk into shirts and disappeared again.

When the Queen came a third time and found all the silk made up in shirts she was mightily pleased and said:

"You are the very woman for my son, for he'll never want a housekeeper while he has you."

Then Nabla and the Prince were betrothed, and on the wedding night there was a gay and a georgeous company in the hall of the Castle. All was mirth and festivity. But as they were about to sit down to a splendid repast there was a loud knock at the door. A servant opened it and there came in an ugly old woman with one foot as big as a pot who, amid the loud laughter of the company, hobbled up the floor and took a seat at the table. She was asked of which party was she, the bride or the groom's, and she replied that she was of the bride's party. When the Prince heard this he believed that she was one of Nabla's poor friends. He went up to her and asked her what had made her foot so big.

"Spinning," she said. "I have been all my life at the wheel and that's what it has done for me."

"Then, by my word," said the Prince, striking the table a great blow, "my wife shall not turn a wheel while I'm here to prevent it!"

As the party were again settling themselves another knock came to the door. A servant opening it let in a woman with one hand as big as a stool. The weight of this hand hanging by her side gave her body a great lean over, so that as she hobbled up the floor the company at the table lay back, laughing and clapping their hands at the funny sight. This woman, taking a seat at the table, was asked by whose invitation she was there, to which she replied that she was of the bride's party. Then the Prince went up to her and inquired what caused her hand to be so big.

"Weaving," she said. "I have slaved at the shuttle all my life; that's what has come on me."

"Then," the Prince said, striking the table a thundering blow, "by my word, my wife shall never throw a shuttle again while I live to prevent it."

A third time the company were ready to begin their repast, when again there came a knock to the door. Everyone looked up; and they saw the servant now admit an ugly old woman with the most monstrous nose ever beheld. This woman likewise took a chair at the table. She was then asked who had invited her—the bride or the groom. She said she was one of the bride's party. Then the Prince, on going up to her, asked her why her nose had come to be so very big.

"It's with sewing," she said. "All my life I have been bending my head over sewing, so that every drop of blood ran down into my nose, swelling it out like that."

Then the Prince struck the table a blow that made the dishes leap and rattle.

"By my word," he said, "my wife shall never either put a needle in cloth again or do any other sort of household work while I live to prevent it."

And the Prince faithfully kept his word. He was always on the lookout to try and catch Nabla spinning, weaving, or sewing, or doing any other sort of work, for he thought she might at any time try to work on the sly.

Poor Nabla, however, never did anything to confirm his uneasiness, but, taking her old mother to stop in the Castle with her, lived happy and contented, and as lazy as the day was long, ever after.

*Scholars of folklore begin to analyse a tale by assigning to it a "type."
For instance, a dragon slayer story is Type 300, a Tom Thumb story
Type 700.*

*They next isolate the "motifs"—which are themes, symbolic inci-
dents, and characters. "Red as blood and white as snow" is Motif Z
65.1, and "Cruel stepmother" is S 31.*

*Perhaps, at their conventions, they keep each other entertained
by reciting numbers and letters aloud.*

*They would certainly have a field day with "The Plaisham," a
story told by Seamus MacManus of Donegal. As you will see, it begins
with an Eternal Triangle, moves quickly to the Three Impossible
Tasks, goes on to the Fairy Helper and the Magic Charm, and ends
with a Goose Girl Parade.*

*But "The Plaisham" is a good joke—and like many jokes, might
lose something in the scientific analysis. The sight of academics lined
up to cross-index its many motifs might just inspire you to shout,
"Drive on the plaisham!"*

THE PLAISHAM

Nancy and Shamus were man and wife, and they lived all alone
together for forty years; but at length a good-for-nothing streel of a
fellow named Rory, who lived close by, thought what a fine thing it
would be if Shamus would die, and he could marry Nancy, and get the
house, farm, and all the stock. So he up and said to Nancy:

"What a pity it is for such a fine-looking woman as you to be
bothered with that ould, complainin', good-for-nothing crony of a man
that's as full of pains and aches as an egg's full of meat. If you were free
of him the morrow, the finest and handsomest young man in the parish
would be proud to have you for wife."

At first Nancy used to laugh at this; but at last, when he kept on at
it, it began to prey on Nancy's mind, and she said to young Rory one
day: "I don't believe a word of what you say. Who would take me if
Shamus was buried the morra?"

"Why," says Rory, "you'd have the pick of the parish. I'd take you
myself."

"Is that true?" says Nancy.

"I pledge you my word," says Rory, "I would."

"Oh, well, even if you would yourself," says Nancy, "Shamus won't be buried to-morrow, or maybe, God help me, for ten years to come yet."

"You've all that in your own hands," says Rory.

"How's that?" says Nancy.

"Why, you can kill him off," says Rory.

"I wouldn't have the ould crature's blood on my head," says Nancy.

"Neither you need," says Rory.

And then he sat down and began to tell Nancy how she could do away with Shamus and still not have his blood on her head.

Now there was a prince called Connal, who lived in a wee sod house close by Nancy and Shamus, but whose fathers before him, ere their money was wasted, used to live in a grand castle. So, next day, over Nancy goes to this prince, and to him says: "Why, Prince Connal, isn't it a shame to see the likes of you livin' in the likes of that house?"

"I know it is," said he, "but I cannot do any better."

"Botheration," says Nancy, "you easily can."

"I wish you would tell me how," says Prince Connal.

"Why," says Nancy, "there's my Shamus has little or nothing to do, an' why don't you make him build you a castle?"

"Ah," says the prince, laughing, "sure, Shamus couldn't build me a castle."

Says Nancy: "You don't know Shamus, for there's not a thing in the wide world he couldn't do if he likes to; but he's that lazy, if you don't break every bone in his body to make him do it, he won't do it."

"Is that so?" says Prince Connal.

"That's so," says Nancy. "So, if you order Shamus to build you a castle an' have it up in three weeks, or that you'll take his life he doesn't, you'll soon have a grand castle to live in," says she.

"Well, if that's so," says Prince Connal, "I'll not be long wanting a castle."

So on the very next morning, over he steps to Shamus's, calls Shamus out, and takes him with him to the place he had marked out for the site of his castle, and shows it to Shamus, and tells him he wants him to have a grand castle built and finished on that spot in three weeks' time.

"But," says Shamus, says he, "I never built a castle in my life. I know nothing about it, an' I couldn't have you a castle there in thirty-three years, let alone three weeks."

"O!" says the prince, says he, "I'm toul' there's no man in Ireland can build a castle better nor faster than you, if you only like to; and if you haven't that castle built on that ground in three weeks," says he, "I'll have your life. So now choose for yourself." And he walked away, and left Shamus standing there.

When Shamus heard this, he was a down-hearted man, for he knew that Prince Connal was a man of his word, and would not stop at taking any man's life any more than he would from putting the breath out of a beetle. So down he sits and begins to cry; and while Shamus was crying there, up to him comes a Wee Red Man, and says to Shamus; "What are you crying about?"

"Ah, my poor man," says Shamus, says he, "don't be asking me, for there's no use in telling you, you could do nothing to help me."

"You don't know that," says the Wee Red Man, says he. "It's no harm to tell me anyhow."

So Shamus, to relieve his mind, ups and tells the Wee Red Man what Prince Connal had threatened to do to him if he had not a grand castle finished on that spot in three weeks.

Says the little man, says he: "Go to the Glen of the Fairies at moonrise the night, and under the rockin' stone at the head of the glen you'll find a white rod. Take that rod with you, and mark out the plan of the castle on this ground with it; then go back and leave the rod where you got it, and by the time you get back again your castle will be finished."

At moonrise that night Shamus, as you may be well assured, was at the rockin' stone at the head of the Glen of the Fairies, and from under it he got a little white rod. He went to the hill where the Prince's castle was to be built, and with the point of the rod he marked out the plan of the castle, and then he went back and left the rod where he got it.

The next morning, when Prince Connal got up out of bed and went out of his little sod hut to take the air, his eyes were opened, I tell you, to see the magnificent castle that was standing finished and with the coping-stones on it on the hill above. He lost no time till he went over to thank Shamus for building him such a beautiful castle; and when Nancy heard that the castle was finished, it was she that was the angry woman.

She went out and looked at the castle, and she wondered and wondered, too, but she said nothing. She had a long chat with Rory that day again, and from Rory she went off to Prince Connal, and says she: "Now, didn't I tell you right well what Shamus could do?"

"I see you did," says Prince Connal, "and it is very thankful to you I am. I'm contented now for life," says he, "and I'll never forget yourself and Shamus."

"Contented!" says she; "why, that place isn't half finished yet."

"How's that?" says Prince Connal.

"Why," says she, "you need a beautiful river flowing past that castle, with lovely trees, and birds singing in the branches, and you should have the ocean roaring up beside it."

"But still," says Prince Connal, says he, "one can't have everything. This is a hundred miles from a river and hundred miles from an ocean, and no trees ever grew on this hill, nor ever could grow on it, and no bird ever sang on it for the last three hundred years."

"Then all the more reason," says she, "why you should have all them things."

"But I can't have them," says Prince Connal.

"Can't you?" says she. "Yes, you can. If you promise to have Shamus's life unless he has you all those things by your castle in three days, you'll soon have all you want," says Nancy.

"Well, well, that's wonderful," says Prince Connal, says he, "and I'll do it."

So he sets out, and goes to Shamus's house, and calls Shamus out to him to tell him that his castle was very bare looking without something about it. Says he: "Shamus, I want you to put a beautiful river flowing past it,with plenty of trees and bushes along the banks, and also birds singing in them; and I want you to have the ocean roaring up by it also."

"But, Prince Connal," says Shamus, says he, "you know very well that I couldn't get you them things."

"Right well I know you can," says Prince Connal, "and I'll give you three days to have all of them done; and if you haven't them done at the end of three days, then I'll have your life." And away goes Prince Connal.

Poor Shamus, he sat down and began to cry at this, because he knew that he could not do one of these things. And as he was crying and crying he heard a voice in his ear, and looking up he saw the Wee Red Man.

"Shamus, Shamus," says he, "what's the matter with you?"

"O," says Shamus, says he, "there's no use in telling you what's the matter with me this time. Although you helped me before, there's not a man in all the world could do what I've got to do now."

"Well, anyhow," says the Wee Red Man, "if I can't do you any good, I'll do you no harm."

So Shamus, to relieve his mind, ups and tells the Wee Red Man what's the matter with him.

"Shamus," says the Wee Red Man, says he, "I'll tell you what you'll do. When the moon's rising to-night, be at the head of the Glen of the Fairies, and at the spring well there you'll find a cup and a leaf and a feather. Take the leaf and the feather with you, and cup of water, and go back to the castle. Throw the water from you as far as you can throw it, and then blow the leaf off your right hand, and the feather off your left hand, and see what you'll see."

Shamus promised to do this. And when the moon rose that night, Shamus was at the spring well of the Glen of the Fairies, and he found there a cup, a leaf, and a feather. He lifted a cup of water and took it with him, and the leaf and the feather, and started for the castle. When he came there, he pitched the cup of water from him as far as he could pitch it, and at once the ocean, that was a hundred miles away, came roaring up beside the castle, and a beautiful river that had been flowing a hundred miles on the other side of the castle came flowing down past it into the ocean. Then he blew the leaf off his right hand, and all sorts of lovely trees and bushes sprang up along the river banks. Then he blew the feather off his left hand, and the trees and the bushes were filled with all sorts and varieties of lovely singing birds, that made the most beautiful music he ever had heard.

And maybe that was not a surprise to Prince Connal when he got up in the morning and went out. Off he tramped to Shamus's to thank Shamus and Nancy, and when Nancy heard this she was the angry woman.

That day she had another long confab with Rory, and from him she went off again to Prince Connal, and asked him how he liked his castle and all its surroundings.

He said he was a pleased and proud man, that he was thankful to her and her man, Shamus, and that he would never forget it to them the longest day of his life.

"O, but," says she, "you're not content. This night you'll have a great gathering of princes and lords and gentlemen feasting in your castle, and you'll surely want something to amuse them with. You must get a plaisham."

"What's a plaisham?" says Prince Connal.

"O" says Nancy, "it's the most wonderful and most amusing thing in the world; it will keep your guests in good humor for nine days and nine nights after they have seen it."

"Well," says Prince Connal, "that must be a fine thing entirely, and I'm sure I would be mightly anxious to have it. But," says he, "where would I get it or how would I get it?"

"Well," says Nancy, "that's easy. If you order Shamus to bring a plaisham to your castle by supper time this night, and promise to have his life if he hasn't it there, he'll soon get it for you."

"Well, if that's so," says Prince Connal, "I'll not be long wanting a plaisham."

So home went Nancy rejoicing this time, for she said to herself that poor old Shamus would not be long living now, because there was no such thing known in the whole wide world as a plaisham; and though Shamus might build castles, and bring oceans and rivers and trees and birds to them, all in one night, he could not get a thing that did not exist and was only invented by Rory.

Well, off to Shamus went Prince Connal without much loss of time, and called Shamus out of his little cabin. He told him he was heartily well pleased with all he had done for him. "But there's one thing more I want you to do, Shamus, and then I'll be content," says he. "This night I give a grand supper to the lords, ladies, and gentry of the country, and I want something to amuse them with; so at supper time you must bring me a plaisham."

"A plaisham! What's that?" says Shamus.

"I don't know," says Prince Connal.

"No more do I," says Shamus, "an' how do you expect me to fetch it to you then?"

"Well," says Prince Connal, says he, "this is all there is to be said about it—if you haven't a plaisham at my castle door at supper time the night, you'll be a dead man."

"O, O," says Shamus, says he, and sat down on the ditch and began to cry, while Prince Connal went off home.

"Shamus, Shamus," says a voice in his ears, "what are you cryin' about now?"

Poor Shamus lifted his head and looked around, and there beside him stood the Wee Red Man.

"O!" says Shamus, says he, "don't mind asking me," he says, "for it's no use in telling you what's the matter with me now. You may build a castle for me," says he, "and you may bring oceans and rivers to it, and trees and birds; but you couldn't do anything to help me now."

"How do you know that?" says the Wee Red Man.

"O, I know it well," says Shamus, says he; "you couldn't give me the thing that never was an' never will be!"

"Well," says the Wee Red Man, says he, "tell me what it is anyhow. If I can't do you any good, sure I can't do you any harm."

So, to relieve his mind, Shamus ups and tells him that Prince Connal had ordered him, within twenty-four hours, to have at his castle door a plaisham. "But," says Shamus, says he, "there never was such a thing as that."

"Sure enough," says the Wee Red Man, "there never was. But still, if Prince Connal wants it, we must try to get it for him. This night, Shamus," says the Wee Red Man, says he, "go to the head of the Glen of the Fairies, to the sciog bush [fairy thorn], where you'll find a bone ring hanging on a branch of the thorn. Take it with you back home. When you get home, young Rory will be chatting with your wife in the kitchen. Don't you go in there, but go into the byre [cowshed], and put the ring in the cow's nose; then lie quiet, and you'll soon have a plaisham to drive to Prince Connal's castle door."

Shamus thanked the Wee Red Man, and that night he went to the head of the Glen of the Fairies, and sure enough, he found the ring hanging from one of the branches of the sciog bush. He took it with him, and started for home. When he looked in through the kitchen window, there he saw Nancy and Rory sitting over the fire, chatting and confabbing about how they would get rid of him; but he said nothing, only went into the byre. He put the ring into the brannet cow's nose, and as soon as the ring went into it, the cow began to kick and rear and create a great tendherary of a noise entirely. Then Shamus got in under some hay in the corner.

It was no time at all until Nancy was out to find what was wrong with the brannet cow. She struck the cow with her fist to quiet her, but when she hit her, her fist stuck to the cow, and she could not get away.

Rory had come running out after Nancy to help her, and Nancy called: "Rory, Rory, pull me away from the cow."

Rory got hold of her to pull her away, but as he did so his hands stuck to Nancy, and he could not get away himself.

Up then jumped Shamus from under the hay in the corner. "Hup, Hup!" says Shamus, says he, "drive on the plaisham."

And out of the byre starts the cow with Nancy stuck to her and Rory stuck to that, and heads toward the castle, with the cow rearing and rowting, and Nancy and Rory yelling and bawling. They made a terrible din entirely, and roused the whole countryside, who flocked out to see what was the matter.

Down past Rory's house the cow went, and Rory's mother, seeing him sticking to Nancy, ran out to pull him away; but when she laid her hand on Rory, she stuck to him; and "Hup, Hup!" says Shamus, says he, "drive on the plaisham."

So on they went. And Rory's father ran after them to pull the mother away; but when he laid his hands on the mother, he stuck to her; and "Hup, Hup!" says Shamus, "drive on the plaisham."

On again they went, and next they passed where a man was cleaning out his byre. When the man saw the ridiculous string of them he flung a graip [fork] and a graipful of manure at them, and it stuck to Rory's father; and "Hup, Hup!" says Shamus, says he, "drive on the plaisham." But the man ran after to save his graip, and when he got hold of the graip, he stuck to it; and "Hup, Hup!" says Shamus, says he, "drive on the plaisham."

On they went, and a tailor came lying out of his house with his lap-board in his hand. He struck the string of them with the lap-board, the lap-board stuck to the last man, and the tailor stuck to it; and "Hup, Hup!" says Shamus, says he, "drive on the plaisham."

Then they passed a cobbler's. He ran out with his heel-stick, and struck the tailor; but the heel-stick stuck to the tailor, and the cobbler stuck to the heel-stick. and "Hup, Hup!" says Shamus, says he, "drive on the plaisham."

Then on they went, and they passed a blacksmith's forge. The blacksmith ran out, and struck the cobbler with his sledge. The sledge stuck to the cobbler, and the blacksmith stuck to the sledge; and "Hup, Hup!" says Shamus, says he, "drive on the plaisham."

When they came near the castle, they passed a great gentleman's house entirely, and the gentleman came running out, and got hold of the blacksmith to pull him away; but the gentleman stuck to the blacksmith, and could not get away himself; and "Hup, Hup!" says Shamus, says he, "drive on the plaisham."

The gentleman's wife, seeing him stuck, ran after her man to pull him away; but the wife stuck to the gentleman; and "Hup, Hup!" says Shamus, says he, "drive on the plaisham."

Then their children ran after them to pull the mother away, and they stuck to the mother; and "Hup, Hup!" says Shamus, says he, "drive on the plaisham."

Then the butler ran to get hold of the children, and he stuck to them; and the footman ran to get hold of the butler, and stuck to him; and the cook ran to get hold of the footman, and stuck to him; and the servants all ran to get hold of the cook, and they stuck to her; and "Hup, Hup!" says Shamus, says he, "drive on the plaisham."

And on they went; and when they came up to the castle, the plaisham was a mile long, and the yelling and bawling and noise that they made could be heard anywhere within the four seas of Ireland. The racket was so terrible that Prince Connal and all his guests and all his servants and all in his house came running to the windows to see what was the matter, at all, at all; and when Prince Connal saw what was coming to his house, and heard the racket they were raising, he yelled to his Prime Minister to go and drive them off with a whip.

The Prime Minister ran meeting them, and took the whip to them; but the whip stuck to them, and he stuck to the whip; and "Hup, Hup!" says Shamus, says he, "drive on the plaisham."

Then Prince Connal ordered out all his other ministers and all of his servants to head it off and turn it away from his castle; but every one of the servants that got hold of it stuck to it; and "Hup, Hup!" says Shamus, says he, "drive on the plaisham."

And the plaisham moved on still for the castle.

Then Prince Connal himself, with all his guests, ran out to turn it away; but when Prince Connal laid hands on the plaisham, he stuck to it; and when his guests laid hands on him, they stuck one by one to him; and "Hup, Hup!" says Shamus, says he, "drive on the plaisham."

And with all the racket and all the noise of the ranting, roaring, rearing, and rawting, in through the castle hall-door drove the plaisham, through and through and out at the other side. The castle itself fell down and disappeared, the bone ring rolled away from the cow's nose, and the plaisham all at once broke up, and when Prince Connal looked around, there was no castle at all, only the sod hut, and he went into it a sorry man.

And all the others slunk off home, right heartily ashamed of themselves, for the whole world was laughing at them. Nancy, she went east; and Rory, he went west; and neither one of them was ever heard of more. As for Shamus, he went home to his own little cabin, and lived all alone, happy and contented, for the rest of his life, and may you and I do the same.

Before Joyce, Shaw, or Wilde, Sheridan or Swift, the satirists of Ireland were renowned. The Celtic kings were generous to every wandering poet, for fear their royal persons would be shamed by cruel and memorable verses made against them. In war, both sides always employed satirists to weaken the enemy with ridicule. So powerful were the rhymed curses (sometimes called ranns) the poets could cast that even nature obeyed them—in the original legend, it was a poet who rhymed the snakes out of Ireland.

As for the characters in our story: the Cat of the Cave, we have met before.

Seanchan was the best known—and feared—of the ancient satirists. Yeats made him the hero of a play, The King's Threshold, in which the bard avenges himself after some regal slight by going on a hunger strike before the gates of the palace—a time-honored Irish method of humiliating an oppressor.

St. Kieran, of Cieran (516–549), founded a great monastic school at Clonmacnoise. It lies in ruins now, south of Athlone. Kieran was famous for his boundless charity. His feast day is September 9.

THE SATIRIST AND THE KING OF CATS

Seanchan the Satirist was a hard man to please. He liked an egg for supper, but he hated an egg boiled too little or too long. A hard egg or a runny one would set him ranting and rhyming against the fire that cooked it and the hen that laid it, so the house would soon be full of sulking smoke and the little bushes around the place shaking and quaking with fugitive hens.

The way he'd cook an egg was this. After he'd set it down in the pot of boiling water, he'd close his eyes and recite out loud a short bitter poem he'd made against misers. And by the time he'd run through the stanzas three times, his egg would be done to a turn.

(It was a trick he'd learned from an egg-loving saint, who would time his eggs by saying Pater Nosters. Seanchan tended to hurry through his prayers, which made for underdone eggs. But his own masterful verses he would declaim with slow care and deliberation.)

On this particular evening, he was standing in the doorway of his little house, which faced west over the bay, and chanting his curse upon the ungenerous, beating time with a ladle, while his supper cooked.

Upon his third repetition of the last word of the satire (which was
gout), he turned and went in to the fire. The boiling pot was empty.
The egg was gone.

Rage and wonder struggled together for possession of Seanchan's
mind. Could some rival satirist have made his meal vanish, by means of
a powerful rhyme against eggs? Had he himself only dreamt the egg?
Was it a fairy egg? Was he the victim of a joke, a robber, a magic spell,
a fit of madness?

Then he heard a little sound, a scratching, scrabbling noise in the
corner of the room. Slowly, he crossed the floor, and peered into the
shadows.

There he could make out tiny rubies, and a bit of pink rope—a
mouse—no, a pair of mice! And between them, his egg! Its shell was
cracked open, and the wee creatures were snout-deep in its sweet white
and yellow juices!

Seanchan the Satirist ground his teeth and clenched his fists. He
strode to the doorway, and once more faced the sun setting over the
bay. And he began a new poem, a string of quatrains, against vermin—
rodents especially, mice, in particular. It was great work.

Behind him in the house, the little thieves looked up from their
booty, trembled, and ran away through their hole in the wall, afraid
and ashamed. Hot with inspiration, Seanchan chanted on.

Cats came into his mind, as a useful rhyme for rats, and quick
cruel bringers of just torment and tragedy to cowardly lice-ridden egg-
stealing mice. . . .

Yet here the poet paused. Cats, indeed! What use were they,
where were they, in time of need? Out cowering in a ditch for fear of
mice! Delinquent hypocrites, not worth the price of their keep, vain,
selfish fickle creatures. . . .

Seanchan by now was roaring his satire into the fast-falling dark.
Carried on the night wind, his harsh words drifted inland, to the banks
of Boyne River, and to the keen ears of Irusan, king of all cats, great Cat
of the Cave.

Irusan was a warrior-king, a berserker-cat of the old school. His
huge body bore many a battle scar, proud signs of his monarchy
attained in combat, and held against all comers. He was quick to anger,
and sudden to avenge any slight upon his honor, or the honor of his
tribe.

When his fighting-rage was upon him, every one of his hairs stood up like a pointed wire, and discharged a shower of sparks around him. His one good eye swelled up to fill the middle of his face like a beacon light. The grass beneath his lashing tail smouldered and withered. His claws, unsheathed, were the jagged spear points of a swift-striking battle line. His enemies were struck dead with fear at the terrible scream he gave out, going into the fray.

And such was his reaction now, as the slanderous words of the distant poet came to him. He leapt out of the mouth of his cave and sent sprawling his two sons, Roughtooth and Growler, who were returning home with a brace of deer in their jaws.

Straight across the middle part of Ireland he ran, bounding over hill and river and lake without pause, till he came to the back of Seanchan's little house.

Up he leapt, like a cloud across the moon, over the thatch he flew, and down upon the ranting poet he pounced. The astonished master of satire could only wriggle and squeak, held fast between the sharp white teeth of the King of Cats.

In a moment, the great beast had turned and galloped back across Galway County, bearing his human prey in his mouth as easy as your tabby might bring a twitching mole in from the garden.

When Irusan reached the banks of the Shannon, he was of two minds whether to jump or swim across. The idea to give Seanchan a dunking pleased him. In he plunged.

The bard, who had fainted away from fright, awoke when the cold water rushed around him and over him, and he recommenced flailing and screaming.

Now the place where they were crossing the river was at Clonmacnoise, where Saint Kieran kept his cell. And among the holy man's many skills and accomplishments was the art of the smith.

By the light of the moon, the saint was hammering away at a long bar of red-hot iron, shaping a doorpost, maybe, or a window frame for his chapel there. The moment he paused to wipe his brow, he heard a great splashing and a pitiful wailing out on the river.

The swimming cat he knew right away, and Seanchan soon after, for saint and satirist had exchanged many conflicting views in the past. It was Kieran himself who'd baptized the bard years ago, in the vain hope he'd turn his poetic skills to some more charitable use.

But whatever his personal feelings were toward Seanchan, the saint knew his duty as a Christian man. He assumed the pose of a spear-man, and launched the flaming bar of iron. It never grazed the terrified poet, but took the cat beneath the ear, and passed through his skull.

Staggering out of the Shannon's waves the beast came, and dropped the bard at the feet of the saint. And while the holy monk revived the wet and shivering poet with a drop of whiskey he kept by him for just such medical emergenices, the Cat of the Cave, wounded as he was, escaped into the night.

And whatever became of him no one knows, but Saint Kieran and Seanchan lived a long time after, and when they died, they went to heaven, and so may all of us.

Here is another functional little tale—it explains how the city of Cork got its name (after King Corc), and how the little lake to its south came to be. A history and geography lesson, as it were, with a moral tacked on for good measure.

But it seems likely that the maiden named Spring Water, who dwells eternally beneath the lough, precedes not only the days when "Saxon foot pressed Irish ground" but also the coming of the Gaels themselves.

And the well to which her father sends her—like every well in Ireland—is "at the world's end"... a doorway into Tir na nOg, the Land of the Ever Young.

FIOR USGA

A little way beyond the Gallows Green of Cork, and just outside the town, there is a great lough of water, where people in the winter go and skate for the sake of diversion. But the sport above the water is nothing to what is under it, because at the very bottom of this lough there are buildings and gardens far more beautiful than any now to be seen. And how they came there was in this manner.

Long before Saxon foot pressed Irish ground there was a great King, called Corc, whose palace stood where the lough is now, in a round green valley that was just a mile about. In the middle of the courtyard was a spring of fair water, so pure and so clear that it was the wonder of all the world. Much did the King rejoice at having so great a curiosity within his palace, but as people came in crowds from far and near to draw the precious water of this spring, he was sorely afraid that in time it might become dry.

So he caused a high wall to be built up around it, and would allow nobody to have the water, which was a very great loss to the poor people living about the palace. Whenever he wanted any for himself he would send his daughter to get it, not liking to trust his servants with the key of the well-door, fearing they might give some of the water away.

One night the King gave a grand entertainment, and there were many great princes present, and lords and nobles without end. There were wonderful doings throughout the palace: there were bonfires, whose blaze reached up to the very sky; and dancing was there, to such

211

sweet music that it ought to have waked up the dead out of their graves; and feasting was there in the greatest of plenty for all who came; nor was anyone turned away from the palace gates, but "you're welcome—you're welcome heartily" was the porter's salute for all.

Now it happened at this grand entertainment there was one young prince above all the rest right comely to behold, and as tall and as straight as ever eye would wish to look on. Right merrily did he dance that night with the old King's daughter, wheeling there, as light as a feather, and footing it away to the admiration of everyone. The musicians played the better for seeing their dancing; and they danced as if their lives depended upon it.

After all this dancing came the supper, and the young prince was seated at table by the side of his beautiful partner, who smiled upon him as often as he wished, for he had constantly to turn to the company and thank them for the many compliments passed upon his fair partner and himself.

In the midst of this banquet one of the great lords said to King Corc, "May it please your majesty, here is everything in abundance that heart can wish for, both to eat and drink, except water."

"Water!" said the King, mightily pleased at someone calling for that of which purposely there was a want. "Water shall you have, my lord, speedily, and that of such a delicious kind that I challenge all the world to equal it. Daughter," said he, "go and fetch some in the golden vessel which I caused to be made for the purpose."

The King's daughter, who was called Fior Usga (which signifies "Spring Water" in English) did not much like to be told to perform so menial a service before so many people, and though she did not venture to refuse the commands of her father, yet she hesitated to obey him, and looked down upon the ground.

The King, who loved his daughter very much, seeing this was sorry for what he had desired her to do, but having said the word he was never known to recall it. He therefore thought of a way to make his daughter go speedily to fetch the water, and this was by proposing that the young prince, her partner, should go along with her.

Accordingly, in a loud voice, he said, "Daughter, I wonder not at your fearing to go alone so late at night; but I doubt not the young prince at your side will go with you."

The prince was not displeased at hearing this and, taking the golden vessel in one hand, with the other he led the King's daughter out of the hall so gracefully that all present gazed after them with delight.

When they came to the sping of water, in the courtyard of the palace, the fair Usga unlocked the door with the greatest care. But stooping down with the golden vessel to take some of the water out of the well, she found the vessel so heavy that she lost her balance and fell in. The young prince tried to save her, but in vain, because the water rose and rose so fast that the entire courtyard was speedily covered with it, and he hastened back almost in a state of distraction to the King.

The door of the well being left open the water, so long confined, rejoiced at obtaining its liberty and rushed forth incessantly, every moment rising higher; it reached the hall of the entertainment sooner than the young prince himself, so that when he attempted to speak to the King he was up to his neck in water. At length the water rose to such a height that it filled the entire green valley in which the King's palace stood, and so the present Lough of Cork was formed.

Yet the King and his guests were not drowned, as would now happen if such an inundation were to take place. Neither was his daughter, the fair Usga, who returned to the banquet hall the very next night after this dreadful event. And every night since then the same entertainment and dancing goes on in the palace in the bottom of the lough, and it will last until someone has the luck to bring up out of it the golden vessel which was the cause of all the mischief.

Nobody can doubt that it was a judgment upon the King for his shutting up the well in the courtyard from the poor people. And if there are any who do not credit my story, they might go and see the Lough of Cork, for there it is to be seen to this day. The road to Kinsale passes at one side of it and when its waters are low and clear the tops of towers and stately buildings may be plainly viewed in the bottom by those who have good eyesight, without the help of spectacles.

The Goban Saor (pronounced "Gubawn Seer") is the subject of many tales throughout Ireland. His name means "Free Maker"—maker in the sense of builder, smith, carpenter, architect. He is related to Wayland Smith, of British folklore, to the Norse Voelund, and to Daedalus of Greek myth.

This adventure of his is taken from Patrick Kennedy's Legendary Fictions. *To it, Mr. Kennedy appended a diagram and instructions for constructing—in scale-model form—the roof support for the round cabin. Despite much patience and many invocations of the supernatural, the present editor was unable to manage it, and has decided to spare the reader the aggravation.*

The Goban Saor's clients nearly always intend to make an end to him, after he has completed his work; but with the aid of his resourceful wife back home, he always escapes, well paid for his labors.

THE GOBAN SAOR

It's a long time since the Goban Saor was alive. Maybe it was him that built the Castle of Ferns; part of the walls are thick enough to be built by any goban, or gow, that ever splintered wood, or hammered red-hot iron, or cut a stone. If he didn't build Ferns, he built other castles for some of the five kings or the great chiefs. He could fashion a spear-shaft while you'd count five, and the spear-head at three strokes of a hammer. When he wanted to drive big nails into beams that were ever so high from the ground, he would pitch them into their place, and, taking a fling of the hammer at their heads, they would be drove in as firm as the knocker of Newgate, and he would catch the hammer when it was falling down.

At last it came to the King of Munster's turn to get his castle built, and to the Goban he sent. Goban knew that, in other times far back, the King of Ireland killed the celebrated architects Rog, Robog, Rodin, and Rooney, that way they would never build another palace equal to his, and so he mentioned something to his wife privately before he set out. He took his son along with him, and the first night they got lodging at a farmer's house. The farmer told them they might leave their beasts to graze all night in any of his fields they pleased. So they entered one field, and says Goban, "Tie the beasts up for the night." "Why," says the son, "I can't find anything strong enough." "Well, then, let us try the next field. Now," says he, "tie up the horses if you can." "Oh, by my word, here's a thistle strong enough this time." "That will do."

The next night they slept at another farmer's house, where there were two young daughters—one with black hair, very industrious; the other with fair complexion, and rather liking to sit with her hands across, and listen to the talk round the fire, than to be doing any work. While they were chatting about one thing and another, says the Goban, "Young girls, if I'd wish to be young again, it would be for the sake of getting one of you for a wife; but I think very few old people that do be thinking at all of the other world, ever wish to live their lives over again. Still I wish that you may have good luck in your choice of a husband, and so I give you three bits of advice. Always have the head of an old woman by the hob; warm yourselves with your work in the morning; and, some time before I come back, take the skin of a newly killed sheep to the market, and bring itself and the price of it home again." When they were leaving the next morning, the Goban said to his son, "Maybe one of these girls will be your wife some day."

As they were going along, they met a poor man striving to put a flat roof over a mud-wall round cabin, but he had only three joists, and each of them was only three-quarters of the breadth across. Well, the Goban put two nicks near one end of every joist, on opposite sides; and when these were fitted into one another, there was a three-cornered figure formed in the middle, and the other ends rested on the mud wall, and the floor they made was as strong as anything. The poor man blessed the two men, and they went on. That night they stopped at a house where the master sat by the fire, and hardly opened his mouth all evening. If he didn't talk, a meddlesome neighbor did, and interfered about everything. There was another chance lodger besides the Goban and his son, and when the evening was half over, the Goban said he thought he would go farther on his journey as it was a fine night. "You may come along with us, if you like," says he to the other man; but he said he was too tired. The two slept in a farmer's house half a mile farther on; and the next morning the first news they heard, when they were setting out, was that the man of the house they left the evening before was found murdered in his bed, and the lodger taken up on suspicion. Says he to his son, "Never sleep a night where the woman is everything and the man nothing." He stopped a day or two, however, and by cross-examining and calling witnesses, he got the murder tracked to the woman and the busy neighbor.

The next day they came to the ford, where a dozen of carpenters were puzzling their heads about setting up a wooden bridge that would neither have a peg nor a nail in any part of it. The king would give a great reward to them if they succeeded, and if they didn't, he'd never give one of them a job again. "Give us a hatchet and a few stocks," says the Goban, "and we'll see if we have any little genius that way." So he squared a few posts and cross-bars, and made a little bridge on the sod; and it was so made, that the greater weight was on it, and the stronger the stream of water, the solider it would be.

Maybe the carpenters weren't thankful, except one envious little, ould bastard of a fellow, that said any child might have thought of the plan (it happened he didn't think of it, though), and would make the Goban and his son drink a cag of whiskey, only they couldn't delay their journey.

At last they came to where the King of Munster kept his court, either at Cashel or Limerick, or some place in Clare, and the Goban burned very little daylight till he had the palace springing up like a flagger. People came from all parts, and were in admiration of the fine work: but as they were getting near the eaves, one of the carpenters that were engaged at the wooden bridge came late one night into the Goban's room, and told him what himself was suspecting, that just as he would be setting the coping-stone, the scaffolding would somehow or other get loose, himself fall down a few stories, and be killed, the king wring his hands, and shed a few crocodile tears, and the like palace never be seen within the four seas of Ireland.

"*Sha gu dheine* [that's it]," says the Goban to himself; but next day he spoke out plain enough to the king. "Please, your Majesty," says he, "I am now pretty near the end of my work, but there is still something to be done before we come to the wall-plate that is to make all sure and strong. There is a bit of a charm about it, but I haven't the tool here—it is at home, and my son got so sick last night, and is lying so bad, he is not able to go for it. If you can't spare the young prince, I must go myself, for my wife wouldn't intrust it to anyone but of royal blood." The king, rather than let the Goban out of his sight, sent the young prince for the tool. The Goban told him some outlandish name in Irish, and bid him make all the haste he could back.

In a week's time, back came two of the poor attendants that were with the prince, and told the king that his son was well off, with the best of eating and drinking, and chess playing and sword exercise, that any prince could wish for, but that out of her sight Goban's wife nor her people would let him, till she had her husband safe and sound inside of his own threshold.

Well, to be sure, how the king fumed and raged! But what's the use of striving to tear down a stone wall with your teeth? He couldn't do without his palace being finished, but he couldn't do without his son and heir. The Goban didn't keep spite; he put the finishing touch on the palace in three days, and, in two days more, himself and his son were sitting at the farmer's fireside where the two purty young girls were.

"Well, my colleen bawn," says he to the one with the fair hair, "did you mind the advice I gave you when I was here last?" "Indeed I did, and little good it did me. I got an old woman's skull from the churchyard, and fixed it in the wall near the hob, and it so frightened everyone, that I was obliged to have it taken back in an hour." "And how did you warm yourself with your work, in the cold mornings?" "The first morning's work I had was to card flax, and I threw some of it on the fire, and my mother gave me such a raking for it, that I didn't offer to warm myself that way again." "Now for the sheep-skin." "That was the worst of all. When I told the buyers in the market that I was to bring back the skin and the price of it, they only jeered at me. One young buckeen said, if I'd go into the tavern and take share of a quart of mulled beer with him, he'd make the bargain with me, and that so vexed me that I turned home at once." "Now, my little *ceann dhu* [dark head], let us see how you fared. The skull?" "Och," says an old woman, sitting close to the fire in the far corner, "I'm a distant relation that was left desolate, and this," says she, tapping the side of her poor head, "is the old woman's skull she provided." "Well, now for the warming of yourself in the cold mornings." "Oh I kept my hands and feet going so lively at my work that it was warming enough." "Well, and the sheep-skin?" "That was easy enough. When I got to the market, I went to the crane, plucked the wool off, sold it, and brought home the skin."

"Man and woman of the house," says the Goban, "I ask you before this company, to give me this girl for my daughter-in-law; and if ever her husband looks crooked at her, I'll beat him within an inch of his life." There were very few words, and no need of a black man to make up the match; and when the prince was returning home, he stopped a day to be at the wedding. If I heard any more of the Goban's great doings, I'll tell 'em some other time.

From Douglas Hyde's Beside the Fire *comes the tale "William of the Tree," at once as straightforward and as mysterious as a dream. And like a dream, it can stand up to any amount of interpretation.*

"Granya Öi," the fairy godmother of the story, is another name for the wise and ancient old woman Cathleen ni Houlihan, the ancient queen and yet more ancient goddess who is Ireland herself.

WILLIAM OF THE TREE

In the time long ago there was a king in Erin. He was married to a beautiful queen, and they had but one only daughter. The queen was struck with sickness, and she knew that she would not be long alive. She put the king under gassa [mystical injunctions] that he should not marry again until the grass should be a foot high over her tomb. The daughter was cunning, and she used to out every night with a scissors, and she used to cut the grass down to the ground.

The king had a great desire to have another wife, and he did not know why the grass was not growing over the grave of the queen. He said to himself: "There is somebody deceiving me."

That night he went to the churchyard, and he saw the daughter cutting the grass that was on the grave. There came a great anger on him then, and he said: "I will marry the first woman I see, let she be old or young." When he went out on the road he saw an old hag. He brought her home and married her, as he would not break his word.

After marrying her, the daughter of the king was under bitter misery at [the hands of] the hag, and the hag put her under an oath not tell anything at all to the king, and not to tell to any person anything she should see being done, except only to three who were never baptised.

The next morning on the morrow, the king went out a hunting, and when he was gone, the hag killed a fine hound the king had. When the king came home he asked the old hag, "Who killed my hound?"

"Your daughter killed it," says the old woman.

"Why did you kill my hound?" said the king.

"I did not kill your hound," says the daughter, "and I cannot tell you who killed him."

"I will make you tell me," says the king.

He took the daughter with him to a great wood, and he hanged

220

her on a tree, and then he cut the two hands and the two feet off her, and left her in a state of death. When he was going out of the wood there went a thorn into his foot, and the daughter said, "That you may never get better until I have hands and feet to cure you."

The king went home, and there grew a tree out of his foot, and it was necessary for him to open the window, to let the top of the tree out.

There was a gentleman going by near the wood, and he heard the king's daughter a-screeching. He went to the tree, and when he saw the state she was in, he took pity on her, brought her home, and when she got better, married her.

At the end of three quarters [of a year], the king's daughter had three sons at one birth, and when they were born, Granya Öi came and put hands and feet on the king's daughter, and told her, "Don't let your children be baptised until they are able to walk. There is a tree growing out of your father's foot; it was cut often, but it grows again, and it is with you lies his healing. You are under an oath not to tell the things you saw your stepmother doing to anyone but to three who were never baptised, and God has sent you those three. When they will be a year old bring them to your father's house, and tell your story before your three sons, and run your hand on the stump of the tree, and your father will be as well as he was the first day."

There was great wonderment on the gentleman when he saw hands and feet on the king's daughter. She told him then every word that Granya Öi had said to her.

When the children were a year old, the mother took them with her, and went to the king's house.

There were doctors from every place in Erin attending on the king, but they were not able to do him any good.

When the daughter came in, the king did not recognise her. She sat down, and the three sons round her, and she told her story to them from top to bottom, and the king was listening to her telling it. Then she left her hand on the sole of the king's foot and the tree fell off it.

The day on the morrow he hanged the old hag, and he gave his estate to his daughter and to the gentleman.

Of this story, Patrick Kennedy writes, "Jemmy Reddy, Father Mur-phy's servant, told it to the occupants of the big kitchen hearth in Coolbawn, one long winter evening, nearly in the style in which it is here given. . . ."

And he did, indeed, attempt to reproduce the brogue, spelling strength "sthrenth" and swords "soords" and so forth.

But for all that, the tale is a "literary" one; the opening sen-tences, indeed, sound like an introduction to King Lear, *and the plot is as complicated and episodic as any Elizabethan dramatist could desire—with little Seven Inches for comic relief.*

It is a tale so full of magic and morality that Victorian Fairy-tale collectors such as Lang and Graves published it in their collections; it is well worth reprinting for another generation.

THE THREE CROWNS

There was once a king, some place or other, and he had three daugh-ters. The two eldest were very proud and uncharitable, but the youngest was as good as they were bad. Well, three princes came to court them, and two of them were the *moral* of the eldest ladies, and one was just as lovable as the youngest. They were all walking down to a lake, one day, that lay at the bottom of the lawn, just like the one at Castleboro', and they met a poor beggar. The king wouldn't give him anything and the eldest princes wouldn't give him anything, nor their sweethearts; but the youngest daughter and her true love did give him something, and kind words along with it, and that was better *nor* all.

When they got to the edge of the lake, what did they find but the beautifulest boat you ever saw in your life; and says the eldest, "I'll take a sail in this fine boat;" and says the second eldest, "I'll take a sail in this fine boat;" and says the youngest, "I won't take a sail in that fine boat, for I am afraid it's an enchanted one." But the others overpersuaded her to go in, and her father was just going in after her, when up sprung on the deck a little man only seven inches high, and he ordered him to stand back. Well, all the men put their hands to their *soords*; and if the same *soords* were only thraneens they weren't able to draw them, for all *sthrenth* was left their arms. Seven Inches loosened the silver chain that fastened the boat, and pushed away; and after grinning at the four men, says he to them, "Bid your daughters and your brides farewell for awhile. That wouldn't have happened you three, only for you want of charity. "You," says he to the youngest, "needn't fear, you'll recover your princess all in good time, and you and she will be as happy as the day is long. Bad people, if they were rolling stark naked in gold, would not be rich. *Banacht lath.*" Away they sailed, and the ladies stretched out their hands, but weren't able to say a word.

Well, they weren't crossing the lake while a cat 'ud be lickin' her ear, and the poor men couldn't stir hand or foot to follow them. They saw Seven Inches handing the three princesses out o' the boat, and letting them down by a nice basket and *winglas* into a draw-well that was convenient, but king nor princes ever saw an opening before in the same place. When the last lady was out of sight, the men found the strength in their arms and legs again. Round the lake they ran, and never drew rein till they came to the well and windlass; and there was the silk rope rolled on the axle, and the nice white basket hanging to it. "Let me down," says the youngest prince; "I'll die or recover them again." "No," says the second daughter's sweetheart, "I'm entitled to my turn before you." And says the other, "I must get first turn, in right of my bride." So they gave way to him, and in he got into the basket, and down they let him. First they lost sight of him, and then, after winding off a hundred perches of the silk rope, it slackened, and they stopped turning. They waited two hours, and then they went to dinner, because there was no chuck made at the rope.

Guards were set till next morning, and then down went the second prince, and sure enough, the youngest of all got himself let down on the third day. He went down perches and perches, while it was as dark about him as if he was in a big pot with the cover on. At last he saw a glimmer far down, and in a short time he felt the ground. Out he came from the big lime-kiln, and lo and behold you, there was a wood, and green fields, and a castle in a lawn, and a bright sky over all. "It's in Tir-na-n-Og I am," says he. "Let's see what sort of people are in the castle." On he walked, across fields and lawn, and no one was there to keep him out or let him into the castle; but the big hall-door was wide open. He went from one fine room to another that was finer, and at last he reached the handsomest of all, with a table in the middle; and such a dinner as was laid upon it! The prince was hungry enough, but he was too mannerly to go eat without being invited. So he sat by the fire, and he did not wait long till he heard steps, and in came Seven Inches and the youngest sister by the hand. Well, prince and princess flew into one another's arms, and says the little man, says he, "Why aren't you eating?" "I think, sir," says he, "it was only good manners to wait to be asked." "The other princes didn't think so," says he. "Each o' them fell to without leave or licence, and only gave me the rough side of their tongue when I told them they were making more free than welcome. Well, I don't think they feel much hunger now. There they are, good *marvel* instead of flesh and blood," says he, pointing to two statues, one in one corner, and the other in the other corner of the room The prince was frightened, but he was afraid to say anything, and Seven Inches made him sit down to dinner between himself and his bride; and he'd be as happy as the day is long, only for the sight of the stone men in the corner. Well, that day went by, and when the next came, says Seven Inches to him: "Now, you'll have to set out that way," pointing to the sun; "and you'll find the second princess in a giant's castle this evening, when you'll be tired and hungry, and the eldest princess tomorrow evening; and you may as well bring them here with you. You need not ask leave of their masters; they're only housekeepers with the big fellows. I suppose, if they ever get home, they'll look on poor people as if they were flesh and blood like themselves."

Away went the prince, and bedad, it's tired and hungry he was when he reached the first castle, at sunset. Oh, wasn't the second princess glad to see him! and if she didn't give him a good supper, it's a wonder. But she heard the giant at the gate, and she hid the prince in a closet. Well, when he came in, he snuffed, and he snuffed, an' says he, "Be [by] the life, I smell fresh mate." "Oh," says the princess, "it's only the calf I got killed to-day." "Ay, ay," says he, "is supper ready?" "It is," says she; and before he ruz from the table he hid three-quarters of the calf, and a cag of wine. "I think," says he, when all was done. "I smell fresh mate still." "It's sleepy you are," says she; "go to bed." "When will you marry me?" says the giant. "You're puttin' me off too long." "St. Tibb's Eve," says she. "I wish I knew how far off that is," says he; and he fell asleep with his head in the dish.

Next day, he went out after breakfast, and she sent the prince to the castle where the eldest sister was. The same thing happened there; but when the giant was snoring, the princess wakened up the prince, and they saddled two steeds in the stables, and *magh go brogh* [the field for ever] with them. But the horses' heels struck the stones outside the gate, and up got the giant and after them he made. He roared and he shouted, and the more he shouted, the faster ran the horses; and just as the day was breaking, he was only twenty perches behind. But the prince didn't leave the castle of Seven Inches without being provided with something good. He reined in his steed, and flung a short, sharp knife over his shoulder, and up sprung a thick wood between the giant and themselves. They caught the wind that blew before them, and the wind that blew behind them did not catch them. At last they were near the castle where the other sister lived; and there she was, waiting for them under a high hedge, and a fine steed under her.

But the giant was now in sight, roaring like a hundred lions, and the other giant was out in a moment, and the chase kept on. For every two springs the horses gave, the giants gave three, and at last they were only seventy perches off. Then the prince stopped again, and flung the second skian behind him. Down went all the flat field, till there was a quarry between them a quarter of a mile deep, and the bottom filled with black water; and before the giants could get round it, the prince and princesses were inside the domain of the great magician, where the high thorny hedge opened of itself to everyone that he chose to let in.

Well, to be sure, there was joy enough between the three sisters, till the two eldest saw their lovers turned into stone. But while they were shedding tears for them, Seven Inches came in, and touched them with his rod. So they were flesh, and blood, and life once more, and there was great hugging and kissing, and all sat down to a nice breakfast, and Seven Inches sat at the head of the table.

When breakfast was over, he took them into another room, where there was nothing but heaps of gold, and silver, and diamonds, and silks, and satins; and on a table there was lying three sets of crowns; a gold crown was in a silver crown, and that was lying in a copper crown. He took up one set of crowns, and gave it to the eldest princess; and another set, and gave it to the second youngest princess; and another, and gave it to the youngest of all; and says he, "Now you may all go to the bottom of the pit, and you have nothing to do but stir the basket, and the peole that are watching above will draw you up. But remember, ladies, you are to keep your crowns safe, and be married in them, all the same day. If you be married separately, or if you be married without your crowns, a curse will follow—mind what I say."

So they took leave of him with great respect, and walked arm-in-arm to the bottom of the draw-well. There was a sky and a sun over them, and a great high wall, covered with ivy, rose before them, and was so high they could not see to the top of it; and there was an arch in this wall, and the bottom of the drawwell was inside the arch. The youngest pair went last; and says the princess to the prince, "I'm sure the two princes don't mean any good to you. Keep these crowns under your cloak, and if you are obliged to stay last, don't get into the basket, but put a big stone, or any heavy thing inside, and see what will happen."

So when they were inside the dark cave, they put in the eldest princess first, and stirred the basket, and up she went, but first she gave a little scream. Then the basket was let down again, and up went the second princess, and then up went the youngest; but first she put her arms round her prince's neck, and kissed him, and cried a little. At last it came to the turn of the youngest prince, and well became him;— instead of going into the basket, he put in a big stone. He drew one side and listened, and after the basket was drawn up about twenty perch, down came itself and the stone like thunder, and the stone was made *brishe* of on the flags.

Well, my poor prince had nothing for it but to walk back to the castle; and through it and round it he walked, and the finest of eating and drinking he got, and a bed of bog-down to sleep on, and fine walks he took through gardens and lawns, but not a sight could he get, high or low, of Seven Inches. Well, I don't think any of us would be tired of this fine way of living for ever. Maybe we would. Anyhow the prince got tired of it before a week, he was so lonesome for his true love; and at the end of a month he didn't know what to do with himself.

One morning he went into the treasure room, and took notice of a beautiful snuff-box on the table that he didn't remember seeing there before. He took it in his hands, and opened it, and out Seven Inches walked on the table. "I think, prince," says he, "you're getting a little tired of my castle!" "Ah," says the other, "if I had my princess here, and could see you now and then, I'd never see a dismal day." "Well, you're long enough here now, and you're wanting there above. Keep your bride's crowns safe, and whenever you want my help, open this snuff-box. Now take a walk down the garden, and come back when you're tired."

Well, the prince was going down a gravel walk with a quickset hedge on each side, and his eyes on the ground, and he thinking on one thing and another. At last he lifted his eyes, and there he was outside of a smith's bawn-gate that he often passed before, about a mile away from the palace of his betrothed princess. The clothes he had on him were as ragged as you please, but he had his crowns safe under his old cloak.

So the smith came out, and says he, "It's a shame for a strong, big fellow like you to be on the *sthra*, and so much work to be done. Are you any good with hammer and tongs? Come in and bear a hand, and I'll give you diet and lodging, and a few thirteens when you earn them." "Never say't twice," says the prince; "I want nothing but to be employed." So he took the sledge, and pounded away at the red-hot bar that the smith was turning on the anvil to make into a set of horse-shoes.

Well, they weren't long powdering away, when a *sthronshuch* [idler] of a tailor came in; and the smith asked him what news he had, he got the handle of the bellows and began to blow, to let out all he had heard for the last two days. There was so many questions and answers at first, that if I told them all, it would be bedtime afore I'd be done. So here is the substance of the discourse; and before he got far into it, the forge was half-filled with women knitting stockings, and men smoking.

"Yous all heard how the two princesses were unwilling to be married till the youngest would be ready with her crowns and her sweetheart. But after the windlass loosened *accidentally* when they were pulling up her bridegroom that was to be, there was no more sign of a well, or a rope, or a windlass, than there is on the palm of your hand. So the *cukeens* that wor courtin' the eldest ladies wouldn't give peace or ease to their lovers nor the king, till they got consent to the marriage, and it was to take place this morning. Myself went down out o' curiosity; and to be sure I was delighted with the grand dresses of the two brides, and the three crowns on their heads—gold, silver, and copper, one inside the other. The youngest was standing by mournful enough in white, and all was ready. The two bridegrooms came in as proud and grand as you please, and up they were walking to the altar rails, when, my dear, the boards opened two yards wide under their feet, and down they went among the dead men and the coffins in the vaults. Oh, such screeching as the ladies gave! and such running and racing and peeping down as there was; but the clerk soon opened the door of the vault, and up came the two heroes, and their fine clothes covered an inch thick with cobwebs and mould.

So the king said they should put off the marriage. "For," says he, "I see there is no use in thinking of it till my youngest gets her three crowns, and is married along with the others. I'll give my youngest daughter for a wife to whomever brings three crowns to me like the others; and if he doesn't care to be married, some other one will, and I'll make his fortune." "I wish," says the smith, "I could do it: but I was looking at the crowns after the princesses got home, and I don't think there's a black or a white smith on the face o' the earth could imitate them." "Faint heart never won fair lady," says the prince. "Go to the palace and ask for a quarter of a pound of gold, a quarter of a pound of silver, and a quarter of a pound of copper. Get one crown for a pattern; and my head for a pledge, I'll give you out the very things that are wanted in the morning." "Ubbabow!" says the smith, "are you in earnest!" "Faith, I am so," says he. "Go! worse than lose you can't."

To make a long story short, the smith got the quarter of a pound of gold, and the quarter of a pound of silver, and the quarter of a pound of copper, and gave them and the pattern crown to the prince. He shut the forge door at nightfall, and the neighbours all gathered in the bawn, and they heard him hammering, hammering, hammering, from that to daybreak; and every now and then he'd pitch out through the window bits of gold, silver, and copper; and the idlers scrambled for them, and cursed one another, and prayed for the good luck of the workman.

Well, just as the sun was thinking to rise, he opened the door, and brought out the three crowns he got from his true love, and such shouting and huzzaing as there was! The smith asked him to go along with him to the palace, but he refused; so off set the smith, and the whole townland with him; and wasn't the king rejoiced when he saw the crowns! "Well," says he to the smith, "you're a married man; what's to be done?" "Faith, your majesty, I didn't make them crowns at all; it was a big *shuler* [vagrant] of a fellow that took employment with me yesterday." "Well, daughter, will you marry the fellow that made these crowns?" "Let me see them first, father." So when she examined them, she knew them right well, and guessed it was her true love that sent

229

them. "I will marry the man that these crowns came from," says she.

"Well," says the king to the eldest of the two princes, "go up to the smith's forge, take my best coach, and bring home the bridegroom." He was very unwilling to do this, he was so proud, but he did not wish to refuse. When he came to the forge, he saw the prince standing at the door, and beckoned him over to the coach. "Are you the fellow," says he, "that made them crowns?" "Yes," says the other. "Then," says he, "maybe you'd give yourself a brushing, and get into that coach; the king wants to see you. I pity the princess." The young prince got into the carriage, and while they were on the way, he opened the snuff-box, and out walked Seven Inches and stood on his thigh. "Well," says he, "what trouble is on you now?" "Master," says the other, "please let me be back in my forge and let this carriage be filled with paving stones." No sooner said than done. The prince was sitting in his forge, and the horses wondered what was after happening to the carriage.

When they came into the palace yard, the king himself opened the carriage door, to pay respect to his new son-in-law. As soon as he turned the handle, a shower of small stones fell on his powdered wig and his silk coat, and down he fell under them. There was great fright and some tittering and the king, after he wiped the blood from his forehead, looked very cross at the eldest prince. "My liege," says he, "I'm very sorry for this accident, but I'm not to blame. I saw the young smith get into the carriage, and we never stopped a minute since." "It's uncivil you were to him. Go," says he, to the other prince, "and bring the young smith here, and be polite." "Never fear," says he.

But there's some people that couldn't be good-natured if they were to be made heirs of Damer's estate. Not a bit civiller was the new messenger than the old, and when the king opened the carriage door a second time, it's a shower of mud that came down on him; and if he didn't fume, and splutter, and shake himself, it's no matter. "There's no use," says he, "going on this way. The fox never got a better messenger than himself."

So he changed his clothes and washed himself, and out he set to the smith's forge. Maybe he wasn't polite to the young prince, and asked him to sit along with himself. The prince begged to be allowed to sit in the other carriage, and when they were half-way, he opened his snuff-box. "Master," says he, "I'd wish to be dressed now according to my rank." "You shall be that," says Seven Inches. "And now I'll bid you farewell. Continue as good and kind as you always were; love your wife, and that's all the advice I'll give you." So Seven Inches vanished; and when the carriage door was opened in the yard—not by the king though, for a burnt child dreads the fire—out walks the prince as fine as hands and pins could make him, and the first thing he did was to run over to his bride, and embrace her very heartily.

Everyone had great joy but the two other princes. There was not much delay about the marriages that were all celebrated on the one day. Soon after, the two elder couples went to their own courts, but the youngest pair stayed with the old king, and they were as happy as the happiest married couple you ever heard of in a story.

IV. WITCHES, VAMPIRES, FETCHES, AND SELKIES

Vampires, Witches, Fetches, and Selkies

Give me your hand! So, keeping close to me,
Shut tight your eyes! Step forward!
—Where are we?

James Stephens
"Slàn Leath"

That the Irish are a superstitious people may be so. They are also a religious people, and that is not the same thing. On New Year's Eve, I had two obligations to my uncle, an Irish priest. The first was to serve his Midnight Mass and stay awake (and alert—there would be a catechism quiz) through a theologically complex (if somewhat rhetorical sermon. He was very keen on Aquinas.

The other was to be the first across the threshold of his house in the New Year, for I was the youngest dark-haired male, and my being first in assured good luck to all, of course. Of course.

Irishmen (and women) of different faiths have died for them, often enough. And Irishmen (and women) of different loyalties have died for their nation, too often. It's not likely any have died for their superstitions.

But they've most of them been lucky enough to meet a ghost or two, to have a tale for the telling. And as for devils—there's little question that there's plenty of them about, and doing their work beautifully. Demonic possession of livestock and hellish interference with the laws of physics accounted for all the minor daily disasters around my grandad's farm, I know. And it was he who taught me to recognize in any black dog seen on the road at twilight a Pooca, that malevolent spirit. (The man was otherwise as rational as any selfavowed socialist.)

There are magic creatures not only in the fields and on the roads, but in the sea as well. Selkies are half human, half seal, and very amorous. Merrows are submarine Fairies. Mermaids abound in the caves, and are said to make good wives—for a while.

Every churchyard and great house has its ghost—Yeats was fond of conjuring them, when visiting. But not all human spirits wandering the night are ghosts. Some are Fetches—the souls and doubles of living men or women "away" from the body; sometimes stolen by fairies, sometimes off on an important errand.

It is the worst of luck to meet your own Fetch, but a widespread folktale concerns a benevolent one. (Yeats, naturally, made a ballad of the tale.) An old priest, Father Gilligan, was summoned to the bedside of a dying parishioner late one night. But he fell back to sleep in his chair at home. When he awoke, and hurried to the deathbed, he was told he had already visited, and administered the last sacraments to the grateful dead man!

It was his Fetch had done it, you see. But who knows if the extreme unction he performed was valid? Superstition is one thing, and religion another. . . .

The middle years of the nineteenth century, in Queen Victoria's glorious reign, were terrible ones for the Irish. Famine was upon the land, and patriotism was brutally suppressed.

But the most brilliant eye and ear surgeon in the British Isles, Sir William Wilde, lived in Dublin, a man dedicated to all things Irish, a renowned antiquarian and student of Gaelic folkways.

The doctor's wife (who published, under the pen name Sperenza, fiercely revolutionary poems) was herself the collector of two volumes of the Ancient Legend, Mystic Charms and Superstitions of Ireland— *from which the tale below is taken.*

So deep and strong was this couple's love for the history and mythology of their homeland that they named their second-born son in honor of Osgar, grandson of Finn McCool. Osgar Fingal Wilde, they called him.

THE HORNED WOMEN

A rich woman sat up late one night carding and preparing wool, while all the family and servants were asleep. Suddenly a knock was given at the door, and a voice called: "Open! Open!"

"Who is there?" asked the woman of the house.

The mistress, supposing that one of her neighbors had called and required assistance opened the door, and a woman entered, having in her hand a pair of wool carders, and bearing a horn on her forehead, as if growing there. She sat down by the fire in silence, and began to card the wool with violent haste. Suddenly she paused and said aloud: "Where are the women? They delay too long."

Then a second knock came to the door, and a voice called as before: "Open! Open!"

The mistress felt herself constrained to rise and open to the call, and immediately a second woman entered, having two horns on her forehead, and in her hand a wheel for spinning the wool.

"Give me place," she said, "I am the Witch of the Two Horns," and she began to spin as quick as lightning.

And so the knocks went on, and the call was heard, and the witches entered, until at last twelve women sat round the fire—the first with one horn, the last with twelve horns. And they carded the thread, and turned their spinning wheels, and wound and wove, all singing

236

together an ancient rhyme, but no word did they speak to the mistress of the house. Strange to hear and frightful to look upon were these twelve women, with their horns and their wheels; and the mistress felt near to death, and she tried to rise that she might call for help, but she could not move, nor could she utter a word or cry, for the spell of the witches was upon her.

Then one of them called to her and said: "Rise, woman, and make us a cake."

Then the mistress searched for a vessel to bring water from the well that she might mix the meal and make the cake, but she could find none. And they said to her: "Take a sieve and bring water in it."

And she took the sieve and went to the well; but the water poured from it, and she could fetch none for the cake, and she sat down by the well and wept. Then a voice came by her and said: "Take yellow clay and moss and bind them together and plaster the sieve so that it will hold."

This she did, and the sieve held the water for the cake. And the voice said again: "Return, and when thou comest to the north angle of the house, cry aloud three times and say, 'The Mountain of the Fenian Women and the sky over it is all on fire.'"

And she did so.

When the witches inside heard the call, a great and terrible cry broke from their lips and they rushed forth with wild lamentations and shrieks, and fled away to Slieve na mon, where was their chief abode. But the Spirit of the Well bade the mistress of the house to enter and prepare her home against the enchantments of the witches if they returned again.

And first, to break their spells, she sprinkled the water in which she had washed her child's feet (the feet-water) outside the door on the threshold; secondly, she took the cake which the witches had made in her absence, of meal mixed with the blood drawn from the sleeping family. And she broke the cake in bits, and placed a bit in the mouth of each sleeper, and they were restored; and she took the cloth they had woven and placed it half in and half out of the chest with the padlock; and, lastly, she secured the door with a great crossbeam fastened in the jambs, so that they could not enter. And having done these things she waited.

Not long were the witches in coming back, and they raged and called for vengeance.

"Open! Open!" they screamed. "Open, feet-water!"

"I cannot," said the feet-water, "I am scattered on the ground and my path is down to the Lough."

"Open, open, cake that we have made and mingled with blood," they cried again.

"I cannot," said the cake, "for I am broken and bruised, and my blood is on the lips of the sleeping children."

Then the witches rushed through the air with great cries, and fled back to Slieve na mon uttering strange curses on the Spirit of the Well, who had wished their ruin; but the woman and the house were left in peace, and a mantle dropped by one of the witches in her flight was kept hung up by the mistress as a sign of the night's awful contest, and this mantle was in possession of the same family from generation to generation for five hundred years after.

Mermaids inhabit not only the warm seas of the tropics, but also the cold North Atlantic. Consider Hans Christian Andersen's Danish specimen, or the schools of them baptised off the Irish coast by that sea-going saint, Brendan the Navigator.

Here is a verbatim report from The Gael, *the Irish-American magazine published in New York at the turn of the century, of one man's attempt to domesticate such a creature.*

THE SHANNON MERMAID

"Sure, (said the old woman), 'twas over there beyond the corner where the river is that the mermaid was caught, and Deny Duggan described her to me, and he the oldest man in Foynes. The man that caught her was one of those who watched the weir over on the Island. They were forever seeing a woman on the point, and they knew it was the mermaid that was ever living in the river, and one day the man saw her sitting on a big stone on the point and she a-combing her fine golden hair back from the forehead of her, and combing it from the rack. And he faced round and crept up behind her when she was not knowing it, and caught her by the two shoulders of her, and brought her to his his house, where his mother lived.

"It was the beautifullest woman ever you see'd, with the golden hair and fair skin of her. Now after a time he took her as his wife, and she had three children to him, and all the time she was doing all the work a woman might do, but never a smile or a laugh out of her, except one day when he was a-doing something with the child on the floor, playing with it, and then she let the sweetest laugh out of her, that ever you heard. Now the man had taken the covering from her that she had the day sitting on the rock, a sort of an oily skin, and he had been told to keep it from her and put it away by way of luck.

"And the house was built so that the fireplace had piers like on each side of it, as in the country houses, and on the top a shelf, and 'twas on this that the man had put away the covering among the nets and sacks. For—she was going about the house doing all the work that a woman might do, but that she could never climb up on a thing, and she afeared even to stand on a chair to reach a thing as might be. But one day—it was seven years from the day he had caught her on the stone and brought her home—she was sitting by the fire with the child, and he just able to walk. He was on her knee sitting, when the man came in looking for the net, and he began to throw things about on the shelf looking for it. Well, he threw down an old sack out of the way of him, and with it sure the covering fell down, and he never seeing it, and it fell behind her so as she couldn't lay hand to it with the child on her knee; so she looked over her shoulder and saw it, and she put the child to stand with the chair, went and took the covering and out of the door with it before the man had time to get down and stop her, and down to the shore she went with a laugh as never you heard with the ringing in it, and into the sea, and she never came back again.

And the three children of her were reared on the island over beyond Deny Duggan's, and 'tis three ages [generations] ago now, for Deny he is the oldest man in Foynes, and when he was young he knew the children of her, and heard of her from a friend of the man that worked with him on the weir."

Bram Stoker, a Dublin man, published Dracula, *his classic tale of supernatural terror, in 1887. Ever since, readers and scholars have wondered about the source of such a horrible and fascinating idea as the vampire—a monster nourished in human blood, who must return to the grave before dawn.*

In 1882 the wandering folktale collector Jeremiah Curtin had recorded the "Tale of the Blood-Drawing Ghost" from Dyeermud Sheehy, a Munster cartman.

So perhaps Stoker first learned the awful secret of the undead's afterlife style not from some quaint and curious volume of Transylvanian necromancy, but riding up beside Dyeermud, on the rocky road between Killarney and Cahirciveen.

Whether or not this Irish vampire is a true fairy, he certainly possesses a leprechaun-like knowledge of buried gold beneath little heaps of stone; and the heroine, Kate, is typical of those plucky Irish girls who kept their wits about them in fairyland, and came back home rich.

THE BLOOD-DRAWING GHOST

There was a young man in the parish of Drimalegue, County Cork, who was courting three girls at one time, and he didn't know which of them would he take; they had equal fortunes, and any of the three was as pleasing to him as any other. One day when he was coming home from the fair with his two sisters, the sisters began:

"Well, John," said one of them, "why don't you get married. Why don't you take either Mary, or Peggy, or Kate?"

"I can't tell you that," said John, "till I find which of them has the best wish for me."

"How will you know?" asked the other.

"I will tell you that as soon as any person will die in the parish."

In three weeks' time from that day an old man died. John went to the wake and then to the funeral. While they were burying the corpse in the graveyard John stood near a tomb which was next to the grave, and when all were going away, after burying the old man, he remained standing a while by himself, as if thinking of something; then he put his blackthorn stick on top of the tomb, stood a while longer, and on going from the graveyard left the stick behind him. He went home and ate

241

his supper. After supper John went to a neighbour's house where young people used to meet of an evening, and the three girls happened to be there that time. John was very quiet, so that ever one noticed him.

"What is troubling you this evening, John?" asked one of the girls.

"Oh, I am sorry for my beautiful blackthorn," said he.

"Did you lose it?"

"I did not," said John; "but I left it on the top of the tomb next to the grave of the man who was buried to-day, and whichever of you three will go for it is the woman I'll marry. Well, Mary, will you go for my stick?" asked he.

"Faith, then, I will not," said Mary.

"Well, Peggy, will you go?"

"If I were without a man for ever," said Peggy, "I wouldn't go."

"Well, Kate," said he to the third, "will you go for my stick? If you go I'll marry you."

"Stand to your word," said Kate, "and I'll bring the stick."

"Believe me, that I will," said John.

Kate left the company behind her, and went for the stick. The graveyard was three miles away and the walk was a long one. Kate came to the place at last and made out the tomb by the fresh grave. When she had her hand on the blackthorn a voice called from the tomb:

"Leave the stick where it is and open this tomb for me."

Kate began to tremble and was greatly in dread, but something was forcing her to open the tomb—she couldn't help herself.

"Take the lid off now," said the dead man when Kate had the door open and was inside in the tomb, "and take me out of this—take me on your back."

Afraid to refuse, she took the lid from the coffin, raised the dead man on her back, and walked on in the way he directed. She walked about the distance of a mile. The load, being very heavy, was near breaking her back and killing her. She walked half a mile farther and came to a village; the houses were at the side of the road.

"Take me to the first house," said the dead man.

She took him.

"Oh, we cannot go in here," said he, when they came near. "The people have clean water inside, and they have holy water, too. Take me to the next house."

She went to the next house.

"We cannot go in there," said he, when she stopped in front of the door. "They have clean water, but there is holy water as well."

She went to the third house.

"Go in here," said the dead man. "There is neither clean water nor holy water in this place; we can stop in it."

They went in.

"Bring a chair now and put me sitting at the side of the fire. Then find me something to eat and to drink."

She placed him in a chair by the hearth, searched the house, found a dish of oatmeal and brought it. "I have nothing to give you to drink but dirty water," said she.

"Bring me a dish and a razor."

She brought the dish and the razor.

"Come, now," said he, "to the room above."

They went up to the room, where three young men, sons of the man of the house, were sleeping in bed, and Kate had to hold the dish while the dead man was drawing their blood.

"Let the father and mother have that," said he, "in return for the dirty water;" meaning that if there was clean water in the house he wouldn't have taken the blood of the young men. He closed their wounds in the way that there was no sign of a cut on them. "Mix this now with the meal; get a dish of it for yourself and another for me."

She got two plates and put the oatmeal in it after mixing it and brought two spoons. Kate wore a handkerchief on her head; she put this under her neck and tied it; she was pretending to eat, but she was putting the food to hide in the handkerchief till her plate was empty.

"Have you your share eaten?" asked the dead man.

"I have," answered Kate.

"I'll have mine finished this minute," said he, and soon after he gave her the empty dish. She put the dishes back in the dresser, and didn't mind washing them. "Come, now," said he, "and take me back to the place where you found me."

"Oh, how can I take you back; you are too great a load; 'twas killing me you were when I brought you." She was in dread of going from the houses again.

"You are stronger after that food than what you were in coming; take me back to my grave."

She went against her will. She rolled up the food inside in the handkerchief. There was a deep hole in the wall of the kitchen by the door, where the bar was slipped in when they barred the door; into this hole she put the handkerchief. In going back she shortened the road by going through a big field at command of the dead man. When they were at the top of the field she asked, was there any cure for those young men whose blood was drawn?

"There is no cure," said he, "except one. If any of that food had been spared, three bits of it in each young man's mouth would bring them to life again, and they'd never know of their death."

"Then," said Kate in her own mind, "that cure is to be had."

"Do you see this field?" asked the dead man.

"I do."

"Well, there is as much gold buried in it as would make rich people of all who belong to you. Do you see the three leachtans [piles of small stone]? Underneath each pile of them is a pot of gold."

The dead man looked around for a while; then Kate went on, without stopping, till she came to the wall of the graveyard, and just then they heard the cock crow.

"The cock is crowing," said Kate; "it's time for me to be going home."

"It is not time yet," said the dead man; "that is a bastard cock."

A moment after that another cock crowed. "There, the cocks are crowing a second time," said she. "No," said the dead man, "that is a bastard cock again; that's no right bird." They came to the mouth of the tomb and a cock crowed the third time.

"Well," said the girl, "that must be the right cock."

"Ah, my girl, that cock has saved your life for you. But for him I would have you with me in the grave for evermore, and if I knew this cock would crow before I was in the grave you wouldn't have the knowledge you have now of the field and the gold. Put me into the coffin where you found me. Take your time and settle me well. I cannot meddle with you now, and 'tis sorry I am to part with you."

"Will you tell me who you are?" asked Kate.

"Have you ever heard your father or mother mention a man called Edward Derrihy or his son Michael?"

"It's often I heard tell of them," replied the girl.

"Well, Edward Derrihy was my father; I am Michael. That blackthorn that you came for tonight to this graveyard was the lucky stick for you, but if you had any thought of the danger that was before you, you wouldn't be here. Settle me carefully and close the tomb well behind you."

She placed him in the coffin carefully, closed the door behind her, took the blackthorn stick, and away home with Kate. The night was far spent when she came. She was tired, and it's good reason the girl had. She thrust the stick into the thatch above the door of the house and rapped. Her sister rose up and opened the door.

"Where did you spend the night?" asked the sister. "Mother will kill you in the morning for spending the whole night from home."

"Go to bed," answered Kate, "and never mind me."

They went to bed, and Kate fell asleep the minute she touched the bed, she was that tired after the night.

When the father and mother of the three young men rose next morning, and there was no sign of their sons, the mother went to the room to call them, and there she found the three dead. She began to screech and wring her hands. She ran to the road screaming and wailing. All the neighbours crowded around to know what trouble was on her. She told them her three sons were lying dead in their bed after the night. Very soon the report spread in every direction. When Kate's father and mother heard it they hurried off to the house to the dead men. When they came home Kate was still in bed; the mother took a stick and began to beat the girl for being out all the night and in bed all the day.

"Get up now, you lazy stump of a girl," said she, "and go to the wake-house; your neighbour's three sons are dead."

Kate took no notice of this. "I am very tired and sick," said she. "You'd better spare me and give me a drink."

The mother gave her a drink of milk and a bite to eat, and in the middle of the day she rose up.

"'Tis a shame for you not to be at the wake-house yet," said the mother; "hurry over now."

When Kate reached the house there was a great crowd of people before her and great wailing. She did not cry, but was looking on. The father was as if wild, going up and down the house wringing his hands.

"Be quiet," said Kate. "Control yourself."

"How can I do that, my dear girl, and my three fine sons lying dead in the house?"

"What would you give," asked Kate, "to the person who would bring life to them again?"

"Don't be vexing me," said the father.

"It's neither vexing you I am nor trifling," said Kate. "I can put the life in them again."

"If it was true that you could do that, I would give you all that I have inside the house and outside as well."

"All I want from you," said Kate, "is the eldest son to marry and Gort na Leachtan [the field of the stone heaps] as fortune."

"My dear, you will have that from me with the greatest blessing."

"Give me the field in writing from yourself, whether the son will marry me or not."

He gave her the field in his handwriting. She told all who were inside in the wake-house to go outside the door, every man and woman of them. Some were laughing at her and more were crying, thinking it was mad she was. She bolted the door inside, and went to the place where she left the handkerchief, found it, and put three bites of the oatmeal and the blood in the mouth of each young man, and as soon as she did that the three got their natural colour, and they looked like men sleeping. She opened the door, then called on all to come inside, and told the father to go and wake his sons.

He called each one by name, and as they woke they seemed very tired after their night's rest; they put on their clothes, and were greatly surprised to see all the people around. "How is this?" asked the eldest brother.

"Don't you know of anything that came over you in the night?" asked the father.

"We do not," said the sons. "We remember nothing at all since we fell asleep last evening."

The father then told them everything, but they could not believe it. Kate went away home and told her father and mother of her night's journey to and from the graveyard, and said that she would soon tell them more.

That day she met John.

"Did you bring the stick?" asked he.

"Find your own stick," said she, "and never speak to me again in your life."

In a week's time she went to the house of the three young men, and said to the father, "I have come for what you promised me."

"You'll get that with my blessing," said the father. He called the eldest son aside then and asked would he marry Kate, their neighbour's daughter. "I will," said the son. Three days after that the two were married and had a fine wedding. For three weeks they enjoyed a pleasant life without toil or trouble; then Kate said, "This will not do for us; we must be working. Come with me tomorrow and I'll give yourself and brothers plenty to do, and my own father and brothers as well."

She took them next day to one of the stone heaps in Gort na Leachtan. "Throw these stones to one side," said she.

They thought that she was losing her senses, but she told them that they'd soon see for themselves what she was doing. They went to work and kept at it till they had six feet deep of a hole dug; then they met with a flat stone three feet square and an iron hook in the middle of it.

"Sure there must be something underneath this," said the men. They lifted the flag, and under it was a pot of gold. All were very happy then. "There is more gold yet in the place," said Kate. "Come, now, to the other heap." They removed that heap, dug down, and found another pot of gold. They removed the third pile and found a third pot of gold. On the side of the third pot was an inscription, and they could not make out what it was. After emptying it they placed the pot by the side of the door.

About a month later a poor scholar walked the way, and as he was going in at the door he saw the old pot and the letters on the side of it. He began to study the letters.

"You must be a good scholar if you can read what's on that pot," said the young man.

"I can," said the poor scholar, "and here it is for you. There is a deal more at the south side of each pot."

The young man said nothing, but putting his hand in his pocket, gave the poor scholar a good day's hire. When he was gone they went to work and found a deal more of gold in the south side of each stone heap. They were very happy then and very rich, and bought several farms and built fine houses, and it was supposed by all of them in the latter end that it was Derrihy's money that was buried under the leach-tans, but they could give no correct account of that, and sure why need they care? When they died they left property to make their children rich to the seventh generation.

According to Sean O'Sullivan (from whose collection The Folklore of Ireland *this tale is taken), more than 150 oral versions of this story have been collected in the last 35 years!*

The tale is almost exclusively found in Gaelic, for it is of a type very difficult to translate, featuring, as it does, in its opening, closing, and descriptive passages, "runs." These are familiar—to the teller and his audience—rhetorical flourishes: time-honored, well-worn clusters of words that the listener can enjoy while the teller catches his breath, or picks up the thread of his story. ("It was a long time ago, and a long time ago it was. . . ." More familiar examples might be "Once upon a time" or "rosy-fingered dawn" or the unfortunate "so, anyway, like, I mean, you know. . . ."

A feature of every version of the tale is the huge and terrifying Great Cat of the Cave, the Big Bad Wolf of Gaelic story-telling, and a figure so familiar that the late Irish humorist Flann O'Brien has no end of fun with it in his hilarious mock folk tale, The Poor Mouth.

THE EVERLASTING FIGHT

It was long ago and a long time ago it was. If I were alive then, I wouldn't be alive now. If I were, I would have a new story or an old one, or I mightn't have any story! Or I might have lost only my back teeth or my front teeth or the furthest back tooth in my mouth!

There was a warrior in Ireland long ago, and his occupation was hunting and fowling on the hillside, listening to the baying of hounds and the clanging of chains, to the whistle of the man from the east and the call of the man from the west, and no sweeter to him would be the storm from the west across the lake than the coming of Conan Maol as he threw stones! One day when the warrior was hunting and fowling with his pack of hounds, he saw three men bearing a box like a coffin on their shoulders. He went towards them and stood in front of them to find out what they had in the box, but they weren't willing to tell him that or where they were taking it to. So he decided to take the box from them, if he were strong enough, and see what was in it. They attacked one another, and it wasn't long until he had beaten them badly and taken the box from them. He then opened it to see what was inside. It was a woman whose like he had never seen, so beautiful was she.

'I'm taking this woman with me,' said he, 'whether ye like it or not!'

'You're not!' said one of the men. 'We'll lose our heads rather than let you take her!'

'I'm taking her and cutting the heads off the three of you as well!' said the warrior.

One of the three was bolder than the other two, so the warrior drew a blow of his sword at him and severed one of his arms.

'Go off home now and take your arm with you!' said the warrior.

He took the woman home that evening and put her into a room until next day, when he intended to take her to a monk or a priest—whichever sort was there at that time—to get married. As soon as he got up next morning, he went to the room where he had left the woman, but she wasn't there. He didn't know where she had gone to, so he said to himself that he would never stop or stay until he found her, wherever in Ireland she might be. He set forth and kept on walking and travelling until the day was drawing to a close; until the white gelding was seeking the shade of the dock-leaf, though the dock-leaf wouldn't stand still for him; and until the sun had sunk into the earth and night was falling. He saw a light far away, and not near him, so he went towards it and entered a house. No sooner had he come in than the young woman for whom he was searching came down from a room. She smothered him with kisses and drowned him with tears, and then dried him with fine, silken towels and with her own hair. There wasn't a man anywhere she thought more of! The arm which he had severed from one of the three men the previous day was lying on a table at the other side of the room. It rose up from the table suddenly and struck him a painful blow on the jaw-bone.

'You wouldn't do that again, arm,' said the warrior, 'if I thought it worth my while to strike you back!'

'Well,' said the young woman, 'the three men who were carrying me yesterday when you took me from them are my three brothers, and when they come home here tonight, they'll kill me and they'll kill you, unless they promise me that they won't harm you. But I must hide you until I get that promise from them.'

She left him, and when he had eaten his supper, she hid him and told him about her brothers. They had to spend every day of their lives, she said, fighting against three waves of enemies, who wanted to take their land from them and banish them.

'My brothers kill them all every day,' said she, 'but they are alive next morning, ready to fight again! And since you cut the arm off one of them, it will take them longer each day to kill the enemy, and they will come home later in the evening.'

That was that! The three brothers came into the house later in the night and sat down to eat their supper. Each one of them said that all he asked for was to have revenge on the man who had cut off the arm of one of them. When they were seated at the table, eating, their sister didn't sit down with them to eat at all. They asked her why she wasn't eating.

'I won't ever eat anything again,' said she, 'unless ye promise me something.'

'We'll promise you anything in the world that we can,' they said, 'except to spare the man who cut the arm off our brother!'

'Ye must promise me whatever I ask for,' said she.

Well, rather than keep her from eating, they promised to do what she wanted, if she ate her food. When they had eaten their supper she told them what she wanted and uncovered the warrior. Each of the three brothers rushed to attack him, but when they remembered their promise to their sister, not to kill or harm him, they sat down again. Next morning, as soon as they had eaten their breakfast, they got ready to leave the house. He asked them where they were going, and they told him about the three waves of enemies they had to fight each day of their lives.

'They are alive again next morning,' they told him, 'although we have been killing them for many years. If we didn't kill them every day, we would soon have to leave this place altogether.'

'I'll go with ye today to see what I can do,' said the warrior. 'I should be able to do at least as well as the one of you that has lost his arm!'

'Stay at home today! Tomorrow will be soon enough for you,' they said.

'I won't,' said he. 'I'll go with ye today to see how these men that ye are killing every day can be alive again next morning.'

He went along with them, although they didn't want him to leave the house that day. They were very friendly towards him, in spite of

the blame they had on him the previous day. They reached the place where the three waves of enemies were waiting for them, armed with swords and every kind of weapon they could get for the fight.

'Ye must sit down now,' said the warrior to the three brothers, 'until I see what I'm able to do against these.'

He made the three sit down. Then he seized his sword and started to cut off the heads of the enemies, and by the end of two hours, not one of them was alive! It used to take the three brothers the whole day and part of the night to do as much!

'Ye are to go home now,' he told the brothers, 'but I won't leave this place until I find out what is making them alive again every night.'

'You mustn't stay,' said the brothers. 'If you stay here and we go home, our sister will say that we killed you, and she will lose her mind.'

'I don't care,' said the wrrior. 'I won't ever leave here until I find out what is making these dead alive again. Go home, and ye can come again tomorrow, if I don't return to the house.'

The three brothers went home, and the warrior remained watching the dead bodies. When night came, he threw heaps of them here and there and lay down between them. It was just midnight when he saw a hag approaching with a small pot in which there was a quill in her hand. She started to throw a dash with the quill of whatever was in the pot on the bodies, and hundreds of them rose up as well and strong and healthy as they had ever been. He kept watching her until she had sprinkled them a few times, and said to himself that, unless he stopped her in time, he would have plenty to do against her and the enemy, if they all came back of life! He attacked them, and it didn't take him long to kill all the men she had revived. Himself and the hag then attacked each other, and he found it harder to overcome her than the three waves of enemies he had killed the previous day. He knocked her down at last and was ready to cut off her head.

'I put geasa on you,' said the hag, 'never to stop or rest until you go to the King of the Bridge and tell him that you killed the Sow and her Litter!'

He cut off her head and set out to find the King of the Bridge. When he came to where he lived, he struck the challenge-pole. He didn't leave a foal in a mare, a calf in a cow, a kid in a she-goat, or a piglet in a sow that he didn't turn around nine times in their skins, with the dint of the blow. The King of the Bridge came out to him.

'I killed the Sow and her Litter tonight,' said the warrior.

'If you did,' said the King of the Bridge, 'you won't ever again kill anybody, after I have finished with you—or else, you're a great warrior."

They attacked each other, wrestling an arm above and an arm below. They made the hard places soft and the soft places hard: they drew springs of fresh water up through the middle of the gray stones by the dint of hatred and anger and strife. They threw out from themselves four showers of battle: a shower of blood from their waists, a shower of frenzy from their swords, a shower of sweat from their brows and a shower of anger from their teeth. So it went on until the day was drawing to a close and a robin alighted on the warrior's shoulder and said:

'O son of the Irish king, you have come to a bad place to die! It will take me many days to cover your dead body with the leaves of the trees.'

A spasm of anger passed through the warrior. He twisted the King of the Bridge around and sank his body to the waist in the earth; with a second twist, he sank him to the apple of his throat; and with the third twist, he shouted:

'Clay over your body, churl!'

'Let it be so!' said the King of the Bridge. 'But I place you under geasa never to halt or rest until you go to the King of the Churchyard and tell him that you have killed the Sow and her Litter and the King of the Bridge.'

The warrior went off and kept travelling until he came to where the King of the Churchyard was. He struck the challenge-pole and didn't leave a calf in a cow, a foal in a mare, a lamb in a ewe, a kid in a she-goat or a piglet in a sow that he didn't turn about nine times in their skins with the sound of the blow! The King of the Churchyard came out to him.

'I killed the Sow and her Litter and the King of the Bridge,' said the warrior.

'You will never again kill anyone, unless you are a better man than I am!' said the King of the Churchyard.

They attacked each other like two mad lions, like two bulls in a field, like two excited rams or two proud enemies that hated each other. They threw out from themselves four showers of battle: a shower of blood from their waists, a shower of frenzy from their swords, a shower of sweat from their brows and a shower of anger from their teeth. So it went on until the day was drawing to a close. They didn't know which of them was the better. Then a robin alighted on the warrior's shoulder and said:

'You have come a long way to die here, and it will take me many days to cover your dead body with the leaves of the trees!'

A spasm of anger passed through the warrior's mind, and he pulled himself together. He gave a twist to the King of the Churchyard and sank him to his waist in the earth; with a second twist, he sank him to the apple of his throat, and with the third twist, he shouted.

'That's clay over your body, churl!'

'It is so, best warrior whom I have ever seen,' said the King of the Churchyard. 'But before you cut off my head, I place you under geasa never to halt or rest until you go to the Great Cat of the Cave and tell him that you have killed the Sow and her Litter, the King of the Bridge and the King of the Churchyard!'

The warrior went off and kept traveling until he reached the place where the Cat of the Cave had made his cave. He entered the mouth of the cave; it was three miles long from mouth to end. So bright was the light that came from the cat's eyes that the warrior could see a small pin that might have fallen on the floor on the darkest night that ever came, even though the cat was a long distance away from him. He kept walking in through the cave, his sword in his hand, ready for the cat, until he reached the very end where the cat was. He looked around everywhere, and then upward towards a ledge high up the cave. He caught sight of a small, little cat, sitting on an arch-way and looking down. From the cat's eyes there shone the brightest and finest light that he had ever seen, and it blinded him when it fell on his own face. He stood in front of the cat and said:

'I have killed the Sow and her Litter, the King of the Bridge and the King of the Churchyard!'

The cat swelled in size until his back reached the roof of the cave. Then he stretched down one of his paws and tore the warrior's body from the waist upwards, and dragged his heart and lungs out on to the floor of the cave. The cat then stretched down his other paw to tear the other side of the warrior's body. As he did so, the warrior caught sight of a black spot under the cat's armpit. He thrust his sword upwards through the spot and pierced his heart. The cat fell down, dead, on to the floor on top of the warrior, who was also dead. So large was the cat's body that it completely covered that of the dead warrior!

That was that! On the following day, the woman and her three brothers went to where the battle used to be fought every day. They found all the enemy lying dead, and so too was the hag who used to bring them back to life. The little pot and the quill lay on the ground beside her. The young woman picked them up and put them in her pocket. They walked on towards where the King of the Bridge lived, as they thought that the warrior might have been killed by him, for they knew that he had always been helping their enemies. They made up their minds to search for the warrior, alive or dead. When they came on the body of the King of the Bridge, they went on to where the King of the Churchyard lived. They found him dead also, and knew that it was the warrior who had killed them all so far. Then they thought that the King of the Churchyard might have sent him to the Great Cat of the Cave, and that he was dead, as the cat had never let anybody escape alive.

They reached the cave of the Great Cat. There was no light within when they entered. They made their way slowly to the end of the cave, and there they found the dead body of the cat. They couldn't see any sign of the warrior, alive or dead. So they turned back again, not knowing where the warrior might be found. The young woman was behind the others and, as she walked along in the dark, her foot struck against the shoe of the warrior, who was lying dead under the cat's body. She shouted to her brothers that he was lying under the body of the cat, and that they should try to release him and bring him back to life with the contents of the pot of the old hag. The four of them tried to lift the cat's body off the warrior, but it was no use—they couldn't even move it. They had to cut the cat's body into pieces with their swords and lay bare what was underneath it. When they dragged the pieces of the cat aside, they put the heart and lungs back into the warrior's body as they had been when he was alive. When they had that done, they rubbed the contents of the pot to his wounds and to his heart and lungs, and he rose to his feet as well as he had ever been.

There weren't in the whole world three men or a young woman

more happy than they, at having found him, and at all their enemies whom they had fought for so long being dead. The warrior and the young woman got married, and they spent seven nights and seven days celebrating. They didn't know whether the first night or the last was the better. Every bite had the taste of honey, and no bite was tasteless!

In Ireland, the young men—sons, husbands, or lovers—die young. Of drink, or rebellion, or in the widow-making sea. The young men leave Ireland for England, or America. The young men become priests, and leave the world.

And, perhaps as a consequence, the figure of a lonely old woman dominates the Irish imagination. In her most debased form, she is the saccharine "Mother Machree," morosely serenaded on St. Patrick's Day. In her most powerful aspect, she is Cathleen ni Houlihan, the old beggar woman of the roads who is, beneath her crone's rags, the magnificent queen, the spirit of Ireland. (She is also known by the name of Shan van Vocht.)

And she is the Old Woman of Beare, a terribly ancient woman of the West, doomed to seven lives, the last of which is eternal. She pities her own fate in a tenth-century poem (translated by Frank O'Connor):

And O God
Once again for ill or good,
Spring will come, and I will see
Everything but me renewed. . . .

Here is a tale told of her to Douglas Hyde.

THE OLD WOMAN OF BEARE

There was an old woman in it, and long ago it was, and if we had been there that time we would not be here now; we would have a new story or an old story, and that would not be more likely than to be without any story at all.

The hag was very old, and she herself did not know her own age, nor did anybody else. There was a friar and his boy journeying one day, and they came in to the house of the Old Woman of Beare.

"God save you," said the friar.

"The same man save yourself," said the hag; "you're welcome, sit down at the fire and warm yourself."

The friar sat down, and when he had well finished warming himself he began to talk and discourse with the old hag.

"If it's no harm of me to ask it of you, I'd like to know your age, because I know you are very old," said the friar.

259

"It is no harm at all to ask me," said the hag; "I'll answer you as well as I can. There is never a year since I came to age that I used not to kill a beef and throw the bones of the beef up on the loft which is above your head. If you wish to know my age you can send your boy up on the loft and count the bones."

True was the tale. The friar sent the boy up on the loft and the boy began counting the bones, and with all the bones that were on the loft he had no room on the loft itself to count them, and he told the friar that he would have to throw the bones down on the floor—that there was no room on the loft.

"Down with them," said the friar, "and I'll keep count of them from below."

The boy began throwing them down from above and the friar began writing down [the number], until he was about tired out, and he asked the boy had he them nearly counted, and the boy answered the friar down from the loft that he had not even one corner of the loft emptied yet.

"If that's the way of it, come down out of the loft, and throw the bones up again," said the friar.

The boy came down, and he threw up the bones, and [so] the friar was [just] as wise coming in as he was going out.

"Though I don't know your age," said the friar to the hag, "I know that you haven't lived up to this time without seeing marvellous things in the course of your life, and the greatest marvel that you ever saw— tell it to me, if you please."

"I saw one marvel which made me wonder greatly," said the hag.

"Recount it to me," said the friar, "if you please."

"I myself and my girl were out one day, milking the cows, and it was a fine, lovely day, and I was just after milking one of the cows, and when I raised my head I looked round towards my left hand, and I saw a great blackness coming over my head in the air. "Make haste," says myself to the girl, "until we milk the cows smartly, or we'll be wet and drowned before we reach home, with the rain." I was on the pinch of my life and so was my girl, to have the cows milked before we'd get the shower, for I thought myself that it was a shower that was coming, but on my raising my head again I looked round me and beheld a woman coming as white as the swan that is on the brink of the waves. She went past me like a blast of wind, and the wind that was behind her, it could not come up with her. It was not long till I saw after the woman two mastiffs, and two yards of their tongue twisted round their necks, and balls of fire out of their mouths, and I wondered greatly at that. And after the dogs, I beheld a black coach and a team of horses drawing it, and there were balls of fire on every side out of the coach, and as the coach was going past me the beasts stood and something that was in the coach uttered from it an unmeaning sound, and I was terrified, and faintness came over me, and when I came back out of the faint I heard the voice in the coach again, asking me had I seen anything going past me since I came there; and I told him as I am telling you, and I asked him who he was himself or what was the meaning of the woman and the mastiffs which went by me.

"I am the Devil, and those are two mastiffs which I sent after that soul."

"And is it any harm for me to ask," says I, "what is the crime the woman did when she was in the world?"

"That is a woman," said the Devil, "who brought scandal upon a priest, and she died in a state of deadly sin, and she did not repent of it, and unless the mastiffs come up with her before she comes to the gates of Heaven the glorious Virgin will come and will ask a request of her only Son to grant the woman forgiveness for her sins, and the Virgin will obtain pardon for her, and I'll be out of her. But if the mastiffs come up with her before she goes to Heaven she is mine."

The great Devil drove on his beasts, and went out of my sight, and myself and my girl came home, and I was heavy, and tired and sad at remembering the vision which I saw, and I was greatly astonished at that wonder, and I lay in my bed for three days, and the fourth day I arose very done up and feeble, and not without cause, since any woman who would see the wonder that I saw, she would be grey a hundred years before her term of life was expired.

"Did you ever see any other marvel in your time?" says the friar to the hag.

"A week after leaving my bed I got a letter telling me that one of my friends was dead, and that I would have to go to the funeral. I proceeded to the funeral, and on my going into the corpse-house the body was in the coffin, and the coffin was laid down on the bier, and four men went under the bier that they might carry the coffin, and they weren't able to even stir the bier off the ground. And another four men came, and they were not able to move it off the ground. They were coming, man after man, until twelve came, and went under the bier, and they weren't able to lift it.

"I spoke myself, and I asked the people who were at the funeral what sort of trade had this man when he was in the world, and it was told me that it was a herd he was. And I asked of the people who were there was there any other herd at the funeral. Then there came four men that nobody at all who was at the funeral had any knowledge or recognition of, and they told me that they were four herds, and they went under the bier and they lifted it as you would lift a handful of chaff, and off they went as quick and sharp as ever they could lift a foot. Good powers of walking they had, and a fine long step I had myself, and I cut out after them, and not a mother's son knew what the place was to which they were departing with the body, and we were going and ever going until night and day were parting from one another, until the night was coming black dark dreadful, until the grey horse was going under the shadow of the docking and until the docking was going fleeing before him.

> The roots going under the ground,
> The leaves going into the air,
> The grey horse a-fleeing apace,
> And I left lonely there.

"On looking round me, there wasn't one of all the funeral behind me, except two others. The other people were done up, and they were not able to come half way, some of them fainted and some of them died. Going forward two steps more in front of me I was within a dark wood wet and cold, and the ground opened, and I was swallowed down into a black dark hole without a mother's son or a father's daughter next nor near me, without a man to be had to keen me or to lay me out; so that I threw myself on my two knees, and I was there throughout four days sending my prayer up to God to take me out of that speedily and quickly. And with the fourth day there came a little hole like the eye of a needle on one corner of the abode where I was; and I was a-praying always and the hole was a-growing in size day by day, and on the seventh day it increased to such a size that I got out through it. I took to my heels then when I got my feet with me on the outside [of the

hole] going home. The distance which I walked in one single day following the coffin, I spent five weeks coming back the same road, and
don't you see yourself now that I got cause to be withered, old, aged,
grey, and my life to be shortening through those two perils in which I
was."

"You're a fine, hardy old woman all the time," said the friar.

Tales of witches and witchcraft are rare in Irish folklore; a wise old woman well-connected with the powers of the Air and the Little People was obviously to be respected, and asked for advice and cures, not ridiculed, tried, and burned.

Biddy Early, an old woman of the west who could see the future in a magic blue bottle, did have occasional run-ins with the parish priest . . . but the local police were more likely to consult her for tips on the races than to arrest her for sorcery.

Even the Wexford Witches in this story of Patrick Kennedy's seem more like fairies than evil crones in league with the devil; for the little red caps they wear are usually a sign of membership among the fairy folk . . . as is their fondness for stolen whiskey punch.

THE WITCHES' EXCURSION

Shemus Rua (Red James) was awakened from his sleep one night by noises in his kitchen. Stealing to the door, he saw half-a-dozen old women sitting round the fire, jesting and laughing, his old housekeeper, Madge, quite frisky and gay, helping her sister crones to cheering glasses of punch. He began to admire the impudence and imprudence of Madge, displayed in the invitation and the riot, but recollected on the instant her officiousness in urging him to take a comfortable posset, which she had brought to his bedside just before he fell asleep. Had he drunk it, he would have been just now deaf to the witches' glee. He heard and saw them drink his health in such a mocking style as nearly to tempt him to charge them, besom in hand, but he restrained himself.

The jug being emptied, one of them cried out, "Is it time to be gone?" and at the same moment, putting on cappeen d'yarrag (a red cap), she added:

> By yarrow and rue,
> And my red cap too,
> Hie over to England.

Making use of a twig which she held in her hand as a steed, she grace-fully soared up the chimney, and was rapidly followed by the rest. But when it came to the housekeeper, Shemus interposed. "By your leave, ma'am," said he, snatching the twig and cap. "Ah, you desateful ould

264

crocodile! If I find you here on my return, there'll be wigs on the green:

> By yarrow and rue,
> And my red cap too,
> Hie over to England.

The words were not out of his mouth when he was soaring above the ridge pole, and swiftly ploughing the air. He was careful to speak no word (being somewhat conversant with witch lore), as the result would be a tumble, and the immediate return of the expedition.

In a very short time they had crossed the Wicklow hills, the Irish Sea, and the Welsh mountains, and were charging, at whirlwind speed, the hall door of a castle. Shemus, only for the company in which he found himself, would have cried out for pardon, expecting to be mummy against the hard oak door in a moment; but, all bewildered, he found himself passing through the keyhole, along a passage, down a flight of steps, and through a cellardoor keyhole before he could form any clear idea of his situation.

Waking to the full consciousness of his position, he found himself sitting on a stillion, plenty of lights glimmering round, and he and his companions, with full tumblers of frothing wine in hand, hobnobbing and drinking healths as jovially and recklessly as if the liquor was honestly come by, and they were sitting in Shemus's own kitchen. The cappeen d'yarrag (red cap) had assimilated Shemus's nature for the time being to that of his unholy companions. The heady liquors soon got into their brains, and a period of unconsciousness succeeded the ecstasy, the headache, the turning round of the barrels, and the 'scattered sight' of poor Shemus. He woke up under the impression of being roughly seized,and shaken, and dragged upstairs, and subjected to a disagreeable examination by the lord of the castle, in his state parlor. There was much derision among the whole company, gentle and simple, on hearing Shemus's explanation, and, as the thing occurred in the dark ages, the unlucky Leinster man was sentenced to be hung as soon as the gallows could be prepared for the occasion.

The poor Hibernian was in the cart proceeding on his last journey, with a label on his back, and another on his breast, announcing him as the remorseless villain who for the last month had been draining the casks in my lord's vault every night. He was surprised to hear himself addressed by his name, and in his native tongue, by an old woman in the crowd. "Ach, Shemus, cappeen d'yarrag?" These words infused hope and courage into the poor victim's heart. He turned to the lord and humbly asked leave to die in his red cap, which he supposed had dropped from his head in the vault. A servant was sent for the head-piece, and Shemus felt lively hope warming his heart while placing it on his head. On the platform he was graciously allowed to address the spectators, which he proceeded to do in the usual formula composed for the benefit of flying stationers: "Good people all, a warning take by me;" but when he had finished the line, "My parents reared me tenderly," he unexpectedly added: "By yarrow and rue," etc., and the disappointed spectators saw him shoot up obliquely through the air in the style of a skyrocket that had missed its aim. It is said that the lord took the circumstance much to heart, and never afterward hung a man for twenty-four hours after his offence.

To us, living in overpopulated cities, in an overpopulated world, the death of an individual has lost meaning. But to the people of a remote village, every death is a death in the family—they need not send to ask for whom the bell tolls.

The dead man—or woman, or child—continues to be a presence in the community, a force, a memory, a personality actually felt . . . a "numinous" presence, which may account for "primitive" people's belief in gods, ghosts, and fairies.

We would call the headless stranger met upon the road in this story a ghost—but Michael Faherty, who told the tale to William Larminie, believed him to be "one of the good people," that is, one of the Sidhe.

Watch how Michael shyly switches from the third person to the first-person singular—how "a man" becomes "I."

THE GHOST AND HIS WIVES

There was a man coming from a funeral, and it chanced as he was coming along by the churchyard he fell in with the head of a man. "It is good and right," said he to himself, "to take that with me now and put it in a safe place." He took up the head and laid it in the churchyard. He went on along the road, and he met a man with the appearance of a gentleman.

"Where were you?" said the gentleman.

"I was at a funeral, and I found the head of a man on the road."

"What did you do with it?" said the gentleman.

"Why so?" said the man.

"That is my head," said he, "and if you did anything out of the way to it, assuredly I would be even with you."

"And how did you lose your head?" said the man.

"I did not lose it at all, but I left it in the place where you found it, to see what you would do with it."

"I believe you are one of the good people," said the man, "and if so, it would be better for me to be in any other place than in your company."

"Don't be afraid, I won't touch you. I would rather do you a good turn than a bad one."

267

"I would like that," said the man. "Come home with me till we get our dinner."

They went home together. "Get up," said the man to his wife, "and make our dinner for us."The woman got up and made dinner for them. Then they ate their dinner. "Come," said the man, "till we play a game of cards."

They were playing cards that evening, and the gentleman slept that night in the house; and on the morning of the morrow, they ate their breakfast together. When two hours were spent—

"Come with me," said the gentleman.

"What business have you with me?" said the man.

"That you may see the place I have at home."

They got up and walked together, till they came to the church-yard. "Lift the tombstone," said the gentleman. He raised the tomb-stone, and they went in. "Go down the stairs,"said the gentleman.

They went down together till they came to the door; and it was opened and they came into the kitchen. There were two old women sitting by the fire. "Rise," said the gentleman to one of them, "and get dinner ready for us." She rose and took some small potatoes.

"Have you nothing for us for dinner but that sort?" said the gentleman.

"I have not," said the woman.

"As you have not, keep them."

"Rise you," he said to the second woman, "and get dinner for us."

She rose and took some meal and husks.

"Have you nothing for us but that sort?"

"I have not," said she.

"As you have not, keep them."

He went up the stairs and knocked at a door. There came out a beautiful woman in a silk dress, and it ornamented with gold from the sole of her foot to the crown of her head. She asked him what he wanted. He asked her if she could get dinner for himself and the stran-ger. She said she could. She laid a dinner before them fit for a king. And when they had eaten and drunk plenty, the gentleman asked if he knew the reason why she was able to give them such a good dinner.

"I don't know," said the man, "but tell me, if it is your pleasure."

"When I was alive, I was married three times, and the first wife I

269

had never gave anything to a poor man except little potatoes; and she must live on them herself till the day of judgement. The second wife, whenever anyone asked alms of her, never gave anything but corn and husks; and she will be no better off herself, nor anyone who asks of her, till the day of judgment. The third wife, who got the dinner for us—she would give us everything from the first."

"Why is that?" said the man.

"Because she never spared of anything she had, but would give it to a poor man; and she will have of that kind till the day of judgement."

"Come with me till you see my dwelling," said the gentleman. There were outhouses, and stables, and woods about the house; and to speak the truth, he was in the prettiest place I ever saw with my eyes. "Come inside with me," said he to the man; and I was not long within when there came a piper, and he told him to play, and he was not long in playing, when the house was filled with men and women. They began dancing. When part of the night was spent, I thought I would go home and sleep. I arose and went home to sleep, and when I awoke in the morning, I could see nothing of the house or anything in the place.

Among sportsmen, Ireland is famous for the game fish in its lakes and streams—trout and salmon, especially. Like many of Ireland's creatures, these fish are often magical—like the Salmon of Wisdom, who inadvertently gave Finn McCool his remarkable thumb—and even their colors and markings are said to be the results of enchantments and adventures long ago.

This story tells how the white trout in the lakes near Cong received the red mark upon their sides, which is there to this day.

Samuel Lover, a musician, playwright, and celebrated painter of portrait miniatures in his day, published the tale in 1834, in his Legends and Stories of the Irish Peasantry.

As to the dialect in which the story is told: Lover was Anglo-Irish, the son of a wealthy Dublin stockbroker, and of the class who, in the words of Yeats, "did not—mainly for political reasons—take the population seriously . . . and created the stage Irishman."

It is a pretty tale, nonetheless, and a funny one, and touched with another quality of Lover's elsewhere praised by Yeats: "the sympathy with peasant life so visible in all his stories."

THE WHITE TROUT: A LEGEND OF CONG

There was wanst upon a time, long ago a beautiful lady who lived in a castle upon the lake beyant, and they say she was promised to a King's son, and they wor to be married, when all of a sudden he was murthered, the crathur (Lord help us), and threwn into the lake above, and so, of course, he couldn't keep his promise to the fair lady—and more's the pity.

Well, the story goes that she went out iv her mind, bekase av loosin' the King's son—for she was tendher-hearted, God help her, like the rest iv us!—and pined away after him, until at last, no one about seen her, good or bad; and the story wint that the fairies took her away.

Well, sir, in coorse o' time, the White Throut, God bless it, was seen in the sthrame beyant, and sure the people didn't know what to think av the crathur seein' as how a white throut was never heard av afor, nor since. For years upon years the throut was there, just where you seen it this blessed minit, longer nor I can tell—aye throth, and beyant the memory o' th' ouldest in the village.

272

At last the people began to think it must be a fairy—for what else could it be? And no hurt nor harm was iver put in the white throut, until some wicked sinners of sojers kem to these parts, and laughed at all the people, and gibed and jeered them for thinkin' o' the likes. One o' them in partic'lar (bad luch to him: God forgi' me for saying it!) swore he'd catch the throut and ate it for his dinner—the blackguard.

Well, what would you think O, the villainy of the sojer? Sure enough he cotch the throut, and away wid him home, and puts in the fryin'-pan, and into it he pitches the purty little thing. The throut squeeled all as one as a christian crathur, and, my dear, you'd think the sojer id split his sides laughin'—for he was a harden'd villain. When he thought one side was done, he turns it over to fry the other, and, what would you think, but the devil a taste of a burn was an it at all. Sure the sojer thought it was a quare throut that could not be briled. "But," says he, "I'll give it another turn by-and-by," little thinkin' what was in store for him, the haythen.

Well, when he thought that side was done he turns it agin, and lo and behold you, the divil a taste more done that side was nor the other. "Bad luck to me," says the sojer, "but that bates the world," says he. "But, I'll thry you agin, my darlint," says he, "as cunnin' as you think yourself."

And so with that he turns it over and over, but not a sign of the fire was on the purty throut. "Well," says he, "my jolly little throut, maybe you're fried enough, though you don't seem overwell dress'd; but you may be better than you look, like a singed cat, and a tit-bit afther all," says he.

With that he ups with his knife and fork to taste a piece o' the throut. But, my jew'l, the minit he puts his knife into the fish, there was a murtherin' screech, that you'd think the life id lave you if you hurd it. Away jumps the throut out av the fryin' pan into the middle o' the flure and an the spot where it fell, up riz a lovely lady—the beautifullest crathur that eyes ever seen, dressed in white, and a band o' gold in her hair, and a sthrame o' blood runnin' down her arm.

"Look where you cut me, you villain," says she, and she held out her arm to him—and, my dear, he thought the sight id lave his eyes.

"Couldn't you lave me cool and comfortable in the river where you snared me, and not disturb me in my duty?" says she.

273

Well, he thrimbled like a dog in a wet sack, and at last he stammered out somethin', and begged for his life, and ax'd her lady-ship's pardon, and said he didn't know she was on duty, or he was too good a sojer not to know bether nor to meddle wid her.

"I was on duty, then," says she. "I was watchin' for my true love that is comin' by wather to me," says the lady, "an' if he comes while I'm away, an' that I miss iv him, I'll turn you into a pinkeen, and I'll hunt you up and down for ever more, while the grass grows or wather runs."

Well, the sojer thought the life id lave him, at the thoughts iv his bein' turned into a pinkeen, and begged for mercy.

And with that says the lady: "Renounce your evil coorses," says she, "you villain, or you'll repint it too late. Be a good man for the futher and go to your duty reg'lar. And now," says she, "take me back and put me into the river again, where you found me."

"Oh, my lady," says the sojer, "how could I have the heart to drownd a beautiful lady like you?"

But before he could say another word, the lady was vanished, and there he saw the little throut an the ground. Well, he put it in a clean plate, and away he runs for the bare life, for fear her lover would come while she was away. And he run, and he run, even till he came to the cave agin, and threw the throut into the river. The minit he did, the wather was as red as blood for a little while, by rayson av the cut, I suppose, until the sthrame washed the stain away; and to this day there's a little red mark an the throut's side, where it was cut.

Well, sir, from that day out the sojer was an altered man, and reformed his ways, and went to his duty reg'lar, and fasted three times a week—though it was never fish he tuk an fastin' days, for afther the fright he got, fish id never rest an his stomach—savin' your presence.

But anyhow, he was an altered man, as I said before, and in coorse o' time he left the army, and turned hermit at last. They say he used to pray evermore for the soul of the White Throut.

The Wildes of Dublin were a markedly unusual couple, even in a city where eccentricity was (and is) the norm. Sir William, the celebrated surgeon, was once accused by a young female patient of having criminally assaulted her. He sued for libel, and lost—thereby setting an unfortunate example of litigiousness for his young son, Oscar. Sir William was unsanitary in his personal habits, even by the low standards of nineteenth-century medical men. A joke among the Dubliners of his time ran, "Why are Sir William Wilde's fingernails black? Because he scratches himself."

His wife, Lady Jane, was a curious figure herself—G.B. Shaw believed her large hands and feet to be symptoms of "Giganticism"— and she was not noted for meticulous housekeeping. She once scolded a maid for stacking the dishes on the coal scuttle. "What do you think the chairs are for?" asked Lady Wilde.

None of which typical Dublin gossip has anything to do with this eerie story, collected by Lady Wilde and published in her book Ancient Cures, Charms and Usages of Ireland.

(The "splendid hall" to which Mary is conveyed seems to be a sort of limbo—the place or state in which Roman Catholics believed the souls of innocent but unbaptized children must spend eternity.)

A LEGEND OF SHARK

On Shark Island there lived some years ago a woman named Mary Callan, with her one and only child. Indeed, she never had another, from the fright she got some weeks after her baby was born, and this was her strange story. Suddenly, at dead of night, she was awoke by the child crying, and starting up, she lit the candle, when to her horror she saw two strange men standing beside her bed, and they threw a mantle over her and drew her out of the house into the dark night; and there at the door she saw a horse waiting, and one of them lifted her up, and then sprang up himself, and they rode away like the wind into the darkness.

Presently they came to a great, black-looking house, where a woman was waiting, who brought her in, and she found herself all at once in a splendid hall lit up with torches and hung with silk. And the woman told her to sit down and wait till she was called, as there was very important business for her to attend to. Now, when the woman left her alone, Mary began to look about her with great curiosity, and a large silver pot on the table filled with sweet-smelling ointment especially attracted her, so that she could not help rubbing some on her hands, and touched her eyes with the fragrant salve.

Then suddenly a strange thing happened, for the room seemed filled with children, but she knew that they were all dead, for some of them were from her own village, and she remembered their names, and when they died. And as she watched them, one of the children came over quite close, and looking fixedly at her, asked: "What brought you here, Mary, to this dreadful place? For no one can leave it until the Judgement Day, and we dwell for ever in sorrow for the life that has been taken from us. And the men went for your child to-night, to bring it here amongst the dead, but when you struck a light they could do no harm; yet they are still watching for it, so hasten back, or it will be too late, and the child will die. And tell my mother that I am with the spirits of the hill, and not to fret, for we shall meet again on the Judgement Day."

"But how can I go out in the darkness?" asked Mary, "for I know not my way."

"Never mind," said the child; "here, take this leaf, and crush it close in your hand, and it will guide you safe from harm." And she placed a green leaf in the woman's hand, and on the instant Mary found herself outside the door of the great house; but a tremor fell on her, for loud voices were heard calling her back, and footsteps seemed to pursue her as she fled away. Then, just as she was sinking to the earth with fright, she grasped the leaf close in her hand, and in a moment she was at her own door, and the footsteps of the pursuers ceased; but she heard a great cry within the house, and a woman rushed out and seized her arm. "Come, Mary," she said, "come quickly. Your child is dying. Something is strangling it, and we cannot help or save him."

Then Mary, wild with fear, sprang to the little bed where lay the child, and he was quite black in the face, as if some one was holding him by the throat; but, quick as thought, Mary took the leaf and crushed it into the child's hand. And gradually the convulsion passed away, and the natural colour came back, and in a little while he slept peacefully in his mother's arms, and she laid him in his bed and watched by him all night; but no harm came, and no evil thing touched him. And in the morning he smiled up at his mother, bright and rosy as ever, and then she knew that the fairy power was broken, and the child was saved by the spell of the leaf that had come to her from the hands of the dead that dwell in the Spirit Land. And Mary made a case for the leaf, and worked it richly, and tied it round her neck to wear for evermore. And from that day the fairies ceased to molest her, and her child grew and prospered, for the spirits of the dead watched over him to keep him safe from harm.

It is the function of many a folk or fairy story, told by the fire or in the nursery, to sound soothing and whimsical—and to convey subversive subject matter. Not only psychologically subversive (as the Freudian critics never tire of reminding us), but politically subversive as well. The tales the old gaffers tell each other, or the children, within earshot of the conquerers often hint at a future rebellion, of a trueborn king or leader now asleep, or in the hills, or underground, who will one day lead his people to freedom.

King Arthur is such a figure. Charlemagne awaits the sound of Roland's horn. and the Earl Fitzgerald is asleep, under the hill.

King Arthur of Britain awaits a summons back from Avalon. Charlemagne of France will return to lead his nation when Roland's horn sounds again. And, in Ireland, the Earl Fitzgerald sleeps under the hill, until the day of his rising. . . .

This tale of the earl's enchantment, as retold by Kennedy, begins with whimsy and ends as a conventional ghost story. But at its heart is a warning—and a promise.

THE ENCHANTMENT
OF GERALD FITZGERALD

In old times in Ireland there was a great man of the Fitzgeralds. The name of him was Gerald, but the Irish, that always had a great liking for the family, called him *Gearoidh Iarla* (Earl Gerald). He had a great castle or rath at Mullaghmast, and whenever the English government were striving to put some wrong on the country, he was always the man that stood up for it. Along with being a great leader in a fight, and very skillful at all weapons, he was deep in the *black art,* and could change himself into whatever shape he pleased. His lady knew that he had this power, and often asked him to let her into some of his secrets, but he never would gratify her.

She wanted particularly to see him in some strange shape, but he put her off and off on one pretence or other. But she wouldn't be a woman if she hadn't perseverance; and so at last he let her know that if she took the least fright while he'd be out of his natural form, he would never recover it till many generations of men would be under the mould. "Oh! she wouldn't be a fit wife for Gearoidh Iarla if she could be easily frightened. Let him but gratify her in this whim, and he'd see

279

what a hero she was!" So one beautiful summer evening, as they were sitting in their grand drawing-room, he turned his face away from her, and muttered some words, and while you'd wink he was clever and clean and out of sight, and a lovely *goldfinch* was flying about the room.

The lady, as courageous as she thought herself, was a little startled, but she held her own pretty well, especially when he came and perched on her shoulder, and shook his wings, and put his little beak to her lips and whistled the delightfullest tune you ever heard. Well, he flew in circles round the room, and played *hide and go seek* with his lady, and flew out into the garden, and flew back again, and lay down in her lap as if he was asleep, and jumped up again.

Well, when the thing had lasted long enough to satisfy both, he took one flight more into the open air; but by my word he was soon on his return. He flew right into his lady's bosom, and the next moment a fierce hawk was after him. The wife gave one loud scream, though there was no need, for the wild bird came in like an arrow, and struck against a table with such force that the life was dashed out of him. She turned her eyes from his quivering body to where she saw the gold-finch an instant before, but neither goldfinch nor Earl Gerald did she ever lay eyes on again.

Once every seven years the Earl rides round the Curragh of Kildare on a steed, whose silver shoes were half an inch thick the time he disappeared; and when these shoes are worn as thin as a cat's ear, he will be restored to the society of living men, fight a great battle with the English, and reign King of Ireland for two score years.

Himself and his warriors are now sleeping in a long cavern under the Rath of Mullaghmast. There is a table running along through the middle of the cave. The Earl is sitting at the head, and his troopers down along in complete armour both sides of the table, and their heads resting on it. Their horses, saddled and bridled, are standing behind their masters in their stalls at each side; and when the day comes, the millers' son that's to be born with six fingers on each hand will blow his trumpet, and the horses will stamp and whinny, and the knights awake and mount their steeds, and go forth to battle.

Some night that happens once in every seven years, while the Earl is riding round the Curragh, the entrance may be seen by any one chancing to pass by. About a hundred years ago, a horse-dealer that was late abroad and a little drunk saw the lighted cavern, and went in. The lights, and the stillness, and the sight of the men in armour cowed him a good deal, and he became sober. His hands began to tremble, and he let fall a bridle on the pavement. The sound of the bit echoed through the long cave, and one of the warriors that was next him lifted his head a little, and said in a deep hoarse voice, "Is it time yet?" He had the wit to say, "Not yet, but soon will," and the heavy helmet sunk down on the table. The horse-dealer made the best of his way out, and I never heard of any other one getting the same opportunity.

In the library of the American Irish Historical Society in New York is a little book called Irish Folklore Tales. *It appears to be about a century old. No editor claims credit for the collection, nor are the tales attributed—although they come, for the most part, from Croker and Kennedy.*

But the story of "The Headless Horseman of Shanacloch" I have not found elsewhere. It is a ghost story about that most traumatic of historical incidents, the Battle of the Boyne River where, on July 12, 1690, King William III of England defeated the combined native Irish and English Catholic troops led by James (the Shemish-a-cocca. of our story).

It is curious to note that the traitor in the tale is a cobbler—a "brogue-maker," as he says. Perhaps his actions are further evidence of leprechauns' vengeance . . . and pleasant to hear that he has been forgiven, and gone to heaven, at last. Would that all ghosts of Irish treachery and combat had been exorcised with him.

THE HEADLESS HORSEMAN OF SHANACLOCH

Long an' merry ago, when Shemish-a-cocca, that lost old Ireland—bad cess to him!—was fighting it with some Orangeman or other that kem from England, with a great army, to destroy the Pope and the Catholics, Shanacloch, that then belonged to the Barrys (the rap M'Adamces), was garrisoned with stout boys, that defended the place for James, and well, in their way, they wor to spill their blood, like ditch-wather, for the bad bird that befouled his own nest. The great guns were planted against the castle over-right us there at Bushy-park, and they roared night and day; but though the bullets battered the walls, and did a power of damage, the boys at Shanacloch ped thim off in their own coin. So, my dear, one dark night they stole upon the castle, being determined by all accounts to take the Barrys at an *amplush*, but they peppered thim with bullets from the portholes; and whin the inimy drew off, they followed thim down the big field to the Bride, and, ma-vrone, the battle-axes of the Barry used to strike off heads and arms like tops o' thistles, and they pursued them into the river, and the Bride, that this blessed night is so muddy an' dark, was thin red with blood. Soon after the English captain hoist his sails, and off with him, horse an' foot, with a flay in his ear. But, as the bodachs

282

wor passing through Bunkilly in their way to Mallow, a man kim against thim, mounted on a black horse, with a great parcel of brogues in a kist.

"Hilloa, frind!" says the captain, "who are you, and where might you be throtting to at that rate?"

"I'm an honest brogue-maker, saving your honour's presence, and carrying this kist of brogues to the garrishon at Shanacloch," says the horseman.

"Will you come back to-night?" says the captain.

"Is it to come back your honour manes? By Jaminie, if I put my eyes on Kippins, the boys wouldn't let me quit tonight. I'll be bail for lashings of whisky there, an' hay and oats galore for this ould baste."

"Harkey, friend," says the captain, "you don't seem to be overbur-thened with money, and if you got a fistful of yellow guineas would you have any objection to do me a trifle of sarvice?"

Well, to make my long story short, the murdhering thraitor agreed for a sum of money to betray the Barrys, and let the inimy in upon him in the dead o' the night. The poor min that wor harrashed and worn out from long watching and constant fighting, took a dhrop extrornary for joy that the English bodachs legged it, and every man went to sleep, when the brogue-maker promised to keep watch till morning. But by the time the min wor dead asleep, the English returned, and the chief of the world opened the gates, and every mother's sowl in the castle was murdered in cold blood. Eighteen Redmonds of the Barrys that were sworn to stand or fall together were stabbed (the Lord save us!) in their sleep. When this massacre was finished the brogue-maker claimed the reward, and requested to be let go, as the daylight was fast approach-ing.

"I'll give you all you bargained for, an' a thrifle over," said the captain; an' when he ped the money down on the nail, he struck off the villain's head for betraying the noble fellows, whose blood flowed through every room of the castle that night.

From that time forward a headless horseman was seen every night riding round Shanacloch, and it is not said that he ever did the laste injury to anybody. In the coorse o' years this very house that I'm telling the story in (God bless all that's in it!) was built upon the Horseman's Walk by the masther's gran'father, and every night he entered the kitchen by the door, and wint out through the opposite wall, that closed after him, as if no Christian sowl passed through it, and they always put out the candle, to allow him to go by unnoticed.

But the night the masther's aunt (God rest her sowl) was marrying, in the middle of the piping an' dancing, the horseman called out at the door—though I wonder how he could, for he had never a head upon him. The people of the wedding didn't hear, or were afeard to answer him, not knowing, poor dear people, what trouble they might be brought to. The headless horseman of Shanacloch was never seen or heard of since. They say his time was out, and his horrible threachery atoned for, and that on this last night he came to thank them for their past kindness to him.

Thanks be to Heaven, spirits and ghosts are going away, very fast, bekase wars and murdhers are at an ind, and the clergy—more power to 'em!—has sent a great many sowls to the Red Say.

V. THE
LITTLE
PEOPLE

The Little People

Up the airy mountain,
  Down the rushy glen,
We dare not go a-hunting
  For fear of little men. . . .

William Allingham
"The Fairies"

They tell the story of a scholar (Yeats told it of himself) searching for evidence of the fairies in the west of Ireland. In some desolate place, the scholar came upon a great red-faced strapping peasant, standing alone in the rain. He approached the man, who was laboring over his potatoes or his fishing net (depending on your version, you see), and, half ashamed of his own arcane pursuits, enquired as to whether the peasant had ever seen any traces of fairies, or such like. "Seen 'em?" boomed the big man. "Amn't I *annoyed* with 'em?"

There are two classes of fairy in Ireland. The first, and most numerous, are the "trooping fairies," the *sidhe*, who live in royal splendor beneath the hills—or beneath the waves. It is thought they are the descendants of the Tuatha De Danaan, for they are very courtly, and beautiful. In their gaiety and wit, their love of music and laughter and ceremony, their sudden temper and boundless generosity, and above all in the air about them of sweet sadness for lost glory, they may well be the Native Spirits of Ireland.

The world-famous leprechauns are another class of creature altogether, being solitary fairies. They are small people, and dark—and may be descended from a still older race, the Fir Bolg, who were conquered long ago by the De Danaan themselves. Their dress (high hat and buckle shoes) is an eighteenth-century style—yet the gold they hoard is "Danish," treasure left behind by the Viking invaders, in the seventh century.

A romantic might hold that the leprechauns represent another—and deeper—spirit of Ireland. Endlessly pictured on travel brochures and St. Patrick's Day cards as harmless and charming and promising of gold, they are in truth full of guile and bile, small and strong and determined—survivors eternally, and eternally . . . solitary.

The leprechauns as Little People first appear in an eleventh-century manuscript, The Death of Fergus. And very little people they are—just about the size of Tom Thumb, or Thumbelina.

It's not impossible that the Irish-born satirist, Jonathan Swift, knew a version of this tale: the reactions of tiny Iubdan (Yu-van) and Esirt to the sight (and especially the smell) of hulking humans are much like those of his hero, Gulliver, to the giant Brobdingnagians; and the "moral"—of pride and vanity leading to humiliation—would have been dear to his savage, indignant heart.

The tale itself seems to be a household, or children's story, grafted onto an heroic legend; in the first part, proud little men fall into porridge pots, and in the second, a magic dragon-slaying sword of kingship is bequeathed to a future hero.

As to the magic shoes of the leprechaun king—which the mortal Fergus is somehow able to put on—remember that the Little People are still reputed to be cobblers of wonderful skill.

FERGUS AND THE KING
OF THE LEPRECHAUNS

At the very time that Fergus, king of Ulster, was holding a feast at his palace, who else would be giving a banquet but Iubdan, king of the Lepra and the Leprachauns?

In his hall under the hill, they sat at the table according to rank, so that Iubdan was at the head of it, with his wife Bebo at the one hand, and Esirt, his chief-poet and wizard, at the other. Now the drink was drawn from the vats, and the carvers stood up to carve; and rich old mellow ale was served to all the company. It wasn't long before the hall was ringing with their shouts and laughter.

There was entertainment, too, at the Leprachaun party: the strong man of the court performed his greatest feat, which was to hew down a thistle with a single stroke of his blade!

Then the king rose up, and held high his drinking horn, and all about him stood up, as well as they could, to do him honor. "Have you ever in all your life," said Iubdan, "seen a king that was better than myself?"

"We have not," they shouted back.

290

"Have you ever seen a strong man the equal of my strong man?"

"We have not."

"Have you seen horses or warriors the like of them gathered here tonight in this house?"

And again they answered him, "We have not, indeed."

"Right again!" said Iubdan. "There's not a hero among us here who isn't the stuff of which kings are made! Proud men of might are we all! Lusty and fierce in battle. . . ."

But here he was interrupted by a burst of laughter from his poet, Esirt. The king asked him would he mind sharing the joke.

Said the poet, "There's a province in Ireland I know, where a single one of its men could take captives and hostages of all four battalions of the Leprachaun!"

"Arrest me that bragging poet there," commanded Iubdan, and it was done. Guards wrestled him to the floor. But Esirt said, "This is a wicked thing you've done, king. It will bear evil fruit. Because of this, you yourself will be five years captive in the palace of Fergus, and leave behind there the greatest of your treasures; and I myself must go to the house of Fergus, and be set floating in his cup of wine, till I am all but drowned. . . ."

The men who had seized Esirt stood away from him then, in awe, for his power was on him—and the poet stood up, alone, before the king.

"Give me leave," he said, "for three days and three nights, to travel to the house of Fergus, and I will bring you proof that I speak the truth."

Then Esirt left them, and went to his own house. He put on his shirt of smooth and delicate silk, and donned his gold-broidered tunic, and his scarlet cloak. On his feet he set two little shoes of white bronze. And he took his poet's wand, and his wizard's hood, and set out by the shortest way to the palace of Fergus, till he knocked on its gates with his wand.

When the gates were opened, the sentry beheld there a man, standing handsome and proud, up to his waist in the close-cut grass of the green. The sentry was struck with amazement, and ran to report this marvel to Fergus and the company. Was he smaller, even they

291

asked, than Aed? (Aed was the poet of Ulster, and a dwarf who could stand up full in the palm of a man's hand.)

The sentry said, "This one could stand up on Aed's hand, I'm telling you!"

There was great laughter at this, and all the court rushed out to see this wonder. They crowded around Esirt, laughing and pushing and shoving for a glimpse of him, till he shouted out, "Huge men that you are, don't all be breathing on me, with your stinking breaths! Stand back now! Further back!"

"Now," he said, "let yon man there, the smallest among you, come to me." And so it was the poet Aed who carried Esirt into the palace, and the Leprachaun stood in the palm of his hand.

To Fergus the king, who asked him his name, he answered, "I am Esirt, son of Beg, son of Buaidgen, chief-poet, wizard, and maker of rhymes to the Lepra and the Leprachauns." Now, the feast was just at its height, and a cup-bearer came to Fergus. "Give a drink to our little guest here," said the king.

But Esirt answered, "I will not eat of your meat, Fergus, nor of your liquor will I drink."

"My, my," said the king. "This is big talk from such a wee, wee man. But if you were dropped into the cup, here, I wonder whether you'd drink any of the liquor, at all!"

The cup-bearer seized Esirt between finger and thumb, and dropped him into the goblet. He thrashed and splashed in it, he sputtered and shouted out, "Poets of Ulster! There are things I could tell you that you dearly need to know! Don't let me drown!"

And so he was lifted out, and wiped clean, and dried with fair satin napkins, while Fergus asked him, "Why would you not drink with us, or eat?"

"I will tell you the reason," sid the little man. But you must hold your anger at it."

"I will, swore the king. And Esirt began singing:

> The Ulster king wears a marriage ring
> Fol de rol de rol
> But the light of his life is his servant's wife
> Fol de rol de day.

And whatever he thinks of my little song,
Fol de rol de rol
Right will be right, and wrong be wrong
Fol de rol de day.

Then Fergus said to him, "You are no child indeed, Esirt, but a man of knowledge. I have, indeed, trifled with the love of my servant's wife, and I am shamed for it."

Said Esirt, "I will eat with you now, if I may; for you have confessed and repented the wrong."

So the feast went on merrily, until Esirt said to all the gathering, "I have made a poem, which I might recite to you, if it please you."

"It is our dearest wish," Fergus answered, and Esirt stood up on the table, at his place, and began to chant;

A king of victories, a king of glory and fame,
Is Iubdan son of Abdan, praise to his name!
His voice is a copper drum sounding;
His cheek is rowan berry bright;
Eyes clear as spring water running;
His color is swan white, sea-foam white.
In peace, Law-maker, Feast-Giver;
But when horses charge down like the waves of the sea,
He is first among his fair host riding,
Death-Bringer then to the brave is he!
Noble and proud the men are all, handsome the women,
That live with him in his palace under the hill—
Great love it is said women bear for Fergus of Ulster.
Iubdan is more beloved still.

When the poet had finished, the men of Ulster, in tribute, heaped gold and treasure on the table, all around him. "I thank you," said the Leprachaun, "for this kindness, which is worthy of your renown. But we who follow my lord have all we need, and in abundance."

But the Ulstermen protested that, saying, "It would dishonor us to take back again gifts we have given, though we had given our very wives or cattle. . . ."

"Then let the gifts be divided up, you poets and scholars of Ulster!" said the bard of the Leprachauns, "two-thirds for yourselves, and a third for the stable boys and jesters of the province."

Three days more and three nights they feasted, till Esirt took his leave of Fergus and the nobles of Ulster. "I will go with you," said Aed, the poet of Ulster, who, dwarf though he was, towered over Esirt. "That you may," said the Leprachaun, "but never say I bid thee come."

So they set out, the pair of poets together, and Aed's step being the longer, he soon called back, "It's a slow walker you are altogether, friend Esirt!" At which the Leprachaun put on such a sprint of running, he was an arrow's flight ahead of his fellow in no time. "Can you not strike a happy medium?" called Aed to him, laughing. "By my word," said the Leprachaun, "I've been three days among you, and never before heard praise of moderation!"

On they went till they came to the sea, at the Strand of the Strong Men. "It's now we must travel over the depths of the sea," said Esirt.

"How shall I do that?" Aed asked him, "and not catch my death of water?"

"A steed of Iubdan's will come to fetch you," Esirt told him, "a trustworthy mount over land and water."

And in no time at all, they marked something among the crests of the waves, moving swiftly toward them. "Upon itself be the evil that thing brings," cried Aed, for he thought it was a bewitched hare he saw moving in the water, there.

But Esirt said, "That is Iubdan's horse, come to fetch us!" And this was the fashion of that horse. Two fierce flashing eyes he had, and a mane of bright scarlet. He had four green legs, and a tail that waved in curls, like smoke. His body was all as golden as the fine-wrought bridle he wore. Esirt was astride him in a flash. "Come up beside me, Aed," he said.

"I will not," said the dwarf. "It's more than yon little beast can do, to carry you alone."

"Ah, man," said the Leprachaun, "stop your complaining will you, and come on! He'll bear us both nicely, whatever the weight of your ponderous wisdom!"

And so they both crossed the open sea on the back of the little horse, and came undrowned to the land of the Leprachauns.

Word went before them to the palace of Iubdan that Esirt had come home, and brought a giant in his company. The king greeted Esirt with a kiss, when they met, and whispered to him, "Friend poet, I trust this giant of yours has not come to destroy us all?"

"He is no giant," Esirt answered him, "but the poet of Ulster, a wizard, and the king's dwarf. He is the smallest man in all his own land, and can lie like a baby in the arms of the warriors there. But while he is here in your kingdom, let you and your subjects take care to stay out from under his feet."

And all the people of the Lepra and Leprachaun came near, but not too near, and gazed up in awe at the size of Aed, the terrible height and width of him.

Then Esirt said to Ibudan the king, "Now it's you who are in my debt, for the treatment you gave me at the feast. I bind you upon your warrior's honor to go yourself to the country where I have been. Every night they make there the 'lord's porridge' for the King of Ulster's breakfast.

"Let yourself be the first one to taste of it this night."

Iubdan went dizzy with fear at that, and asked his wife Bebo would she bear him company. "I will," she said, "but it was an evil day when you had that poet arrested." The pair of them mounted Iubdan's golden horse, and made their way to the palace of Fergus, and inside it.

Bebo whispered to him to search the place for that porridge pot in a hurry, so they could be away before the people were up and about.

And it wasn't long before they came upon the great cauldron of porridge, hanging over the fire. Iubdan stood up on his toes, and reached for it. He backed off and took a running jump for it. But he never reached its rim at all. "Get up on your horse," said Bebo, "and climb up from there to the lip of the pot." And he did that, and there he was, hanging over the edge of the pot; but his arms were too short to reach the shank of the ladle that was down in the porridge. Down and over he stretched, his foot slipped, and the next he knew he was in it, up to his navel. No ropes or chains fashioned by mortal man or Leprachaun could have bound his legs firmer than that stuff he was stuck in.

"You're a long time at your breakfast," Bebo called out to him.

"Bebo," his voice came to her, "I'm stuck fast. I'm done for. Save yourself, Bebo! Take the horse with you back to Lepraland!"

"Never say it," she answered. "I'll not leave the place till I see what becomes of you, husband."

And so the servants of Fergus soon discovered them, the queen of the Leprachauns beneath the porridge pot, and the king within it; and with much laughter, they were carried in to Fergus.

"But this is not the same wee man who was here before," said Fergus, squinting down at him. "Who are you, mannikin, and where are you from, at all?"

"I am Iubdan, king over the Lepra and the Leprachaun, and this woman with me is Bebo the queen; and I never told a lie."

"Let them be taken out," said Fegus, "and given for playthings to the children of the household. . . ."

But Iubdan said to him, "If it please you, sir, their great thumbs would bruise us, and the breath of them make us sick. If you keep us in your care, we will never leave your palace without permission. My word upon it."

So, by the command of Fergus, they were carried to a fair and private room, and a trusty servant with them, to see to their needs.

And for a year and a day, it was the chief recreation and delight of all the people of Ulster to look upon the little couple, and listen to their words.

But at the end of that time, the folk of the Leprachaun, seven battalions strong, came in quest of their king and queen, making camp on the green before the gates. When Fergus and the nobles of Ulster came out to them, they promised a rich ransom to redeem the royal pair.

"What ransom?" asked Fergus.

"Every year, without ploughing or sowing, we will fill this plain with waving corn."

"I will not give you back your little king for the likes of that," answered Fergus.

"We will do you a turn of mischief tonight," they told him.

"What mischief is that?"

"There's not a cow in all Ulster will give milk in the morning," they told him.

"That you may do, or you may not do," said Fergus. "But I will not give up your king to you."

And on the morn, when they had made good their threat, and not a drop of sweet milk was to be had the length and breadth of Ulster, they spoke again with Fergus, swearing they would make good the spoil they had done in return for their king and queen.

Again he refused them, and they vowed and did another deed of vengeance, defiling that night the water of every well and stream and river.

The third morning, and the fourth, Fegus denied them their desire, and the third night they burned all the stores of grain in the province, and the fourth night they snipped the ears from every stalk of corn in Ulster.

And a fifth time Fergus told them, "I will not give your king up to you," till they vowed another vengeance against him.

"In the night we will shave your women's hair, and your men's hair, and shame and disgrace will be on them all, forever!" they said.

At that, Fergus replied, "Do it, and on my oath, I will kill your king and your queen both for you!"

Now Iubdan heard all of this, for he was behind the king, held in a bird-cage of wicker a servant carried. He shouted out, "That's not the way of it at all! Great king, give me leave to speak to my people!" And Fergus gave orders for him to be brought forth before the army of Leprachauns, who set up a mighty shout, seeing him.

But Iubdan said to them, "For the love you bear me, and the loyalty you owe me, undo now all the evil you have done, and make good all you have spoiled; for I may not be bought, or bartered, or taken from here by force. It was the poet Esirt who prophesied that I would be kept captive in this place, until I had left behind the choicest thing of all my treasures."

Then, turning to Fergus, he said to him, "Of all my possessions choose you now a single one, for so it must be. Choose with care," he said and he began to name them, and number them:

"Take my spear, O take my spear, for many are your enemies, Fergus, and it is a hundred-slayer!

297

"Take my shield, O take my shield, for in its shelter none can be wounded!

"My sword, and O my sword! There's no better blade in the hand of any prince, throughout all Ireland!

* "Take my belt, O take my belt! It is of gold and silver linked, and no sickness may touch the man it goes 'round!

"My cauldron take, then, my magic cauldron! Though stones be put into it, out of it comes meat fit for princes!

"Take my harp, O my sweet-stringed harp! All of itself it plays, without a finger upon it, and its music is a charm upon women!

"Take my shears, that are never dull, or my needle of gold take, or even my shoes. . . ."

"What power is in the shoes?" said Fergus.

And although his shoes were his chiefest treasure, Iubdan was obliged to answer him, "Alike he may walk on land and on sea, who wears them."

So of all that Iubdan possessed, Fergus made his choice, and that was the shoes of white bronze.

Then Iubdan and his queen were released to the folk of the Lepra and the Leprachaun, and they bade Fergus farewell, and departed for their own land, although all Ulster grieved to see them go.

But that is not the end of the story.

Fergus had reason to choose the shoes of the Leprachaun for his ransom. There was a monster that lived in the lake nearby, and one time when Fergus was swimming there, the beast rose up against him. The lake began to boil, and she shot up out of the water and across the sky, as big as a rainbow. Fergus swam for shore, but as he reached it, the monster's breath touched him, and withered him into a crooked, squint-eyed man, with his mouth twisted round the side of his face.

He never knew it, of course, and because he was their king, no one ever spoke of it to him, and the queen saw to it that all mirrors were kept from him.

But a day came when the king and queen took to arguing over some trifle, and he gave her a blow in anger. Said she, "You'd be better employed showing your mighty wrath to the monster in the lake, that twisted your mouth up the side of your face, than you are beating women."

THE LITTLE PEOPLE

Then Fergus called for a mirror, and in it he saw his poor twisted face. He swore vengeance against the monster in the Lake; and that is why of all Iubdan's things, he chose the shoes that could go upon water.

The people of Ulster went out in boats and barges onto the lake, to accompany Fergus, and when they were in the midst of it, the monster rose up among them. She hurled herself down across the boats, and broke them into twigs, and the people in them were sent howling into the water, and swimming desperately for shore.

There Fergus bid them sit and watch, while he alone went to deal with the beast. He put on the shoes he'd got from the Leprachaun, and ran straight into the lake, making straight for the monster. She bared her fangs, like a wolf-hound threatened. Her eyes blazed like two torches kindled. She put out her sharp claws, like spear points in the battle line, and threw her head back so her neck bent like a drawn bow.

Good luck to the man fated to fight such a huge-headed, long-toothed dragon as that!

Fergus charged on, heedless, and the pair of them came together in the midst of the lake. They so flogged the water that the trout in it leaped up and flung themselves on the shore, for the white sandy lake bottom was churned up to the surface.

Now the water was white as new milk; now it was all turned crimson with the froth of blood. And the dragon, rising out of the water as tall as an oak, turned and fled before the onslaught of Fergus.

But he followed after, and dealt her blow after blow, till she died; and with the sword that was in his hand, the *Caladbolg*, the best blade in Ireland, he cut her all to pieces; and to the shore, where the Ulstermen stood waiting, he brought her heart.

He himself had taken many a wound, from tooth and from claw, and he fell down before them, stretched out upon the shore, with his life's blood spilling out of him.

Around him stood the Ulstermen, weeping; and the poet Aed, newly returned from Lepraland, made over him this verse:

Dig you now the grave of Fergus
Carve you his name on the Ogham stone

Never by enemies defeated,
By his vanity was he overthrown.

Fergus gave the sword *Caladbolg* into Aed's keeping.
"This is the sword of Ulster's true king," he said.

"Let men remember it, and its story, until another Fergus is in Ulster, who is worthy to bear it." And he died then.

And the sword *Caladbolg* was the weapon wielded in future days by Fergus Mac Roy, champion of the Red Branch knights of Ulster.

In 1913, after attending a lecture on the customs of the newly discovered pygmies of Africa, Elizabeth Andrews decided to gather what information she could on the "Pygmies" of her own region, the leprechauns of Ulster.

She published her findings in an informal and charming book, Ulster Folklore. *Throughout, she remains, while not exactly a believer, open-minded about the caves and mounds and circles of stones which her informants assure her are the homes of the Gentry. One story she was told illustrates the belief that the Gentry have difficulty reproducing, and require both mortal mates and midwives.*

MIDWIFE TO THE GENTRY

There was an old woman at Glenties. She had no children herself, her only daughter having died some years previous, but she was a great hand at helping the women around there to give birth, when their time came.

One dark wet night a little man came knocking at her door and asked her would she come with him, to help his wife. She didn't like to go, it being so late, but he was beside himself, pleading and saying it wasn't far to go. In the end, she consented.

He led her a short way into the mountains, to his dwelling, and he brought her in to his wife, and who was she but the old woman's daughter she'd thought was dead all the while!

The little man left them together, and the daughter begged the old woman not to tell him who she was. And she gave her mother a ring, so she'd know when to meet her again.

"After the baby's born," the daughter said, "himself will offer you a reward. Don't take it. Ask him instead for the child. At first he'll refuse, but if you beg, he'll give in."

Well, the baby was born, a little red-headed boy, and the midwife refused the handful of gold pieces the little man held out to her.

What payment would she take, he asked her. The child itself, said she. Never, he said, but she asked him would he deny a lonely old woman the company of a child, and she promised she'd care for it, and keep it safe, and in the end he agreed.

And back home the old woman went in the morning, with her red-headed grandson. The daughter was well pleased, and she whispered to the old woman before she left that they'd meet again soon, when the fair was held on the hill behind Glenties.

"But mind, now, mother," she said, "never speak a word to my husband, if you see him again."

After that, they had many a happy meeting together on the hill, the old woman, her daughter and the child. It was the ring she'd been given that warned the old woman when they were to meet.

But one day came when the ring called out to her, and she bundled up the boy, and rushed out to the hill. And when she saw her daughter standing there beside the little man, she never thought at all, but greeted them both, and went and shook his hand!

A terrible anger took hold of the little man, and he blew a breath of air in the old woman's eyes, so she'd never see the Gentry again.

And when she looked, the ring was gone, and her daughter, too, and the red-headed boy.

There is a story of fairy kindness that is told in every part of the world (in Japan it is called Kabutori) and, naturally, in every part of Ireland. Douglas Hyde heard it in the west, in Connacht; Croker collected it in midland Tipperary; and our version, by Patrick Kennedy, comes from Wexford, in the east.

Fairies are great singers and dancers, and that is because (depending on your view of their nature) they either love music or are condemned to it.

The wee dancers in this tale seem to be obliged to sing and dance eternally, and glad of any change to their tune, an endless repetition of the days of the week. Croker appends to his version of the story this "unique specimen of fairy song," as he calls it:

THE PALACE IN THE RATH

Everybody from Boncady to Enniscorthy knows the rath [a fortified place surrounded by a wall or ditch] between Tombrick and Munfin. Well, there was a poor, honest, quiet little creature, that lived just at the pass of Glenamoin, between the hill of Coolgarrow and Kilachdiarmid. His back was broken when he was a child, and he earned his bread by making cradles, and bosses, and chairs, and beehives, out of straw and briers. No one in the barony of Bantry or Scarawalsh could equal him at these. Well, he was a sober little fellow enough, but the best of us may be overtaken. He was coming from the fair of Enniscorthy one fine summer evening, up along the beautiful shady road of Munfin; and when he came near the stream that bounds Tombrick, he turned into the fields to make his road short. He was singing merrily enough, but by degrees he got a little stupefied; and when he was passing the dry, grassy ditch that surrounds the rath, he felt an inclination to sit and rest himself.

It is hard to sit awhile, and have your eyes a little glassy, and the things seeming to turn round you, without falling off asleep; and asleep my poor little man of straw was in a few minutes. Things like droves of cattle, or soldiers marching, or big flakes of foam, on a flooded river were pushing on through his brain, and he thought the drums were playing a march, when he woke up, and there in the face of the steep bank that was overgrown with bushes and blackthorn, a passage was open between nice pillars, and inside was a great vaulted room, with arches crossing each other, a hundred lamps hanging from the vault, and thousands of nice little gentlemen and ladies, with green coats and gowns, and red sugar-loaf caps, dancing and singing, and nice little pipers and fiddlers, perched up in a little gallery by themselves, and playing music to help out the singing.

He was a little cowed at first, but as he found no one taking notice of him, he stole in, and sat in a corner, and thought he'd never be tired looking at the fine little people figuring, and cutting capers, and singing. But at last he began to find the singing and music a little tedious. It was nothing but two short bars and four words, and this was the style:

Yae Luan, yae Morth—
Yae Luan, yae Morth.

The longer he looked on, the bolder he grew, and at last he shouted at the end of the verse:

Agus Dha Haed-yeen.

Oh, such cries of delight as rose up among the merry little gentry! They began the improved song, and shouted it until the vault rang:

> Yae Luan, yae Morth—
> Yae Luan, yae Morth,
> Yae Luan, yae Morth,
> Agus Dha Haed-yeen.°

After a few minutes, they all left off the dance and gathered round the boss maker, and thanked him for improving their tune. "Now," said the chief, "if you wish for anything, only say the word, and, if it is in our power, it must be done." "I thank you, ladies and gentlemen," says he, "and if you'd only remove this hump from my back, I'd be the happiest man in the Duffrey." "Oh, easy done, easy done!" said they. "Go on again with the dance, and you come along with us." So they went on with:

> Yae Luan, Yae Morth—
> Yae Luan, Yae Morth,
> Yae Luan, Yae Morth,
> Agus Dha Haed-yeen.

One fairy taking the new friend by the heel, shot him in a curve to the very roof, and down he came the other side of the hall. Another gave him a shove, and up he flew back again. He felt as if he had wings; and one time when his back touched the roof, he found a sudden delightful change in himself; and just as he touched the ground, he lost all memory of everything around him.

Next morning he was awakened by the sun shining on his face from over Slieve Buie, and he had a delightful feel down along his body instead of the disagreeable *cruith* he was accustomed to. He felt as if he could go from that to the other side of the stream at one step, and he burned little daylight till he reached Glenamoin. He had some trouble to persuade the neighbours of the truth of what had happened; but the

°Monday, Tuesday/Monday, Tuesday/Monday, Tuesday/and Wednesday.

wonder held only nine days; and he had like to lose his health along with his hump, for if he only made his appearance in Ballycarney, Castle Dockrell, Ballindaggin, Kilmeashil, or Bonclody, ten people would be inviting him to a share of a tumbler of punch, or a quart of mulled beer.

The news of the wonderful cure was talked of high and low, and even went as far as Ballynocrish, in Bantry, where another poor *anga-shore* of a humpback lived. But he was very unlike the Duffry man in his disposition; he was as cross as a brier, and almost begrudged his right hand to help his left. His poor old aunt and a neighbor of hers set out one day, along with him, along the Bunclody road, passing by Kil-lanne and the old place of the Colcoughs at Duffrey Hall, till they reached Temple-shambo. Then they kept along the hilly by-road till they reached the little man's house near the pass.

So they went up and told their business, and he gave them a kind welcome, and explained all the ins and outs of his adventure; and the end was, the four went together in the heel of the evening to the rath, and left the little lord in his glory in the dry, brown grass of the round dyke, where the other met his good fortune. The little ounkran never once thanked them for all the trouble they were taking for him. He only whimpered about being left in that lonesome place, and bade them to be sure to be with him at the flight of night, because he did not know what way to take from it.

At last, the poor cross creature fell asleep; and after dreaming about falling down from the rocks, and being held over the sea by his hump, and then that a lion had him by the same hump, and was running away with him, and then that it was put up for a target for soldiers to shoot at, the first volley they gave awoke him, and what was it but the music of the fairies in full career. The melody was the same as it was left them by the hive-maker, and the tune and dancing was twice as good as it was at first. This is the way it went:

> Yae Luan, yae Morth—
> Yae Luan, yae Morth,
> Yae Luan, yae Morth,
> Agus Dha Haed-yeen.

But the new visitor had neither taste nor discretion; so when they came about the third time to the last line, he croaked out:

Agus Dha-Yaerd-yeen
Agus Dha Haen-ya.°

It was the same as a cross fiddler that finds nobody going to give him anything, and makes a harsh back-screak of his bow along one of the strings. A thousand voices cried out, "Who stops our dance? Who stops our dance?" and all gathered round the poor fellow. He could do nothing but stare at them with his poor, cross, frightened face; and they screamed and laughed till he thought it was all over with him.

But it was *not* over with him.

"Bring down that hump," says the king; and before you could kiss your hand it was clapped on, as fast as the knocker of Newgate, over the other hump. The music was over now, the lights went out, and the poor creature lay till morning in a nightmare; and there the two women found him, at daybreak, more dead than alive. It was a dismal return they had to Ballynocrish; and the moral of my story is, that you should never drive till you first try the virtue of leading.

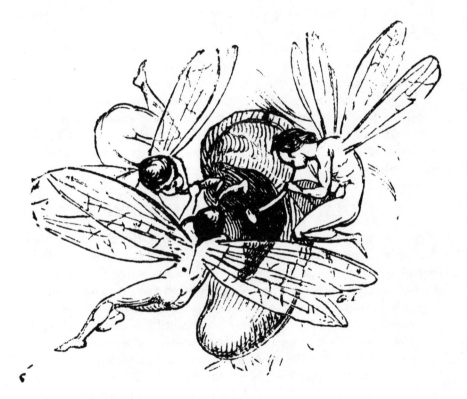

Fir Darrig means The Red Man. According to Yeats, this creature wears a red cap and coat and busies himself with practical joking, especially with gruesome joking. "This he does, and nothing else." Like the leprechaun, Fir Darrig is a "solitary fairy," and it is unusual to find him (as we do in the tale of Diarmid Bawn) associating with a whole troop of Little People.

In Donegal, he is the largest of the fairies. In Munster, where Crofton Croker gathered this tale, he is as tiny as the rest.

Possibly he is a descendant, or a much-diminished version, of the Dagda, "The Red Man of All Knowledge," once King of the Sidhe and father of Angus.

The Clurican, yet another solitary fairy, has a great fondness for liquor. Fir Darrig seems to share the Irish addiction, mortal and otherwise, for tobacco—hence his joining in the expedition to Jamaica.

The "gospel" hung about Diarmid's neck, which saves his life, is a text of Scripture blessed by a priest and worn about, sewn into a little cloth bag, to ward off sickness and evil. Belief in the efficacy of a text of Holy Writ is a custom in many cultures no more, nor less, superstitious than nineteenth-century Irish peasants.

DIARMID BAWN, THE PIPER

One stormy night Patrick Burke was seated in the chimney corner, smoking his pipe quite contentedly after his hard day's work; his two little boys were roasting potatoes in the ashes, while his rosy daughter held a candle to her mother, who, seated on a siesteen, was mending a rent in Patrick's old coat; and Judy, the maid, was singing merrily to the sound of her wheel, that kept up a beautiful humming noise just like the sweet drone of a bagpipe. Indeed, they all seemed quite contented and happy; for the storm howled without, and they were warm and snug within by the side of a blazing turf fire. "I was just thinking," said Patrick, taking the dudeen from his mouth and giving it a rap on his thumb-nail to shake out the ashes; "I was just thinking how thankful we ought to be to have a snug bit of a cabin this pelting night over our heads, for in all my born days I never heard the like of it."

"And that's no lie for you, Pat," said his wife; "but, whisht! what noise is that I hard?" and she dropped her work upon her knees, and looked fearfully towards the door.

"The Vargin herself defend us all!" cried Judy, at the same time rapidly making a pious sign on her forehead, "if 'tis not the banshee!"

"Hold your tongue, you fool," said Patrick, "it's only the old gate swinging in the wind," and he had scarcely spoken, when the door was assailed by a violent knocking. Molly began to mumble her prayers, and Judy proceeded to mutter over the muster-roll of saints; the youngsters scampered off to hide themselves behind the settle-bed; the storm howled louder and more fiercely than ever, and the rapping was renewed with redoubled violence. "Whisht, whisht!" said Patrick; "what a noise ye're all making about nothing at all. Judy aroon, can't you go and see who's at the door?" for notwithstanding his assumed bravery, Pat Burke preferred that the maid should open the door.

"Why, then, is it me you're speaking to?" said Judy, in a tone of astonishment; "and is it cracked mad you are, Mister Burke; or is it, maybe, that you want me to be rund away with, and made a horse of, like my grandfather was?—the sorrow a step will I stir to open the door, if you were as great a man as you are, Pat Burke."

"Bother you, then! and hold your tongue, and I'll go myself." So saying, up got Patrick, and made the best of his way to the door. "Who's there?" said he, and his voice trembled mightily all the while. "In the name of Saint Patrick, who's there?"

" 'Tis I, Pat," answered a voice which he immediately knew to be the young squire's. In a moment the door was opened, and in walked a young man with a gun in his hand and a brace of dogs at his heels.

"Your honour's honour is quite welcome, entirely," said Patrick, who was a civil sort of a fellow, especially to his betters. "Your honour's honour is quite welcome; and if ye'll be so condescending as to demean yourself by taking off your wet jacket, Molly can give ye a bran new blanket, and ye can sit forenent the fire while the clothes are drying."

"Thank you, Pat," said the squire, as he wrapped himself in the proffered blanket.

"But what made you keep me so long at the door?"

"Why, then, your honour, 'twas all along of Judy, there, being so much afraid of the good people; and a good right she has, after what happened to her grandfather—the Lord rest his soul!"

"And what was that, Pat?" said the squire.

"Why then, your honour must know that Judy had a grandfather; and he was ould Diarmid Bawn, the piper, as personable a looking man as any in the five parishes he was; and he could play the pipes so sweetly, and make them spake to such perfection, that it did one's heart good to hear him. We never had nay one, for that matter, in this side of the country like him, before or since, except James Gandsey, that is own piper to Lord Headly—his honour's lordship is the real good gentleman—and 'tis Mr. Gandsey's music that is the pride of Killarney lakes. Well, as I was saying, Diarmid was Judy's grandfather, and he rented a small mountainy farm; and he was walking about the fields one moonlight night, quite melancholy-like himself for want of the tobaccy; because why, the river was flooded, and he could not get across to buy any, and Diarmid would rather go to bed without his supper than a whiff of the dudeen. Well, your honour, just as he came to the old fort in the far field, what should he see—the Lord preserve us!—but a large army of the good people, 'coutered for all the world just like the dragoons! 'Are ye all ready?' said a little fellow at their head, dressed out like a general. 'No,' said a little curmudgeon of a chap all dressed in red, from the crown of his cocked hat to the sole of his boot. 'No, general,' said he; 'if you don't get the Fir Darrig a horse he must stay behind, and ye'll lose the battle.'

"'There's Dairmid Bawn,' said the general, pointing to Judy's grandfather, your honour, 'make a horse of him.'

"So with that master Fir Darrig comes up to Diarmid, who, you may be sure, was in a mighty great fright; but he determined, seeing there was no help for him, to put a bold face on the matter; and so he began to cross himself, and to say some blessed words, that nothing bad could stand before.

"'Is that what you'd be after, you spalpeen?' said the little red imp, at the same time grinning a horrible grin; 'I'm not the man to care a straw for either your words or your crossing.' So, without more to do, he gives poor Diarmid a rap with the flat side of his sword, and in a moment he was changed into a horse, with little Fir Darrig stuck fast on his back.

Away they all flew over the wide ocean, like so many wild geese, screaming and chattering all the time, till they came to Jamaica; and there they had a murdering fight with the good people of that country.

Well, it was all very well with them, and they stuck to it manfully, and fought it out fairly, till one of the Jamaica men made a cut with his sword under Diarmid's left eye, and then, sir, you see, poor Diarmid lost his temper entirely, and he dashed into the very middle of them, with Fir Darrig mounted upon his back, and he threw out his heels, and whisked his tail about, and wheeled and turned round and round at such a rate that he soon made a fair clearance of them—horse, foot, and dragoons. At last Diarmid's faction got the better, all through his means; and then they had such feasting and rejoicing, and gave Diarmid, who was the finest horse amongst them all, the best of everything.

"'Let every man take a hand of tobaccy for Diarmid Bawn,' said the general; and so they did; and away they flew, for 'twas getting near morning, to the old fort back again, and there they vanished like the mist from the mountain.

"When Diarmid looked about the sun was rising, and he thought it was all a dream, till he saw a big rick of tobaccy in the old fort, and felt the blood running from his left eye; for sure enough he was wounded in the battle, and would have been kilt entirely, if it wasn't for a gospel composed by Father Murphy that hung about his neck ever since he had the scarlet fever; and for certain it was enough to have given him another scarlet fever to have had the little red man all night on his back, whip and spur for the bare life. However, there was the tobaccy heaped up in a great heap by his side; and he heard a voice, although he could see no one, telling him 'that 'twas all his own, for his good behaviour in the battle; and that whenever Fir Darrig would want a horse again he'd know where to find a clever beast, as he never rode a better than Diarmid Bawn.' That's what he said, sir."

"Thank you, Pat," said the squire; "it certainly is a wonderful story, and I am not surprised at Judy's alarm. But now, as the storm is over, and the moon shining brightly, I'll make the best of my way home." So saying, he disrobed himself of the blanket, put on his coat and, whistling his dogs, set off across the mountain; while Patrick stood at the door, bawling after him, "May God and the blessed Virgin preserve your honour, and keep ye from the good people; for t'was of a moonlight night like this that Diarmid Bawn was made a horse of, for the Fir Darrig to ride."

313

Whatever they may be—fallen angels, or remnants of the proud Tuatha de Danaan, ghosts, or mortals who have gone "away" and live wild in the hills—the Little People seldom wish us well.

This story of a leprechaun and his mocking laughter was recorded in County Galway, in 1937, and published in Sean O'Sullivan's Irish Folktales. *According to Mr. O'Sullivan, there are seventy-eight distinct versions of this tale in the folklore archives of University College, Dublin, which makes it a very popular story indeed.*

THE THREE LAUGHS OF THE LEIPREACHAN

There was a farmer long ago, and he used to get up very early in the morning and go out to see how his livestock and crops were after the night. One fine morning when he went out, he heard a noise as if somebody were hammering. He looked around and saw a huge mushroom growing. He was surprised at its size and went to take a closer look at it. What should he see under the mushroom but a leipreachan, who was making a pair of shoes. People say that the leipreachan is a shoemaker. The farmer ran and seized hold of him.

"I have been a long time looking for you," said the farmer; "and you'll never leave my hands until you tell me where I can get riches."

They say that when the Danes were in Ireland, they hid a lot of money in the earth, and only the leipreachan knows where it is.

"Oh, I can't tell you that," cried the leipreachan. "I don't know where they hid it."

"You'll have to tell me," said the farmer, "or I'll cut off your head."

"Well, I can't tell you," said the leipreachan.

The farmer brought him home and put him into a trunk. He left him there for seven years. One day when the farmer was out walking by the shore, he found a balk of timber washed in by the tide. He sold it to another man, and when he returned home, the leipreachan laughed inside the trunk. The farmer didn't take any notice of this, but when the seven years were up, he took him out of the trunk.

"I'll put you in for seven more years," said he, "and, if you don't tell me where I can get riches, I'll cut off your head."

314

"Do, if you wish. I can't tell you where you'll find it," said the leipreachan.

One day soon afterward, a poor man who was passing by came in. The farmer was at his breakfast, and he invited the poor man to sit down and eat something.

"No, thank you, I'll be going," said the poor man.

He hadn't gone far when he broke his leg. The leipreachan laughed again, but the farmer took no notice. When the second seven years were up, the farmer went to the trunk again and took out the leipreachan.

"If you don't tell me where I can get those riches, I'll cut off your head," said he.

"Do, if you wish. I can't tell you," said the leipreachan.

The farmer locked him in the trunk once more. Some time after that, the leipreachan overheard the farmer saying that he was going to a fair. Now at that time, anyone who had money used to hide it in the earth, fearing it might be stolen from him. There were lots of thieves in those days. (Indeed, we have some, even today.) When the farmer was getting ready to leave, he went to the hiding place to get some of his money. Weren't the thieves watching him taking it! He went off to the fair, and when he returned home, the leipreachan laughed. The farmer jumped up and took the leipreachan out of the trunk.

"That's the third time you have laughed since I caught you," said he. "What made you laugh each time?"

"There are many things which a person would be better off for not knowing," said the leipreachan.

"Enough of that coaxing talk," said the farmer. "Tell me why you laughed."

"Well," said the leipreachan, "you remember the day you found the balk of timber at the edge of the sea?"

"I do," said the farmer.

"That balk was full of money, and the man to whom you sold it has been rich ever since."

"That's true enough," said the farmer. "Now, tell me why you laughed the second time."

"Ah, let me go," said the leipreachan.

"I won't until you tell me," said the farmer.

"Well," said the leipreachan, "you remember the day a poor man came in and you invited him to eat something, and he refused? When he turned down the food, he turned down his luck, and he hadn't gone far when he broke his leg. Had he waited for a bite of food, the danger would be over."

"Tell me now about your third laugh."

"I won't. Better for you not to know," said the leipreachan.

They started to argue, and finally the farmer took hold of the leipreachan's head and told him that he'd sweep it off unless he told him why he laughed the last time.

"Very well," said the leipreachan. "When you were getting ready for the fair, you went to the hiding place in the field to get some money. You took some of it with you. But there was a thief watching you, and when you had gone off to the fair, he went to the place and stole the rest of it."

The farmer jumped up, and out he ran to search for his money. He went around like a madman from one place to another. If he didn't know that it had been stolen, he mightn't have lost his reason.

When Crofton Croker, first of the Irish fairy-tale collectors, told his friend Thomas Keightley what he was about, it gave Keightley a grand idea.

What the brothers Grimm had just done for Germany, what Walter Scott was accomplishing in Scotland and Croker in Ireland, he would do—for the world!

Keightley was an Irish barrister who had moved to London for his health. Like any Victorian gentleman with a notion, he managed to work it up into a thoroughgoing obsession, and taught himself numerous obscure languages in his pursuit of fairy lore from all places and times.

In 1828 he published The Fairy Mythology, *an amazing potpourri of anecdotes, reflections, classical tags, verse translations, speculations, and tales . . . all this thirty years before Bullfinch's* Age of Fable, *and sixty years before Frazier's* Golden Bough!

Although Keightley wrote of Little People from ancient Persia to Iceland, he did not neglect those of his native land, as in this tale "which we ourselves heard from the peasantry of Kildare in our boyhood."

THE LEPRECHAUN IN THE GARDEN

There's a sort o' people that every body must have met wid sumtime or another. I mane thim people that purtinds not to b'lieve in things that in their hearts they *do* b'lieve in, an' are mortially afeard o' too. Now Failey Mooney was one o' these. Failey (iv any o' yez knew him) was a rollockin', rattlin', divil-may-care sort ov chap like—but that's neither here nor there; he was always talkin' one nonsinse or another; an' among the rest o' his fooleries, he purtinded not to b'lieve in the fairies, the Leprechauns, an' the Poocas, an' he evin sumtimes had the impedince to purtind to doubt o' ghosts, that every body b'lieves in, at any rate. Yit sum people used to wink an' luk knowin' whin Failey was gostherin', fur it was obsarved that he was mighty shy o' crassin' the foord o' Ahnamoe afther nightfall; an' that whin onst he was ridin' past the ould church o' Tipper in the dark, tho' he'd not enough o' pottheen into him to make any man stout, he med the horse trot so that there was no keepin' up wid him, an' iv'ry now an' thin he'd throw a sharp luk-out ovir his lift shouldher.

317

Well, one night there was a parcel o' the neighbours sittin' dhrinkin' an' talkin' at Larry Reilly's public-house, an' Failey was one o' that party. He was, as usual, gittin' an wid his nonsince an' baldherdash about the fairies, an' swearin' that he didn't b'lieve there was any live things barrin' min an' bastes, an' birds and fishes, an' sich like things as a body cud see, an' he wint on talkin' in so profane a way o' the good people, that som o' the company grew timid an' begun to crass thimsilves, not knowin' what might happin', whin an ould woman called Mary Hogan wid a long blue cloak about her, that was sittin' in the chimbly corner smokin' her pipe widout takin' the laste share in the conversation, tuk the pipe out o' her mouth, an' threw the ashes out o' it, an' spit in the fire, an' turnin' round, luked Failey straight in the face. "An' so you don't b'lieve there's sich things as Leprechauns, don't ye?" sed she.

Well, Failey luked rayther daunted, but howsumdivir he sed nothin'. "Why, thin, upon my throth, an' it well becomes the likes o' ye, an' that's nothin' but a bit uv a gossoon, to take upon yer to purtind not to b'lieve what yer father, an' yer father's father, an' his father afore him, nivir med the laste doubt uv. But to make the matther short, seein' 's b'lievin' they say, an' I, that might be yer gran'mother, tell ye there is sich things as Leprechauns, an' what's more, that I mysilf seen one o' thim—there's fur ye, now!"

All the people in the room luked quite surprised at this, an' crowded up to the fireplace to listen to her. Failey thried to laugh, but it wouldn't do, nobody minded him.

"I remimber," sed she, "some time afther I married the honest man, that's now dead and gone, it was by the same token jist a little afore I lay in o' my first child (an' that's many a long day ago), I was sittin', as I sed, out in our little bit o' a gardin, wid my knittin' in my hand, watchin' sum bees we had that war goin' to swarm. It was a fine sunshiny day about the middle o' June, an' the bees war hummin' and flyin' backwards an' forwards frum the hives, an' the birds war chirpin' an' hoppin' an the bushes, an' the buttherflies war flyin' about an' sittin' an the flowers; an' ev'ry thing smelt so fresh an' so sweet, an' I felt so happy, that I hardly knew whare I was. Well, all uv a suddint, I heard among sum rows of banes we had in a corner o' the gardin, a n'ise that wint tick tack, tick tack, jist fur all the world as iv a brogue-maker was puttin' an the heel uv a pump. 'The Lord presarve us," sed I to

318

mysilf, 'what in the world can that be?' So I laid down my knittin', an' got up, an' stole ovir to the banes, an' nivir believe me iv I didn't see, sittin' right forenint me, in the very middle of thim, a bit of an ould man, not a quarther so big as a newborn chid, wid a little cocked hat an his head, an' a dudeen in his mouth, smokin' away; an' a plain, ould-fashioned, dhrab-coloured coat, wid big brass buttons upon it, an his back, an' a pair o' massy silver buckles in his shoes, that a 'most covered his feet they war so big, an' he workin' away as hard as ivir he could, heelin' a little pair o' pumps. The instant minnit I clapt my two eyes upon him I knew him to be a Leprechaun, an' as I was stout an' fool-hardy, sez I to him, 'God save ye honist man! that's hard work ye're at this hot day.' He luked up in my face quite vexed like; so wid that I med a run at him an' cotch hould o' him in my hand, an' axed him whare was his purse o' money! 'Money?' sed he, 'money annagh! an' whare on airth id a poor little ould crathur like mysilf git money?' 'Come, come,' sed I, 'none o' yer thricks upon thravellers; doesn't every body know that Leprechauns, like ye, are all as rich as the divil him-silf." So I pulled out a knife I'd in my pocket, an' put on as wicked a face as ivir I could (an' in throth, that was no aisy matther fur me thin, fur I was as comely an' good-humoured a lukin' girl as you'd see frum this to Ballitore)—an' swore by this and by that if he didn't instantly gi' me his purse, or show me a pot o' goold, I'd cut the nose aff his face. Well, to be shure, the little man did luk so frightened at hearin' these words, that I a'most found it in my heart to pity the poor little crathur. 'Thin,' sed he, 'Come wid me jist a couple o' fields aff, an' I'll show ye whare I keep my money.' So I wint, still houldin' him fast in my hand, an' keepin' my eyes fixed upon him, whin all o' a suddint I h'ard a whiz-z behind me. 'There! there!' cries he, 'there's yer bees all swarmin' an' goin' aff wid thimsilves like blazes.' I, like a fool as I was, turned my head round, an' whin I seen nothin' at all, an' luked back at the Lepre-chaun, an' found nothin' at all in my hand—fur whin I had the ill luck to take my eyes off him, ye see, he slipped out o' my fingers jist as iv he was med o' fog or smoke, an' the sarra the fut he ive come nigh my garden agin."

The alphabet we use is simply not up to the task of capturing the sound of spoken Irish. (Which accounts for the apparently lunatic spellings of Irish names and places. Ask anyone christened Sean why it's pronounced that way.)

But then, our poor twenty-six letters can't even represent the sound of an Irishman speaking English, and any writer attempting to transcribe Irish dialogue might well despair.

George Bernard Shaw, a Dubliner, left his considerable fortune for research on "a proposed British Alphabet," based on phonetics, to solve the problem.

Old stories written in "brogue" are today slightly embarrassing to the Irish, in the way that Uncle Remus *tales are to the blacks of America. There is something patronizing about them.*

"Barney Noonan and the Little People" is taken from D.R. McAnally's Irish Wonders, *published in 1887. It's a little bit like that somewhat later Irish tall tale,* Finnegans Wake—*you have to read it aloud, to make any sense of it, at all.*

BARNEY NOONAN AND THE LITTLE PEOPLE

" "There was sorraa betther boy in the country than Barney Noonan. He'd work as reg'lar as a pump, an' liked a bit av divarshun as well as annybody when he'd time for it, that wasn't aften, to be sure, but small blame to him, for he wasn't rich be no manner o' manes. He'd a power av ragard av the good people an' when he wint be the rath beyant his field, he'd pull off his caubeen an' take the dudheen out av his mouth, as p'lite as a dancin' masther, an' say, 'God save ye, ladies an' gintlemen,' that the good people always heard though they niver showed thimselves to him. He'd a bit o' bog, that the hay was on, an' afther cuttin' it, he left it for to dhry, an' the sun come out beautiful an' in a day or so the hay was as dhry as powdher an' ready to put away.

"So Barney was goin' to put it up, but, it bein' the day av the fair, he thought he'd take the calf an' sell it, an' so he did, an' comin' up wid the boys, he stayed over his time, bein' hindhered wid dhrinkin' an' dancin' an' palaverin' at the gurls, so it was afther dark when he got home an' the night as black as a crow, the clouds gatherin' on the tops av the mountains like avil sper'ts an' crapin' down into the glens like

disthroyin' angels, an' the wind howlin' like tin thousand Banshees, but
Barney didn't mind it all wan copper, being' glorified wid the dhrink
he'd had. So the hay niver enthered the head av him, but in he wint an'
tumbled in bed an' was shnorin' like a horse in two minnits, for he was
a bach'ler, God bless him, an' had no wife to gosther him an' ax him
where he'd been, an' phat he'd been at, an' make him tell a hundred
lies about not gettin' home afore. So it came on to thunder an' lighten
like as all the avil daymons in the univarse were fightin' wid cannons in
the shky, an' by an' by there was a clap loud enough to shplit yer skull
an' Barney woke up.

" 'Tattheration to me,' says he to himself, 'it's goin' for to rain an'
me hay on the ground. Phat'll I do?' says he.

"So he rowled over on the bed an' looked out av a crack for to see
if it was ralely rainin'. An' there was the biggest crowd he iver seen av
little men an' wimmin. They'd built a row o' fires from the cow-house
to the bog an' were comin' in a shtring like the cows goin' home, aitch
wan wid his two arrums full o' hay. Some were in the cow-house, resay-
vin' the hay; some were in the field, rakin' the hay together; an' some
were shtandin' wid their hands in their pockets beways they were the
bosses, tellin' the rest for to make haste. An' so they did, for every wan
run like he was afther goin' for the docther, an' brought a load an'
hurried back for more.

"Barney looked through the crack at thim a crossin' himself ivery
minnit wid admiration for the shpeed they had. 'God be good to me,'
says he to himself, 'i' is not ivery gossoon in Leitrim that's got haymak-
ers like thim,' only he never spake a word out loud, for he knewn very
well the good people 'udn't like it. So they brought in all the hay an' put
it in the house an' thin let the fires go out an' made another big fire in
front o' the dure, an' begun to dance round it wid the swatest music
Barney iver heard.

"Now be this time he'd got up an' feelin' aisey in his mind about
the hay, begun to be very merry. He looked on through the dure at
thim dancin', an' by an' by they brought out a jug wid little tumblers
and begun to drink summat that they poured out o' the jug. If Barney
had the sense av a herrin', he'd a kept shtill an' let thim dhrink their fill
widout openin' the big mouth av him, bein' that he was as full as a
goose himself an' naded no more; but when he seen the jug an' the
tumblers an' the fairies drinkin' away wid all their mights, he got mad

an' bellered out like a bull, 'Arra-a-a-h now, ye little attomies, is it dhrinkin' ye are, an' never givin' a sup to a thirsty mortial that always thrates yez as well as he knows how,' and immejitly the fairies, an' the fire, an' the jug all wint out av his sight, an' he to bed agin in a timper. While he was layin' there, he thought he heard talkin' an' a cugger-mugger goin' on, but when he peeped out agin, sorra a thing did he see but the black night an' the rain comin' down an' aitch dhrop the full av a wather-noggin. So he wint to slape, continted that the hay was in, but not plazed that the good people 'ud be pigs entirely, to be afther dhrinkin' undher his eyes an' not offer him a taste, no, not so much as a shmell at the jug.

"In the mornin' up he gets an' out for to look at the hay an' see if the fairies put it in right, for he says, 'It's a job they're not used to.' So he looked in the cow-house an' thought the eyes 'ud lave him when there wasn't a shtraw in the house at all. 'Holy Moses,' says he, 'phat have they done wid it?' an' he couldn't consave phat had gone wid the hay. So he looked in the field an' it was all there; bad luck to the bit av it had the fairies left in the house at all, but when he shouted at thim, they got tarin' mad an' took all the hay back agin to the bog, puttin' every shtraw where Barney laid it, an' it was as wet as a drownded cat. But it was a lesson to him he niver forgot, an' I go bail that the next time the fairies help him in wid his hay he'll kape shtill an' let thim dhrink thimselves to death if they plaze widout sayin' a word."

Here, from Crofton Croker's original collection of Irish folktales, is the archetypal leprechaun story, little man in a cocked hat, trickery, treasures, and all. (A Cluricaune is a leprechaun from Cork, a little more inclined to the drink than his fellows elsewhere—but a leprechaun, all the same.)

"The Danes," whose gold the Little People of Ireland are believed to guard, are the Vikings, who raided and pillaged Ireland on a regular and ferocious schedule from the year 795 until their defeat by King Brian Boru at Clontarf (near Dublin) in 1014.

It is a tradition in both Ireland and Scotland that "the Danes" had a recipe for making beer from heather—the Cluricaune of our story claims to know the secret—and that they left buried treasure behind them.

And indeed, the bogs yield up, from time to time, marvelous artifacts of beaten gold, including, in one case, a marvelously wrought scale-model Viking warship.

THE FIELD OF BOLIAUNS

Tom Fitzpatrick was the eldest son of a comfortable farmer who lived at Ballincollig. Tom was just turned of nine-and-twenty when he met the following adventure, and was as clever, clean, tight, good-looking a boy as any in the whole county Cork. One fine day in harvest—it was indeed Lady-day in harvest, that everybody knows to be one of the greatest holidays in the year—Tom was taking a ramble through the ground, and went sauntering along the sunny side of a hedge, thinking in himself, where would be the great harm if people, instead of idling and going about doing nothing at all, were to shake out the hay, and bind and stook the oats that were lying on the ledge, especially as the weather had been rather broken of late, when all of a sudden he heard a clacking sort of noise a little before him, in the hedge. "Dear me," said Tom, "but isn't it now really surprising to hear the stonechatters singing so late in the season?" So Tom stole on, going on the tops of his toes to try if he could get a sight of what was making the noise, to see if he was right in his guess. The noise stopped; but as Tom looked sharply through the bushes what should he see in a nook of the hedge but a brown pitcher, that might hold about a gallon and a

324

half of liquor; and by-and-by a little wee diny dony bit of an old man, with a little *motty* of a cocked hat stuck upon the top of his head, a deeshy daushy leather apron hanging before him, pulled out a little wooden stool, and stood up upon it, and dipped a little piggin into the pitcher, and took out the full of it, and put it beside the stool, and then sat down under the pitcher, and begin to work at putting a heel-piece on a bit of a brogue just fitting for himself. "Well, by the powers," said Tom to himself, "I often heard tell of the Cluricaune; and, to tell God's truth, I never rightly believed in them—but here's one of them in real earnest. If I go knowingly to work, I'm a made man. They say a body must never take their eyes off them, or they'll escape."

Tom now stole on a little further, with his eye fixed on the little man just as a cat does with a mouse, or, as we read in books, the rattle-snake does with the birds he wants to enchant. So when he got up quite close to him, "God bless your work, neighbour," said Tom.

The little man raised up his head, and "Thank you kindly," said he.

"I wonder you'd be working on the holiday?" said Tom.

"That's my own business, not yours," was the reply.

"Well, may be you'd be civil enough to tell us what you've got in the pitcher there?" said Tom.

"That I will, with pleasure," said he; "it's good beer."

"Beer!" said Tom. "Thunder and fire! where did you get it?"

"Where did I get it, is it? Why, I made it. And what do you think I made it of?"

"Devil a one of me knows," said Tom, "but of malt, I suppose; what else?"

" 'Tis there you're out. I made it of *heath*."

"Of heath!" said Tom, bursting out laughing; "sure you don't think me to be such a fool as to believe that?"

"Do as you please," said he, "but what I tell you is the truth. Did you ever hear tell of the Danes?"

"And that I did," said Tom; "weren't them the fellows we gave such a licking when they thought to take Limerick from us?"

"Hem!" said the little man, drily, "is that all you know about the matter?"

"Well, but about them Danes?" said Tom.

"Why all the about them there is, is that when they were here they taught us to make beer out of the heath, and the secret's in my family ever since."

"Will you give a body a taste of your beer?" said Tom.

"I'll tell you what it is, young man, it would be fitter for you to be looking after your father's property than to be bothering decent quiet people with your foolish questions. There now, while you're idling away your time here, there's the cows have broke into the oats, and are knocking the corn all about."

Tom was taken so by surprise with this that he was just on the very point of turning round when he recollected himself; so, afraid that the like might happen again, he made a grab at the Cluricaune, and caught him up in his hand; but in his hurry he overset the pitcher, and spilt all the beer, so that he could not get a taste of it to tell what sort it was. He then swore what he would not do to him if he did not show him where his money was. Tom looked so wicked and so bloodyminded that the little man was quite frightened; so, says he, "Come along with me a couple of fields off, and I'll show you a crock of gold."

So they went, and Tom held the Cluricaune fast in his hand, and never took his eyes from off him, though they had to cross hedges and ditches, and crooked bit of bog (for the Cluricaune seemed, out of pure mischief, to pick out the hardest and most contrary way), till at last they came to a great field all full of boliaun buies (rag-weed), and the Cluricaune pointed to a big boliaun, and says he, "Dig under that boliaun, and you'll get the great crock all full of guineas."

Tom in his hurry had never minded the bringing a spade with him, so he thought to run home and fetch one; and that he might know the place again he took off one of his red garters, and tied it round the boliaun.

"I suppose," said the Cluricaune very civilly, "you have no further occasion for me?"

"No," says Tom; "you may go away now, if you please, and God speed you, and may good luck attend you wherever you go."

"Well, good-bye to you, Tom Fitzpatrick," said the Cluricaune, "and much good may it do you, with what you'll get."

So Tom ran, for the dear life, till he came home and got a spade, and then away with him, as hard as he could go, back to the field of boliauns; but when he got there, lo, and behold! not a boliaun in the field but had a red garter, the very identical model of his own, tied about it; and as to digging up the whole field, that was all nonsense, for there was more than forty good Irish acres in it. So Tom came home again with his spade on his shoulder, a little cooler than he went; and many's the hearty curse he gave the Cluricaune every time he thought of the neat turn he had served him.

VI. THE LIVING TRADITION

The Living Tradition

Cast your mind on other days
That we in coming days may be
Still the indomitable Irishry.

W. B. Yeats
"Under Ben Bulben"

Ireland is a civilized country now, with television and inflation. The storytellers appear on the television and are probably underpaid, what with the inflation.

Sir William Wilde was assured, before the end of the last century (by one Darby Doolin) that "what betune them national boords and Godless Colleges and other sorts of larnin' . . . sarra wan of the Gintry (cross about us!) will be found in the country . . . in no time." So much for the leprechauns.

When the old songs and dances are performed, it is usually as a show for the ticket-buying tourists.

New tales, or variations on old ones, are gathered like rare wild flowers by scholars and filed away in libraries and journals in Dublin, or Germany.

And the chances are that if you were to ask a contemporary Irishman for an old tale, he'd treat you to the same look you'd get from an Apache from whom you requested a rain dance. (The further away—in miles and generations—from Ireland, the less true this is. Especially on St. Patrick's Day.)

But in truth, not even the most up-to-date forward-thinking Irish person can resist "the backward look." The Past is alive and well in Ireland: the historical Past—of old glories and old wrongs—and the better, older Past—of High Deeds and heroes, of the hosting of the Sidhe, and Giants and Little People, and useful curses and tales by the fireside, when the world was new.

And the memory of those myths and the telling of those tales are yet (despite the dairy products, woolens, and light machinery) Ireland's leading export—and her lasting glory.

This story, collected by Douglas Hyde for his Legends of Saints and Sinners, *concerns the origin of the Cross of Cong, an important symbol of faith and nationhood.*

In much the same spirit that the Druids had set standing stones by the roadside, the early Christians of Ireland set crosses, symbols of the new faith, but of a peculiarly Celtic design: there is a circle around the intersection of the two cross beams.

The Cross of Cong was fashioned in 1123. It is of oak, plated with copper, and ornamented with gold filagree. It was originally commissioned to house a relic of the "true Cross" . . . a lingering example of the famous gold-working and enameling skilles of the ancient Celts.

It was long lost and discovered (stored away in a trunk) only in the last century, and is now proudly exhibited at the national Museum in Dublin.

The "Dove's Hole" mentioned in the tale remains a tourist attraction in Cong, County Mayo. But of the Stone of Truth there is, alas, no trace—or, maybe, it's just as well. . . .

THE STONE OF TRUTH OR THE MERCHANT OF THE SEVEN BAGS

There was a man in it, hundreds and hundreds of years ago, whose name was Paidin O Kerwin and he was living close to Cong in West Connacht. Paidin was a strange man; he did not believe in God or in anything about him. It's often the priest thought to bring him to Mass, but it was no use for him, for Paidin would not take the advice of priest or bishop. He believed that man was like the beast, and he believed that when man died there was no more about him.

Paidin lived an evil life; he used to be going from house to house by day, and stealing in the night.

Now, at the time that St. Patrick was in West Connacht seeking to make Christians of the Pagans, he went down one day upon his knees, on a great flag stone, to utter prayers, and he left after him a great virtue in the same stone, for anybody who might speak above that stone, it was necessary for him to tell the clear truth, he could not tell a lie, and for that reason the people gave the name to that flag of the Stone of Truth.

Paidin used always to have a great fear of this stone, and it's often he intended to steal it. One night when he found an opportunity he hoisted the stone on his back, took it away with him, and threw it down into a great valley between two hills, seven miles from the place where it used to be, and the rogue thought that he was all right; but the stone was back in its old place that same night without his knowing.

Another night after that he stole the geese of the parish priest, and as the people doubted him, they said that they would bring him to the Stone of Truth. Paidin was laughing in his own mind, for he knew that he had the stone stolen; but great was the surprise that was on him when he saw the stone before him in its own place. When he was put above the stone he was obliged to tell that he had stolen the geese, and he got a great beating from the priest. He made a firm resolution then that if he got an opportunity at the stone again, he would put it in a place that it would never come out of.

A couple of nights after that he got his opportunity again, and stole the stone a second time. He threw it down into a great deep hole, and he went home rejoicing in himself. But he did not go a quarter of a mile from the place until he heard a great noise coming after him. He looked behind him and he saw a lot of little people, and they dressed in clothes as white as snow. There came such fear over Paidin that he was not able to walk one step, until the little people came up with him, and they carrying the Stone of Truth with them. A man of them spoke to him and said: "O accursed Paidin, carry this stone back to the place where you got it, or you shall pay dearly for it."

"I will and welcome," said Paidin.

They put the stone upon his back and they returned the road on which they had come. But as the devil was putting temptation upon Paidin, he went and threw the stone into a hole that was deeper than the first hole, a hole which the people made to go hiding in when the war would be coming. The stone remained in that hole for more than seven years, and no one knew where it was but Paidin only.

At the end of that time Paidin was going by the side of the church-yard, when he looked up at a cross that was standing there, and he fell into a faint. When he came to himself, there was a man before him and he clothed as white as the snow. He spoke to him and said: 'O accursed Paidin, you are guilty of the seven deadly sins, and unless you do penance you shall go to hell. I am an angel from God, and I will put a penance on you. I will put seven bags upon you and you must carry them for one and twenty years. After that time go before the great cross that shall be in the town of Cong, and say three times, 'My soul to God and Mary,' spend a pious life until then, and you will go to heaven. Go to the priest now, if you are obedient (and ready) to receive my counsel."

"I am obedient," said Paidin, "but the people will be making a mock of me."

"Never mind the mock, it won't last long," said the angel.

After this conversation a deep sleep fell upon Paidin, and when he awoke there were seven bags upon him, and the angel was gone away. There were two bags on his right side, two bags on his left side, and three others on his back, and they were stuck so fast upon him that he thought that it was growing on him they were. They were the colour of his own skin, and there was skin on them. Next day when Paidin went among the people he put wonder on them, and they called him the Merchant of the Seven Bags, and that name stuck to him until he died.

Paidin began a new life now. He went to the priest, and he showed him the seven bags that were on him, and he told him the reason that they were put on him. The priest gave him good advice and a great coat to cover the seven bags with; and after that Paidin used to be going from house to house and from village to village asking alms, and there used never be a Sunday or holiday that he would not be at Mass, and there used to be a welcome before him in every place.

About seven years after that Paidin was going by the side of the hole into which he had thrown the Stone of Truth. He came to the brink of the hole, went down on his two knees and asked God to send him up the stone. When his prayer was ended he saw the stone coming up, and hundreds of white doves round about it. The stone was rising and ever rising until it came into Paidin's presence on the ground, and then the doves went back again. The next day he went to the priest and told him everything about the Stone of Truth, and the way it came up out of the hole. "I will go with you," said the priest, "until I see this great wonder." The priest went with him to the hole and he saw the Stone of Truth. And he saw another thing which put great wonder on him; thousands and thousands of doves flying round about the mouth of the hole, going down into it and coming up again. The priest called the place Poll na gColum or the Doves' Hole, and that name is on it until the present day. The blessed stone was brought into Cong, and it was not long until a grand cross was erected over it, and from that day to this people come from every place to look at the Doves' Hole and the old people believed that they were St. Patrick's angels who were in those doves.

The Stone of Truth was for years after that in Cong, and it is certain that it did great good, for it kept many people from committing crimes. But it was stolen at last, and there is no account of it from that out.

Paidin lived until he was four score years of age, and bore his share of penance piously. When the one and twenty years that the angel gave him were finished, and he carrying the seven bags throughout that time, there came a messenger in a dream to say to him that his life in this world was finished, and that he must go the next day before the Cross of Cong and give himself up to God and Mary. Early in the morning he went to the preist and told him the summons he had got in the night. People say that the priest did not believe him, but at all events he told Paidin to do as the mesenger had bidden him.

Paidin departed, and left his blessing with his neighbours and relations, and when the clock was striking twelve, and the people saying the Angelical Salutation, Paidin came before the cross and said three times, "My soul to God and to Mary," and on the spot he fell dead.

That cross was in the town of Cong for years. A bishop, one of the O'Duffy's, went to Rome, and he got a bit of the true Cross and put it into the Cross of Cong. It was there until the foreigners came and threw it to the ground. The Cross of Cong is still in Ireland, and the people have an idea that it will yet be raised up in the town of Cong with the help of God.

The Pot of Broth, *a one-act comedy on which Yeats and Lady Gregory collaborated, has been a popular "curtain-raiser" at the Abbey Theater since 1902.*

The aristocratic founders of Ireland's National Theater were resolved to preserve and give new life to all the folk traditions of their homeland, and liked to present a double bill, in which a peasant joke would precede a mythical, mysterious tragedy. The Pot of Broth *often was the opener for such famous plays as* Cathleen ni Houlihan *or* Deirdre.

Despite being adopted by the gentry, the tale itself remained popular with the common people. As a lad in County Limerick, Kevin Danaher heard the story told by Old Dick Denihan in the 1930s. . . .

THE SOUP STONE

There was a poor travelling man going the roads, and it is often he was cold and hungry. Well, one day he was saying to himself that a drink of hot soup would do him all the good in the world, and he knew a farmer's house where the woman was kind of soft, and he made up his mind to try his luck there. Down with him to the brink of the river and he picked up a nice round stone about the size of an apple, and in with him to the farmer's house, and asked the woman would she give him a pan and a small drop of clean warm water, and so she did. And he was washing and cleaning the stone until he had it shining.

'You have great washing of the stone, my poor man,' says she.

'And why not I, ma'am, and it a soup stone,' says he.

'Is it how you could make soup of it?' says she.

'It is, indeed, and the best of soup,' says he.

'Glory be to God, and could anyone do it?' says she.

'Not a sign of bother on them to do it, but to watch the one that knows how to make it,' says he.

'Why then, I'd be greatly obliged to you,' says she, 'and there is the pot and there is the fire, and plenty water.'

He put down about half a gallon of water in the pot, and the stone inside in it. And the two of them were watching it.

'A shake of salt and pepper would do it no harm,' says he. She gave him the pepper and the salt. After a while, and the water began to boil:

336

'It isn't thickening so well,' says he, 'a shake of flour would do it no harm.' She put a good handful of white flour in the pot. 'And that bone of a leg of mutton that you're going to throw to the dogs,' says he, 'would do it no harm at all, but great good, maybe.' She had no notion of throwing it to the dogs, and plenty meat on it, but she wouldn't give it to say that she was keeping it for her husband's supper, and down it went into the pot. 'There will be great strength in it now,' says he, 'but a few potatoes would do it no harm.' It was herself that peeled half a dozen of the potatoes, and down with them. It was boiling up now, and getting fine and thick. 'Do you know what,' says he, 'I'm thinking that a couple of them fine big onions would put a finish on it.' No sooner said than done, and the soup boiled away for half an hour or so. ''Tis ready now,' says she, getting two piggins and filling out the soup into them, about a quart in each. I tell you it went down sweetly. 'That is a fine soup,' says she, 'and I'm much obliged to you for showing me how to make it.' 'What did I tell you?' says he, 'but that you could make the finest of soup out of a soup stone?' He rested himself for a while, and had a smoke of her husband's tobacco. And off he went. And the foolish woman never stopped boasting of how she could make soup out of a stone, and all the neighbours laughing behind their hand at her. But I'd say it was a long time before the travelling man came around that part of the country again.

The national sport of Ireland is hurling, a game that looks, to the outsider, like a combination of field hockey and a gang war.

The heroes of myth and legend, such as Cuchulain and Finn McCool, performed prodigious feats on the hurling field, and as boys with the curved sticks in their hands learned the fierce swordsmanship that would make them great warriors in their prime.

As it is now played, there are fifteen players to a team, and actual manslaughter is discouraged. But originally, contests were between towns or clans or "factions," with as many men to a side as that side could muster, and anything (except throwing the ball or carrying it in the hand) went.

This tale of an international, supernatural hurling match was gathered by Liam Mac Coisdeala, in 1935, in Galway, but appears to concern the time of the potato famine.

THE FAIRY HURLING MATCH

There was a great strapping young man, a married man, a farmer, lived over east of the lake some time ago, when the times were even harder than these times. Sean Walsh was his name, and month after month the poor man hadn't the money to pay the rent for his house and fields, until one day Blake, the landlord, came round to take away all his cattle, and left him there with only one lean little beast.

And that very night, a fog came up, and the animal didn't come home. Sean's wife told him to go out, and look for it on the mountains.

"I won't," said he. "That's the end of our cattle, and the end of us."

Whatever his wife's answer was to that, it wasn't long before Sean was out searching the mountainside. He hadn't walked far when he saw, coming toward him through the fog, the finest man he'd ever seen.

"God to you," said the stranger.

"God and Mary to you," said Sean.

Then the stranger said, "I've come to you, Sean Walsh, for I need your help this night."

"I can't give it just now," said Sean. "I'm looking for an animal of mine that's missing."

"That beast is safe and at home," said the stranger, as if there were no doubt of that fact. "Now come along with me."

They walked on a fair bit.

"Don't you know who I am?" asked the stranger. "I'm chief of the fairy host of Connacht. Ourselves will be playing a hurling game against the fairy host of Scotland this night, and if the Scots win it, they'll take away with them all the harvest of Ireland, but if we win, we'll keep it."

"I'm with you," said Sean.

"Good man," said the fairy. "I've picked yourself out of all the hurlers of Ireland for this game. The Scots have a good strong hurler to help them, a one-eyed blacksmith who's strong as a bull. If that one knocks you down, you're a dead man, I tell you."

Sean Walsh and the fairy chief came down into a glen as the fog was lifting, and by moonlight and starlight they saw the two teams gathered. The Irish fairies wore green caps, of course, and the Scots wore red.

Then the stranger handed Sean a stout ash hurley and a cap of green and sent him running out on the field, just as the ball was thrown in the air for the game to begin.

Right away, Sean swung his hurley and hit the one-eyed Scot a terrific clout over the ear. The man went down. Sean raised the ball on the blade of his stick and ran down field, knocking down the fairies of Scotland as he went. They scattered like chickens in front of a fox. The havoc he caused was terrible, I tell you.

After the Irish fairy host had won the game, the fairy chief of Connacht said to Sean, "It's grand work you've done this night. Now, here's a stallion for you. Catch him by the mane, and hold him until he whinnies three times, and looks as if he had it in his mind to eat you. Let him loose then, and see what happens.

Sean was afraid, but he held onto the stallion's mane till the great beast whinnied three times, and then let him go free. Now, the fairy host of Scotland had a stallion of their own, and the two animals attacked each other, screaming and kicking and biting. It was fearful to watch them at it, until the Irish stallion killed the other.

Then the chief of the Connacht fairies came up to Sean once more, and handed him a scythe. "Take this now," he said, "and wield it as hard as ever you can, against the wind."

Sean took hold of the scythe, and drew it hard against the east wind, which blew stronger and then again stronger on his face. He planted his feet and swung the blade, sweeping it against that howling wind, and the sweat was running down his body, though the night was cold, until the wind was still.

The fairy host of Ireland raised a great cheer, and the chief of Connacht came to Sean again. "Great work, Sean Walsh!" he said to him. "You've won the day! Oh man, if only you could see the work you've done here!"

"What I've done is small use to me if I can't see it," said Sean.

Then the fairy pulled a wisp of long grass, and braided it and wound it into a ring. "Put that to your eye," he said. "Look through it, and see all you've done."

Sean put it against his eye and looked. The heights of the mountains and the deep of the glen were scattered and heaped and speckled with the people he'd killed.

"Take the ring from your eye now, or you'll be rooted in this place forever, on account of the many you've killed," said the fairy. "Now, here's a letter for you. Take it back to Blake the landlord, and tell him you got it from me."

Well, then.

Sean took the letter and walked away, and he never looked back till he came to Blake's big house. It was a servant that answered the door, and he said he'd take the letter in to Blake. It wasn't long before he came back, and led Sean into the landlord.

"Where did you get this letter?" said Blake.

"From the finest man I ever laid eyes on."

"It looks very like the writing of a son of mine," said Blake. "But my son died long years ago."

"That man is your son, right enough," said Sean, and he told the landlord how his son was now chief of the fairy host of Connacht.

The letter told Blake to let Sean have his cows back, and his piece of land rent-free for evermore. And he did that.

And they say that when Sean Walsh died, a long time after all that, you could hear the fairy host shouting for him in the air for a mile around Galway that night.

And that's a true story, I tell you!

341

In the middle of the seventeenth century, a sudden, savage uprising by the Irish against their English rulers was even more savagely put down by the invading armies of Oliver Cromwell. After Cromwell's victories, and under his rule, Ireland first became a conquered province, a colony of natives without human rights—without, in fact, humanity. Cromwell distributed the land he took from the defeated Catholic landowners in rebellious Ulster to his Puritan followers; the Ulster nobility was offered the choice of "hell or Connaught," which is to say, they could move south, or die.

After three hundred years, Cromwell's name is still hated and feared in Catholic Ireland. It is actually invoked by mothers of rambunctious infants as a synonym for devil *or* bogeyman.

Here is a recent story of the wicked Cromwell, recorded in Galway and published in O'Sullivan's The Folklore of Ireland.

CROMWELL AND O'DONNELL

The hatred which Cromwell's ruthless deeds in Ireland in 1649–50 aroused in the hearts of the Irish people is reflected in this and other tales from oral tradition. The prophet (sometimes named Mac Amhlaoimh), who foretells the future for Cromwell and others, figures in other versions of this tale also. Some versions tell that Cromwell died in Ireland, that the Irish soil refused to receive his body, and that it drifted on the sea until it finally sank to the bottom of the Irish Sea, causing it to be very rough ever since!

There was a man here in Ireland long ago. He was a gentleman by the name of O'Donnell and he was very friendly with a monk in the district. One day the monk told him that there was a great change to come over Ireland; that England would take over Ireland, and that a leader of the name of Cromwell would be throwing the Irish people, who had land, out on the road and would be settling his own people from England in their place.

"The best plan for you," said the monk to O'Donnell, "is to go off over to England. The man they call Cromwell is a cobbler. You must travel around England, with a notebook, and ask every man you meet to sign his name in the book, promising that he won't ever take your land or dwelling-place off you. Keep on travelling like that until you go to where Cromwell is living."

That was that! O'Donnell crossed over to England and he was travelling around with his book, pretending to be a bit simple, asking everyone he met to sign his book that he would never take his land or dwelling-place off him. He kept going till he came to Cromwell's house. He went in and asked Cromwell to put a side-patch on one of his shoes. When the job was done, he handed a guinea to Cromwell.

"A thousand thanks to you! That's good payment," said Cromwell.

"Now," said O'Donnell, "I hope that you will sign this book that you will never take my land or dwelling-place off me."

"Why wouldn't I promise you that?" said Cromwell.

He took hold of the book and signed in it that he would never take his land or dwelling-place off O'Donnell in Ireland. When he had done that, O'Donnell went back to Ireland.

Some years later, there was a great change in England. Cromwell rose up high and took the power from the king. Then he came to Ireland. He was throwing the people out of their land, whether they were noble or lowly, and killing them. He arrived at O'Donnell's house and struck a blow on the door.

"Out with you from here!" he shouted. "You're here long enough!"

"I hope you won't put me out until you and myself have dinner together," said O'Donnell.

"What sort of dinner have you?" asked Cromwell.

"Roast duck," said O'Donnell.

"That's very good," said Cromwell. "I like that."

Cromwell went into the house and the two of them started eating the dinner. When they had eaten, O'Donnell took out his book and showed it to Cromwell.

"Do you recognize that writing?" said O'Donnell.

"I do, 'tis mine," said Cromwell. "How did you know that I'd be coming to Ireland or that I'd rise so high?"

It was no use for O'Donnell to hide it; he had to tell the truth to Cromwell.

"There was a holy monk in this place," said he, "and it was he that told me that a great change would come in Ireland and that it was a cobbler in England by the name of Cromwell who would come here and put me out of my land."

"You must send for that holy monk for me," said Cromwell, "and if he doesn't come, I'll cut the head off him!"

O'Donnell went off and found the monk and brought him back to Cromwell.

"How did you get this knowledge?" asked Cromwell.

"I got it from Heaven," replied the monk.

"Now you must tell me how long I will live," said Cromwell.

"You will live as long as you wish to," said the holy monk.

"I'll live for ever then!" said Cromwell.

There was another big gentleman from England along with Cromwell.

"And how long will I live? Will I get a long life?" he asked.

"If you pass the door of the next forge you meet on the road alive," said the monk, "you'll live a long time."

"Ah, I'll live for ever so!" said the gentleman.

That was that! Cromwell didn't evict O'Donnell; he left him where he was, and went away. Himself and the English gentleman and their troop of soldiers went along, and when they were passing by a forge, Cromwell said;

"There's a shoe loose on one of our horses. But luckily we're near this forge!"

He jumped off his horse and entered the forge. The smith was inside.

"Hurry up and put a shoe on this horse for us!" said Cromwell.

The poor smith was trembling with terror. He hurried here and there about the forge, looking for a good piece of iron. He was afraid that he wouldn't be able to get a piece good enough for Cromwell and his army. Cromwell himself was searching around also, and he spied an old gun-barrel stuck above one of the rafters of the forge.

"Here's a piece of iron that's good!" he said.

He pulled down the old gun and shoved the barrel of it into the fire—he was well used to working in forges too, for his father was a smith. He started to blow the bellows. The English gentleman was standing outside the door. It wasn't long till the shot went off through the mouth of the gun and it struck the gentleman on his vest pocket and went out through his body at the other side. It killed him. Cromwell ran out when he heard the noise outside, jumped up on his horse, dug the spurs into it and raced for Dublin. As he was galloping along the road,

344

whom did he see, walking ahead of him, but the holy monk! When the monk saw Cromwell coming towards him, he tried to run down and hide himself under the arch of a bridge.

"Come up out of that, you devil!" shouted Cromwell. "If I have to go down to you, I'll cut the head off you!"

The monk came up to him.

" 'Tisn't from you I was hiding at all," said the monk, "but from the man behind you."

"What man is behind me?" asked Cromwell.

"He's sitting behind you on the horse," said the monk.

Cromwell looked behind him and he saw the Devil at his back. All he did was dig his spurs into his horse and race for Dublin. He went back to England and never returned to Ireland again. After spending a while in England, he grew restless. The King of Spain died, and his son, who hadn't much sense or knowledge about ruling a country, took his place. Cromwell decided on a plan which seemed very good to him. He wrote a letter to the young Spanish king, inviting him to England, and offered him his daughter in marriage. When the king got the letter, he sent for his advisors and told them about it.

"That's a plan of Cromwell's," said they, "to try to get into this country and take over the kingdom. Write a letter back to him and say that you'd like such a marriage arrangement, but you want a year to think the matter over; when the year is out, you might like the offer very much. You must be strengthening your army during the year, and at the end of it, write to him and say that you don't wish to marry the Devil's daughter!"

Cromwell happened to be shaving himself when he got the letter at the end of the year. He had one side of his face shaved, when the letter was handed to him. When he read the piece about the Devil's daughter, he cut his throat with the razor and fell dead.

About the time when Cromwell killed himself, a ship was entering Liverpool, and the captain saw, coming towards him in the air, a fiery coach drawn by dogs, and they crying out: "Clear the way for Oliver Cromwell!"

There has been lively commerce between Ireland and America since Brendan the Navigator was (so many believe) the first European to set foot in the New World, in the sixth century.

Enormous numbers of Irish families emigrated to America to escape the famine, the "Great Hunger" of the 1850's; but others, as the American Irish Historical Society will proudly and loudly tell you (if you give them half a chance) were signers of the Declaration of Independence, generals, teachers, priests, outlaws, and politicians before them. Wasn't Scarlett O'Hara herself born in a house named after the palace of the High King, Tara?

For its part, America gave Ireland potatoes, tobacco, and Aemmon de Valera, all of which became national obsessions. This is a story about tobacco. It was collected in 1950, by R. M. Dorson, and first published in the Journal of American Folklore *(LXVII).*

SEAN PALMER'S VOYAGE TO AMERICA
WITH THE FAIRIES

Sean Palmer—he lived in Rinneen Ban. He had a small farm and owned a fishing boat—he fished during the summer season. He was married and had three children growing up. Now Sean was very fond of tobacco—he was a very hard smoker and would prefer to go without his meals any day than to go without a smoke of his clay pipe, and at that time shops were few and far between. The country folk had to depend on huckstering egg-women who visited them once a month perhaps, to buy their eggs, to supply their various household needs— tobacco, soap, needles, pins, etc., which they exchanged for the housewives' eggs. They sold tobacco for a penny a finger. The middle finger of the right hand from the top of the knuckle was the measure. It was called "a finger of tobacco."

Now it so happened that on this certain occasion to which our story refers, the egg-woman who used to visit Rinneen Ban was not as punctual as was customary with her, and Sean Palmer had to go without his usual smoke. As with all heavy tobacco smokers, this enforced abstention from the nerve-soothing weed had a very serious effect on Sean's usually active and industrious disposition. For two days he sat on the hob by the kitchen fire, grumbling and grousing and cursing the egg-woman roundly for her delay in supplying him with his favourite weed.

On the evening of the third day, after he had made about the twentieth trip from the hob to the kitchen door in the hope that the egg-woman would sooner or later make her appearance, he spoke thus to his wife: "Mary," said he, "I can't stand it any longer! The end of my patience is exhausted. I think I'll set off to Sean [Murphy] The Locks for a finger of tobacco. There will be no living in this house with me if I have to spend the night without a smoke of tobacco."

Sean The Locks kept a little shop about a quarter of a mile to the south of the present village of Waterville—there was no village then— and sold tobacco and groceries.

"The potatoes are boiled, Sean," said his wife, "and you may as well sit over to the table and eat your supper before you start off."

"Yerrah, woman," said Sean, "I cannot see the table, nor can I see the potatoes. I am stark blind for the want of a smoke. I will start off this very minute for Sean The Locks' shop, and the potatoes can wait until I come back."

He arose from his seat on the hob, grasped his blackthorn stick, and set off for Sean The Locks' shop, dressed only in his sleeve-waist-coat, and flannel drawers. He had neither shoes nor stockings on his feet, as men wore shoes only when going to Mass or to the local town on a fair or market day at that time. As he approached the quay—there is a little quay on the roadside at the bottom of Rinneen Ban, where fishing boats came to shore and landed their catches of fish—it is how there were two men on the road before him, standing, and he made toward them.

"That is Sean Palmer," said one of the men to the other. "I know what is the matter with him, and where he is going. He has no tobacco," said he, in Sean's hearing. They knew Sean was listening to them.

When Sean came within speaking distance of the two men, he saluted them, and they returned his salutation.

"I presume you have got no tobacco, Sean," said one of the men; "and do you see those two men down there? Go down to them and you will get your fill of tobacco from them."

There was a little boat pulled up alongside the quay below, and two men in her. Sean hesitated for a moment.

"I suppose it is rather late to go to Sean The Locks' shop, now," he said, "and my supper is on the table, awaiting my return. Even if I only got one pipeful from them, sufficient to satisfy my craving till morning, I'd be very well pleased." "Go on down," said one of the men, "and you'll get plenty tobacco."

Sean went down to the quay and stood on the pier. The boat was pulled close in beside the quay. There were two men in her. Sean addressed them very politely and said he would be ever so grateful if they would kindly give him a smoke of tobacco.

"That you shall get, and plenty, and to spare," said one of the men. "Step into the boat and be seated. Come in," said he.

As Sean was stepping into the boat, he chuckled with delight at the idea of having had such good luck.

"By gor," said he to himself, "isn't it I that have struck the good luck. It is an old saying, and a true one, that a hound let loose is better than a hound on the leash."

"Here you are, Sean," said one of the men who was in the boat, "take that and smoke to your satisfaction," handing him his own pipe, which was red [i.e., lighted] and in full steam.

Sean took the pipe from him, thanked him, and sat on the center thwart of the little boat, puffing great blasts of smoke from his pipe. He was almost enveloped in tobacco smoke. He sat there puffing eagerly at the pipe, oblivious of his surroundings and oblivious of everything like a man in a trance. "Oh, man alive!" said he to himself. "Isn't it the oil of the heart. 'Tis the grandest pipe of tobacco I have ever smoked in my life."

It was not very long until the two men in the boat made a sign to their two companions who were still standing on the roadway, bidding them to come down and get into the boat at once, and so they did, and no sooner had they stepped aboard than the sails were raised close to Sean's ear, and the order was given: "To sea with you boys!" and the little boat shot out from the quayside and away to sea with her.

"By gor," said Sean to himself, "you have high notions like the poor man's cabbage [an old saying or cant-word] whatever destination you are bound for."

Neither Sean nor any of the four boatmen spoke a word for some time nor interfered with one another in any way, and in the meantime the boat was racing along, skimming over the surface of the sea like a shot from a gun, and it was not very long until Sean saw lights—the lights of houses, he presumed.

"Yerrah," said Sean to one of the men, "are not those the lights of Lohar houses?"

"Och! God help you," replied one of the men. "Wait awhile and you shall see much finer houses than your Lohar houses."

"By the cross of the ass," said Sean, "surely they are the Lohar houses, and there is Rinneen Ban to the west."

"Och! God help you," said another of the men. "Do you not know where you are now? You are beside New York Quay!" said he. "See the ships and the people and the grand houses. Step ashore now, Sean," said he.

Sean stared in confusion at the sight that met his eyes, and it took him some time to regain his usual composure. However, he stepped ashore, as he was bade to do by the man in the boat, and he mixed with the crowds of people on the quay, but they were all complete strangers to him. He knew none of them, and he imagined they were all staring at him.

"Oh, good heavens," said he to himself, "no wonder they are all staring at me with nothing on me but my sleeve-waistcoat and my flannel drawers and without a shoe or a stocking on my feet. Why did I not put on my frieze coat when I was leaving the house?"

A man passed close by him as he stood there on the quay, gazing at the crowds. "Upon my conscience," said the man as he passed him by, "but that fellow bears a very close resemblance to Sean Palmer of Rinneen Ban. "

"By heaven," said Sean to himself, "that fellow certainly is in America. Andy Pickett from Rinneen Ban. Sure I knew him well before he came over here, and if he is in America, I am in America also. I suppose he did not recognize me."

"Make no mistake about it," said one of the men who brought him over in the boat. "You really are in America. Now, Sean," said he, "you have a brother here in New York, have you not?"

"I have," said Sean, "but New York is a big place, and how could a poor greenhorn like me find out where he lives?"

"Never mind," said the man, "come along and we shall find him."

Two of the men accompanied Sean, and the other two men

remained in charge of the boat. They walked along through the main streets of New York, Sean and his two companions, until they came to one of the side streets. The two men suddenly stopped in front of a tenement.

"Your brother Paddy lives in this house," said one of them to Sean. "Knock at the door and tell the people of the house that you want to see Paddy Palmer."

Sean did as he was bade. He knocked at the door, and one of the servants came in response to his knock.

"Does Paddy Palmer from Rinneen Ban live here?" Sean asked the servant.

"Yes, he does," the servant replied. "Come right in to his room." Sean followed the servant upstairs to an upper room. "This is his room, now," said the servant. "You can step right in," and he left him.

Sean stepped into the room, and when Paddy saw him dressed in a sleeve-waistcoat, flannel drawers, and without shoes nor stockings on his feet, he thought he belonged to the other world—that he was dead and that this was his spirit which had come to visit him.

"Good heavens, Sean!" he exclaimed. "Was it how you died?"

"No, faith," replied Sean, "but I am very much alive."

"And when did you come to America?" asked Paddy.

"I landed on the quay about a quarter of an hour ago," Sean replied.

"And when did you leave home?" asked Paddy.

"I left Rinneen Ban about a half hour ago," said Sean.

"And what brought you over, or were there many people on the boat coming over?" asked Paddy.

"Wait a minute until I tell you my story," said Sean. "I ran short of tobacco, and I started off just after nightfall for Sean The Locks' shop to get some tobacco, and when I reached Rinneen Ban quay [repeats his experience]. As I stood there on the quay, gaping at the crowds as they passed to and fro, Andy Pickett from Rinneen happened to pass by. 'My soul from the devil!' said he, as he passed along. 'That fellow resembles Sean Palmer from Rinneen Ban very closely!'

"Well, one of the men asked me if I had a brother here in New York. I said, yes. I have. So they brought me along here."

"Sit down just for a moment until I order some supper for you," said Paddy; "and while you are eating, I'll go out to the store next door

350

and fetch you some tobacco, and when I come back I shall give you my best suit of clothes. You look terrible in those old duds you are wearing. I can buy myself another new suit tomorrow."

Sean sat down when the supper came and started eating, and he had just finished as Paddy came back, carrying a fairly large box of tobacco under his arm.

"Now Sean," said he, "you have a half-year's supply of tobacco in this box," putting his hand in his trousers' pocket at the same time and producing a bundle of dollars. "And here are a few dollars for you," said he, "which I intended sending you at Christmas, but as you happen to be on the spot now, you will save me the trouble of sending it along to you."

'Pon my word, he gave him a very good present, Paddy did.

"Well," said Sean, "you have given me a very decent present, Paddy, and I am very thankful to you, and now I must be going. The two men are out there on the street waiting for me; so I cannot delay any further."

Paddy wrapped up his best suit in a sheet of brown paper together with the box of tobacco and handed the parcel to Sean.

"Goodbye now, Sean," said he; "and God speed you."

Sean stepped out into the street. His two companions of the boat were standing there waiting for him.

"My word, Sean," said one of them; "you have not fared too badly by your visit."

"By my soul!" replied Sean. "You bet I haven't. I have a bundle of dollars to the value of even pounds together with a large box of tobacco and a fine suit of clothes!"

"Give me the bundle now, Sean," said the man, "and I will put it on the boat." Sean handed him the parcel and the man set off toward the boat with it; and said the other man, addressing Sean: "Sean," said he, "haven't you got a sister up in Boston?"

"I have, by gor," said Sean, "I have a sister somewhere in the States—probably in Boston."

"Yes, she is in Boston," replied the man. "I know the house where she lives, and if you wish to visit her, I will accompany you there, and we shall find her out. The other man will catch up with us. Come right along," said he.

"By my soul," said Sean, "I'd like very much to see my sister Cait. Why shouldn't I?"

They started off and reached Boston in less than no time. As they were going through the city of Boston, Sean's companion stopped suddenly in front of one of the houses in the main street, in front of the door.

"Well, Sean," said he, "here we are in Boston, and your sister Cait lives here in this house. Go over and knock at the door and inquire if she is in, that you want to see her."

Sean went over and knocked at the door. The door was opened by a middle-aged woman, in answer to Sean's knock. "Whom do you want to see?" the woman asked.

"I want to see Cait Palmer," said Sean.

"I am Cait Palmer," said she.

"Good God, Cait," said he, "do you not know your brother Sean from Rinneen Ban?"

"Yerrah, Sean," said she, "and when did you die?" She thought that it was from the other world he had come, when she saw the sleeve-waistcoat and the flannel drawers on him, and he barefooted.

"By my soul!" said Sean, "I am not dead. I am very much alive," said he. "I have come all the way from Rinneen Ban to see you. I have been down in New York with Paddy since I arrived in the States, and he will tell you the whole story when you meet him."

"Wisha, Sean," said she, "and when did you leave Rinneen Ban?"

"I left there about suppertime tonight," said he. "I started off for Sean The Locks' shop to get some tobacco; but it would take too long to tell you the whole story now. Paddy will tell you all about it when you see him. I had supper with him down in New York. God bless poor Paddy. He was very kind to me. He gave me a big box of tobacco, a grand new suit of his own clothes, and a bundle of dollars to take home with me."

Cait opened her purse and handed him a twenty-dollar bill.

"Here, Sean," said she, "take that. It is all the money which I have got on me at present; but I shall not forget you at Christmastime. I will send you a check at Christmas."

Sean bade his sister goodbye and stepped out into the street, where his two companions were still standing, waiting for his return.

"Well, Sean," said one of the men to him, "how did you get on with your sister Cait?"

"By my soul!" replied Sean, "I did very well. She gave me a twenty-dollar bill."

The three then set off again for New York, and as they were approaching the city, Sean stopped suddenly. "Good heavens!" he exclaimed. "Where is my pipe? It must have fallen from my mouth, or I must have left it behind in Boston. I should have handed it back to the man who gave it to me, and now it is lost, and what a fine pipe it was."

"Never mind about the pipe," said one of his companions. "Don't worry about it, we shall get another pipe."

As they were going through New York, one of the men said, "By the way, Sean, I suppose you knew Cait 'Strockaire' O'Shea from the top of Lohar?"

"I did indeed," said Sean. "We were very close friends before she emigrated to America. As a matter of fact, I had a great notion to marry her at one time."

"Would you like to see her?" asked the man. "She lives here in this lane. I know the house where she lives."

"Ah, I don't think I should," said Sean. "My clothes are very shabby, and I would feel ashamed to meet her in this rig-out."

"Don't let that prevent you from seeing her," said the man who asked the question. "I'll run down and fetch your new suit from the boat, and you can exchange it for your old duds. We are in no hurry. We have got plenty of time."

The man started off for the boat and was back again with the new suit to Sean in less than no time.

"Come along now, Sean," said he, "and peel off every stitch of your old clothes from the skin out and put this suit on you."

He handed Sean the suit, and the other companion took Sean aside. He took him into a dark corner of the alley, and Sean put the new suit on.

His two companions then directed Sean to the house in the lane where Cait "Strockaire" O'Shea lived. Sean knocked on the door and was admitted by Cait, who recognized her old neighbor as soon as she laid eyes upon him. She gave him a *cead mile failte* and asked him how long was he in America and when he came over.

353

"I have been here during the past few years," replied Sean. He did not want to let her know that he had only just come over that night. "And I am going back to Ireland again," said he; "so I decided to call to see you before I go back."

"That was very kind of you indeed, Sean," said she; "and when are you sailing for Ireland?"

"I am sailing this very night," replied Sean. "I shall be leaving in a few hours' time."

"Ah, Sean," said she, "had I known in time that you were going back to Ireland I would have booked my passage on that boat along with you."

She opened her purse and handed Sean a fifteen-dollar bill. "Take this little present to my brother Con," said she—her brother Con "Strockaire" O'Shea, who lived in the top of Lohar—"and here is a little gift for yourself," said she, handing him a five-dollar bill. "You can drink my health on the boat when you are crossing. By the way, Sean," said she, "did you marry ever since?"

"I say marry to you," replied Sean. He gave her no direct answer.

"Perhaps, Sean," said she, "we may both splice it up yet."

"You could never tell," replied Sean as he bade her goodbye; "stranger things might happen."

Sean stepped out into the street, where his two companions were still standing waiting for him.

"Well, Sean," said they, "how did you get on with Cait "Strockaire"?

"We got on fine," replied Sean. "We had a very pleasant chat and she gave me fifteen dollars to take home to her brother Con, who lives on the top of Lohar, and five dollars for myself, to drink her health going over on the boat."

"Come along now, Sean," said his two companions, "our time is running short. We must make off the boat."

They started off for the quay—New York Quay—and they made off the boat, and the other two men were waiting for them at the boat, where they had left her. They told Sean to come aboard, and he did. They spread their sails by the quayside and loosed the mooring rope.

One of the men spoke in a low tone to the fourth man, who was at the steer, "There is no time to spare now. Give her all the canvas she can take." And the little boat bounded out from New York Quay like a falling star.

They were not very far out to sea when Sean felt the missing pipe being shoved between his teeth.

"My soul from the devil," he exclaimed; "is this not the missing pipe?"

"Never mind," said one of the men, "but see if it is still red, and if it is, puff away at it to your heart's content."

The pipe was still red, and soon Sean saw the puffs of smoke coming out of his mouth. "Ah," he exclaimed, "it is an old saying and a true one that a lucky man only needs to be born."

That was well and good, and it was not very long until Sean saw land appearing in the distance, and very soon he was able to distinguish the houses on the mainland.

"Bless my soul," said he to one of the men. "Are they the Lohar houses which I can see in the distance?"

"Yes, they are," replied the man.

"Well, I give this little boat the lead for good speed," said Sean. "I thought we were only a few miles out from New York, and here we are now within a few oars' length of Rinneen Ban quay."

The boat swept in toward the quay like a rushing wave, her forward part resting on dry sand.

"Step out of the boat, Sean," commanded one of the men; "you are landed safe and sound on Rinneen quay."

Sean took up his parcel and stepped ashore, and as he turned around to thank the crew, there was no trace or tidings of the crew or of their boat to be seen anywhere, as if the sea had swallowed them up.

As Sean walked up the road from the pier, he heard the cocks crowing in the houses above. When he reached home, he knocked loudly at the kitchen door.

"Get up and open the door for that rascal of a father of yours," said Sean's wife to her eldest daughter. They had retired long since and were sound asleep. "He has spent the night card playing in Sean The Locks' shop, I presume."

The little girl got up and opened the door, and when she saw the strange man dressed in an elegant Yankee suit, the likes of which she had never before seen, complete with panama hat, and wearing a pair of well-shined glacé kid shoes, she shrank back in fear before the stranger and rushed back to the bedroom, screaming and calling her mammy that there was a strange man in the kitchen. Her mother got out of bed, dressed, and came up in the kitchen. She knew Sean at once, of course—Sean had thrown some bog deal on the fire in the meantime, and it lighted up the kitchen.

The wife looked at Sean for some time and surveyed him from head to foot, and when she recovered her composure, "Good lord, Sean," said she, "where have you been all this night or where did you get that fine suit of clothes which you have on your bones?"

"I did," replied Sean; "I got it over in New York from my brother Paddy."

She looked at him again more closely. She thought he had lost his reason.

"And see here again," said he, "as proof that I have been in New York, see this fine box of tobacco which I got from Paddy. A full half-year's supply," said he. "And see here again," said he, putting his hand in his trousers' pocket and pulling up a fistful of dollars. "There's some money which he gave me to take home with me. I was up in Boston also, and I visited my sister Cait and she gave me some money, and on the way back to New York, I visited our old neighbor Cait "Strockaire" O'Shea from the top of Lohar—and 'tis she that is looking fine and strong—and she gave me a twenty-dollar bill to bring home with me to her brother Con and a five-dollar bill for myself to drink her health coming over on the boat."

Sean's wife took up the tobacco box and examined it. She had a little education and was able to read and write, and she saw the words "New York" in large characters on the lid and the date of the month on which the tobacco was packed.

"By gor, Sean," said she, "your story is a true one. This box came from New York sure enough, but how in the name of heaven did you manage to get there and back again and in such a short time too?"

So Sean told her the whole story, as I have already told it to you, and next morning when Sean got up and out of bed—he didn't get up too early, I suppose, as he felt tired after the voyage of the previous night—he ate his breakfast and dressed himself up in his grand new suit of clothes, shoes, and panama hat, and strolled out around the little farm. And when the neighbors saw the well-dressed stranger, they were wondering who he was. Nobody knew Sean when he was dressed up in the suit of fine clothes. After awhile they approached closer to Sean to find out who he was. It was only then that they recognized Sean.

In the course of time letters came from America to Sean's neighbors in Rinneen Ban and the top of Lohar—from Andy Pickett and Cait "Strockaire" O'Shea, telling them that they had seen Sean Palmer in America and that they had spoken to him.

So that is now the story of Sean Palmer for you, and the tobacco, and his voyage to America with the fairies.

This is Crofton Croker's telling of an old Killarney legend, or, in fact, of three legends, one laid on top of the other. The Prince O'Donaghue is here described as a Norman knight in armor. So, he is, first of all, remembered as one of those English earls who came to Ireland before Elizabeth's time—those gallant, half-mad, brawling chieftains who became "more Irish than the Irish" and led the Gaelic-speaking peasants, their fellow Catholics, in many a failed uprising against the growing English Protestant power.

But O'Donaghue is also often the name given, in the southwest part of Ireland, to the local fairy chieftain, the king of the Little People who had, themselves, been driven "underground" long ago by the Gaels.

And, before and behind those two figures, can we not see, riding upon the water, "preceded by the huge wave that curled and foamed up as high as the horse's neck," the Celtic sea god himself, Manannan Mac Lir?

THE LEGEND OF O'DONOGHUE

In an age so distant that the precise period is unknown, a chieftain named O'Donoghue ruled over the country which surrounds the romantic Lough Lean, now called the Lake of Killarney. Wisdom, beneficence, and justice distinguished his reign, and the prosperity and happiness of his subjects were their natural results. He is said to have been as renowned for his warlike exploits as for his pacific virtues; and as a proof that his domestic administration was not the less rigorous because it was mild, a rocky island is pointed out to strangers, called "O'Donoghue's Prison," in which this prince once confined his own son for some act of disorder and disobedience.

His end—for it cannot correctly be called his death—was singular and mysterious. At one of those splendid feasts for which his court was celebrated, surrounded by the most distinguished of his subjects, he was engaged in a prophetic relation of the events which were to happen in ages yet to come. His auditors listened, now wrapt in wonder, now fired with indignation, burning with shame, or melted into sorrow, as he faithfully detailed the heroism, the injuries, the crimes, and the miseries of their descendants. In the midst of his predictions he rose slowly from his seat, advanced with a solemn, measured, and majestic tread to

the shore of the lake, and walked forward composedly upon its unyield-
ing surface. When he had nearly reached the centre he paused for a
moment, then, turning slowly round, looked toward his friends, and
waving his arms to them with a cheerful air of one taking a short farewell, disappeared from their view.

The memory of the good O'Donoghue has been cherished by suc-
cessive generations with affectionate reverence; and it is believed that
at sunrise, on every May-day morning, the anniversary of his departure, he revisits his ancient domains; a favoured few only are in general
permitted to see him, and this distinction is always an omen of good
fortune to the beholders; when it is granted to many it is a sure token of
an abundant harvest—a blessing, the want of which during this prince's
reign was never felt by his people.

Some years had elapsed since the last appearance of O'Donoghue.
The April of that year had been remarkably wild and stormy; but on
May-morning the fury of the elements had altogether subsided. The air
was hushed and still; and the sky, which was reflected in the serene
lake, resembled a beautiful but deceitful countenance, whose smiles,
after the most tempestuous emotions, tempt the stranger to believe that
it belongs to a soul which no passion has ever ruffled.

The first beams of the rising sun were just gilding the lofty summit
of Glenaa, when the waters near the eastern shore of the lake became
suddenly and violently agitated, though all the rest of its surface lay
smooth and still as a tomb of polished marble; the next moment a foaming wave darted forward and, like a proud high-crested war-horse
exulting in his strength, rushed across the lake toward Toomies Mountain. Behind this wave appeared a stately warrior fully armed,
mounted upon a milk-white steed; his snowy plume waved gracefully
from a helmet of polished steel, and at his back fluttered a light blue
scarf. The horse, apparently exulting in his noble burden, sprung after
the wave along the water, which bore him up like firm earth, while
showers of spray that glittered brightly in the morning sun were dashed
up at every bound.

The warrior was O'Donoghue; he was followed by numberless
youths and maidens, who moved lightly and unconstrained over the
watery plain, as the moonlight fairies glided through the fields of air;
they were linked together by garlands of delicious spring flowers, and
they timed their movements to strains of enchanting melody. When

O'Donoghue had nearly reached the western side of the lake, he suddenly turned his steed, and directed his course along the wood-fringed shore of Glenaa, preceded by the huge wave that curled and foamed up as high as the horse's neck, whose fiery nostrils snorted above it. The long train of attendants followed with playful deviations the track of their leader, and moved on with unabated fleetness to their celestial music, till gradually, as they entered the narrow strait between Glenaa and Dinis, they became involved in the mists which still partially floated over the lakes, and faded from the view of the wondering beholders; but the sound of their music still fell upon the ear, and echo, catching up the harmonious strains, fondly repeated and prolonged them in soft and softer tones, till the last faint repetition died away, and the hearers awoke as from a dream of bliss.

Kevin Danaher, a member of the Irish Folklore Commission, lecturer at University College, a writer, collector, and editor, is the very best kind of "expert."

In such books as Gentle Places and Simple Things, In Ireland Long Ago, *and* The Year in Ireland, *he describes and celebrates folk-ways and traditions with neither cold, scholarly abstraction nor weepy one-of-the-boys blarney, but with thoroughness—and love.*

The story of "The World Under the Ground" he first heard from his own great-grandmother, although, as he tells us, it is "well known and wide spread."

In fact, it will remind readers not only of many of Grimm's stories, such as "Mother Holly," but also of Alice in Wonderland.

We have kept Danaher's spellings, but for those of you reading aloud, an hAbhann may be pronounced "Evan" and Nóirín as "Noreen."

THE WORLD UNDER THE GROUND

Long ago there was a farmer living over alongside the river, and Seán na hAbhann was the name that everyone called him. He was well off until his wife died, and he was left with the one child, a lovely little girl about fifteen years old, named Nóirín.

Well, what ever misfortune was down on him, he married again, and that was the woman that wore him down with misery. She was the hard virago, without grace or goodness, and she had a daughter that was as bad as herself, one age to Nóirín. They were doing their best, the two of them, to turn the father against Nóirín with the dint of lies and villainy, but it was no good for them because Seán na hAbhann was so fond of his dead wife's child. When it failed them with the father to get Nóirín put out of the place my two villains thought to get rid of her another way, and one day when she was lifting a bucket of water from the deep well they came behind her and gave her a shove, so that she fell in and sank, and then away home with them, and every screech and *ulagón* out of them, that she was drowned in the well and they not able to save her in time.

Nóirín thought that she was finished with this world for ever, and the water choking her, but where did she come to her senses but lying on a bank of grass in the middle of a meadow with the sun shining and

361

the place all full of flowers. She got up on her feet and walked over to the hedge of the field to see where was she at all. The hedge was so weak with age that it would not hold up a blackbird and when she tried to cross over into the next field, the hedge spoke to her and said: 'Take care! I am old and weak, do not break me!' 'Indeed and I will take care,' says Nóirín; I will not touch a twig or a leaf of you,' and with that she jumped right over the hedge without touching it. 'I am thankful to you, girl,' says the hedge, 'and I will make it up to you some day.'

Nóirín was travelling on through the fields until she came to a baker's oven and it was going at full heat with a great fire under it. I tell you that she was surprised when the oven called her. 'Come here, nice little girl, and take out the cakes of bread. I am too hot and I am in dread they will be burnt, for they are baking this last seven years and no one to take them out.' So she took out the cakes and laid them down on a soft mossy bank. 'May God reward you,' says the oven, 'and good luck to you on your road, and take one of the cakes for fear you would be hungry.' She took one of the cakes and she was eating it going along.

On she went through the fields and it was not long until she came to where a poor old woman was sitting on a *túrtóg* and she crying with the hunger. It was lucky that she had most of the cake left—it was a very big cake, as round as the top of a forty-gallon keg—and she gave a quarter of it to the old woman, and the old woman gave her all the blessing you could think of, and promised to help her if she ever could.

On with Nóirín until she came to a grove of trees, and there was a flock of sparrows there and the poor creatures weak with the hunger. 'What about a small cut of the bread for us,' said the sparrows, 'and we without a full meal for the last seven years.' 'Oh, God help us, you must be starved,' says Nóirín, and she breaking a quarter of the cake out on the ground for them. 'May God reward you,' said the sparrows, 'and if ever we have the chance, you can be sure that we will not forget you.'

She was not long on the road until she came to an apple tree and it bending down with the weight of the ripe apples. 'Will you have pity on me,' says the apple tree, 'and give me a good shake. I am so loaded down with the apples that I am in dread my branches will break.' She gave the tree a shake, and a right good shake, and a very big load of apples fell down and she made a nice heap of them under the tree. 'May God reward you,' says the tree, 'and I will repay you some day, if I can. But now take as many of the red juicy apples as you like.' Nóirín took a few of the apples and on she went.

It was not long until she was crossing out over a high ditch when she came on a big ram and his wool tangled in the briers and the bushes. 'Girl, dear,' says the ram. 'Is there any chance you would shear me? I am tangling in everything and my wool all dirty from dragging along the ground, and I not sheared for the last seven years.' There was a shears lying on top of the ditch, and it was not long until the ram was sheared. 'I am thankful to you,' says the ram, 'and I hope that some day I will be able to repay you.'

Off with Nóirín again, and what did she see but a cow and her udder trailing on the ground, she had so much milk. 'Would you milk me, little girl?' says the cow, 'I wasn't milked for seven years.' So Nóirín milked the cow and the cow promised to repay her some day. It was not long until she met a horse, and his bridle was tangled in a bush. 'Hi, little girl, says the horse, 'will you untangle my bridle, and I will make it up to you some day.' And she untangled the reins and the bridle so that the horse could go away free.

She was travelling on across the fields until she came to the road, and she was going along the road until she came to a little house by the side of it, and it was the only house she could see anywhere, and the night was beginning to fall, so she plucked up her courage and in she went to ask for a night's shelter. There was no one inside but two women, a mother and her daughter, and it would be hard to tell which one of them was the ugliest to look at, with teeth like the prongs of a rake on them and yellow skins. The only difference between them was that the old hag had a wispy beard on her like a goat's *meigeal*, and the daughter had not. They gave Nóirín a lump of stale grey bread and a can of water for her supper, and a sop of straw to put under her lying on the ground. But she was hungry and tried, and she ate the bread and slept soundly on the straw.

The next morning when she woke, the women told her that they were the only people living in the World Under the Ground, and that the best thing she could do would be to stay in service with them working as a servant girl and that she would be well paid for it when she was leaving them at the end of the year. And Nóirín agreed to this, for she had no where else to turn.

The next morning she was up at the break of day, and the first thing she had to do was to milk the cows, and that would be no bother to her, and her father having thirty milking cows at home; she was well used to cows. But the minute she was inside the gate of the paddock where the old hag's cows were then they started to run around wild, trying to jump out over the ditch and to puck Nóirín with their horns. The poor girl did not know what to do or where to turn; she was in dread of her life, that they would trample her, when she heard a voice: "Open the gate and let me in the paddock!" and there was the cow that she had milked, the cow that was seven years without milking. And Nóirín opened the gate, and that cow was not long quietening the other cows; she had them as tame as day-old lambs in a minute. And Nóirín milked them, and it is she was proud coming back to the house with all the milk. But it was no smile or laugh that the hag or her daughter had for her, for they thought that if they could fault her in her work they could cheat her out of her wages. Nóirín worked away all day, but she got no word of praise or kindness from the women.

The next morning she was up again at the break of day, and the first job she got to do this day was to wash woollen thread, and while she was washing the thread in the stream the old hag came out with two skeins of wool, a short black skein and a long white skein. And she told her that she would have to hold washing them in the stream until the black one changed to white and the white one turned to black. She began, and she held washing them for an hour or more, but she might as well be idle, for there was no change coming in the wool. She sat down on the bank and the tears began to come with her, and it would be hard to blame her. But it was not long until she heard a footstep, and when she lifted her head who should be there but the old woman that she gave the share of the cake to. "Stop your crying now, girl dear," says the old woman, "and take your two hanks of wool and draw the white one with the stream and at the same time draw the black one against the stream." Nóirín jumped up and did what she was told, and while you would be looking around you the black one was white and the white one was black. Off home to the hag's house with her, and her task done to perfection. And the two women, the hag and her daughter, had eyes as big as saucers on them with the dint of astonishment, but they pretended nothing although they were boiling with rage and disappointment that they could not blame Nóirín or find fault with her.

The next morning as soon as Nóirín had finished whatever scraps they gave her for her breakfast, the *cailleach* handed her a sieve and told her to go down to the stream and bring back the full of it of water. Nóirín went off and she was sitting on the bank and the tears beginning to come with her when a whole flock of small birds flew down and sat on her head and her shoulders and her hands. It was the sparrows that she had fed with the bread, and they without a meal for seven years, and they began to sing, and there were words with the song:

'Stuff the sieve with moss
And plaster it with clay,
And then you can take
The water away.'

That was enough for Nóirín. She stuffed moss into the holes in the sieve and plastered it nicely with yellow clay, and home with her and the sieve full to the brim of water. And if the women were disappointed the day before, they were mad with the rage today, but they still pretended nothing, only watched their chance to cheat her.

It went on like that, the women giving her hard tasks to do, and she doing them with the help of her friends, until at last the patience broke on the hag and her daughter and they told Nóirín to take her wages and be off with herself. And she was to take her wages like this; she was to go into the room and there were three caskets on the table, a beautiful gold casket and a fine silver casket and a dirty little lead casket. And before Nóirín could put her hand on any one of them, she heard this fluttering at the window, and there were the sparrows.

'Leave the gold,
And leave the silver.
But take the lead,
And you'll be saved.

That was the song they had at the window. So Nóirín took the lead casket and put it under her shawl, and away with her, making back along the way she came to the house the first day. But it was not long until she heard the screeching and the calling behind her, for the hag and her daughter saw the gold and the silver caskets left behind, and the lead casket gone, and after her with them and sparks from their heels. Nóirín was running for her life, but they were overtaking her when who did she see but the cow that was not milked for seven years. "Come here behind me," says the cow, "and I'll put them astray.' And when the women came up the cow called to them: "Over that ditch and away with her," and the women cleared the ditch in one leap and off with them in the other direction. On with Nóirín then, but it was not long until they were on her track again, and she was gasping for breath with the dint of the running when she heard the call—"in under the heap of wool with you, girl!" and there was the ram and the seven years' growth of wool in one big heap alongside him. In under the wool with Nóirín and away with the two women again and sparks from their heels.

On with Nóirín again and this time she got as far as the apple tree and the big heap of apples under it. And the horse that she had freed and he grazing under the tree. "In under the apples with you!" says the tree, and the horse worked the hooves on the heap until she was well covered. It was not a minute until the women were there again and "Where is she? Where is she?" out of them. "It is up in that tree she is," says the horse, and away up the apple tree with them, but the tree moved the branches so that it was easy for them to climb up but very hard for them to come down, and by the time they were on the ground, Nóirín was gone a good bit of the road. The next thing she came to was the hedge, and she in dread that she would never be able to jump it. But the hedge opened a gap when she was coming and closed up again just when the two hags were going through it. And it was full of all sorts of briers and bushes, and by the time they tore themselves out of the hedge it was nightfall, and they were all raggedy and torn from the thorns and the briers. So they went away home, and they were not in any nice temper. But by that time Nóirín was at the very spot where she had landed when she fell down the well, and she was so tired and worn out that she fell down dead asleep. And when she opened her eyes again where did she find herself but lying alongside the well near her father's house. And the lead casket was safe alongside her hand.

Off home with her running, and the first person she met was her father. And wasn't he delighted to see her, and he thinking she was drowned in the well, according to the story of the stepmother. But it was the sour face the stepmother had before her, and the scolding and the screeching, so that in the end Nóirín could not stand it any more, and she told her father that she was going to live in a little cabin that they had down the fields. And she spent a good part of the day sweeping and cleaning the little cabin. And in the evening she thought of the lead casket, and she opened it. It was then that the eyes opened on her, for it was so full of gold and jewels that the shine of it nearly blinded her. And as fast as she took anything out of it, it was full again. She was drawing gold and jewels and money, and silk carpets and curtains and clothes out of it until she had the cabin shining like a palace.

There was one of the neighbours crossing the field, and he wondered to see the smoke from the chimney of the cabin, and over with him to see who was there. He was so blinded by all the wealth that he did not recognize Nóirín, and what he told everyone was that a queen was after coming to live in the cabin, and that she had a palace made of it. And they were all coming to see the queen, and Nóirín made them all welcome, for there was food and drink in plenty coming from the lead casket, too. And Nóirín told them all how she got the riches and escaped from the hags. And when the stepmother and the daughter heard about it, they made up the plan to get riches for themselves, too. The stepmother wanted the daughter to go and the daughter wanted the mother to go, until finally, and they arguing and fighting at the brink of the well, the old woman gave the daughter a shove, and away down with her.

She came to herself, the same as Nóirín, but it was not the same as Nóirín she conducted herself. She broke down the hedge and laughed at the oven that was full of bread. She threw stones at the sparrows and made fun of the apple tree and the horse and ram and the cow. When she came to the house of the old hag and her daughter she was full of talk of all she was going to do for them. You would think that she was going to work all round her, but it was not long until the two hags were well tired of her, she was so lazy and so slovenly. And if they were not satisfied with a neat little girl like Nóirín, it would be hard for them to have anything to do with a *straoil* like this one. And finally they took her into the room, and showed her the two caskets that Nóirín left behind her. And nothing would do her but to take the gold casket. And the hags let her go but they gave her a good beating first. And she had no easy journey home, for the cow pucked her, and the ram hit her, and the horse kicked her, and the tree let down a big load of hard green apples on top of her, and the birds pecked her and pulled wisps out of her hair, and it like a bush by this time, and finally, when she came to the hedge she was half the day tearing herself through it.

Finally she came to the place under the well, and she threw herself down and fell asleep, and she woke up alongside the well and her old mother waiting for her. And away home with the two of them; they could not wait to open the casket. But it is they were sorry they ever opened it, for what came out but frogs and lizards and serpents and every kind of a crawling thing: And away with them running mad through the country and they screeching at the top of their voices and the creepy-crawlies after them. And that was the last that anyone ever saw of them.

Nóirín and her father settled down in the old home, and they had it like a palace with all the things out of the lead casket, and they without a trouble in the world, except for the number of visitors that were coming to see all the grand things in the house. And it was not long until the son of the king came to see all the grand things, and when he saw Nóirín nothing would do him but to make a match with her. And they were married, and what was in the country of people came to the wedding. And if they were not happy, it was no fault of Nóirín's.